W9-CLY-966

THE SOCIOLOGY OF ECONOMIC LIFE

second edition

Neil J. Smelser

IES

The new edition of this best-selling book has been revised and expanded to stress the current thinking about the interplay between economic and social forces. Though chapter headings remain the same, little of the original content has been retained; the second edition identifies advances in our knowledge of the workings of economy and society, while indicating the remaining areas of ignorance and uncertainty.

Like the previous edition, this edition explores the similarities and differences between economics and sociology. It ties together a mass of widely scattered empirical studies within a single analytic framework.

Interesting material on factory life, the factory and the community, and labor-management conflict is combined with discussions of economic change and progress and a comparative analysis of markets and consumption. The informed analysis of the sociological causes and consequences of economic growth contains special reference to the newly developing nations and portrays

PRENTICE-HALL
FOUNDATIONS OF MODERN SOCIOLOGY SERIES

Alex Inkeles, Editor

THE SCIENTIST'S ROLE IN SOCIETY
Joseph Ben-David

DEVIANCE AND CONTROL
Albert K. Cohen

MODERN ORGANIZATIONS
Amitai Etzioni

THE FAMILY
William J. Goode

SOCIETY AND POPULATION, Second Edition
David M. Heer

WHAT IS SOCIOLOGY? An Introduction to the Discipline and Profession
Alex Inkeles

THE SOCIOLOGY OF SMALL GROUPS
Theodore M. Mills

SOCIAL CHANGE, Second Edition
Wilbert E. Moore

THE SOCIOLOGY OF RELIGION
Thomas F. O'Dea

SOCIETIES: Evolutionary and Comparative Perspectives
Talcott Parsons

THE SYSTEM OF MODERN SOCIETIES
Talcott Parsons

THE AMERICAN SCHOOL: A Sociological Analysis
Patricia C. Sexton

THE SOCIOLOGY OF ECONOMIC LIFE, Second Edition
Neil J. Smelser

SOCIAL STRATIFICATION: The Forms and Functions of Inequality
Melvin M. Tumin

THE SOCIOLOGY OF ECONOMIC LIFE

in detail the setting in which economic life is grounded. The book also provides a broad historical perspective that reviews the dominant figures in the history of economic-sociological thought.

Neil J. Smelser, Ph.D., is University Professor of Sociology of the University of California. He is co-author with Talcott Parsons of *Economy and Society: A Study in the Integration of Economic and Social Theory* and is the author of other works in the field of economic sociology.

second edition

THE SOCIOLOGY OF ECONOMIC LIFE

NEIL J. SMELSER
University of California, Berkeley

Prentice-Hall, Inc., Englewood Cliffs, New Jersey

Library of Congress Cataloging in Publication Data

SMELSER, NEIL J

The sociology of economic life.

(Prentice-Hall foundations of modern sociology series)

Bibliography: p.

Includes index.

1. Economics. 2. Sociology. 3. Economic development—Social aspects. I. Title.

HM35.S55 1976 301.5'1 75-19130

ISBN 0-13-821579-0

ISBN 0-13-821561-8 pbk.

Printed in the United States of America

10 9 8 7 6 5 4 3 2 1

Prentice-Hall International, Inc., London

Prentice-Hall of Australia, Pty. Ltd., Sydney

Prentice-Hall of Canada, Ltd., Toronto

Prentice-Hall of India Private Limited, New Delhi

Prentice-Hall of Japan, Inc., Tokyo

Prentice-Hall of Southeast Asia (Pte.) Ltd., Singapore

CONTENTS

PREFACE TO THE SECOND EDITION

About ten years after the first edition of this book appeared (1963), Prentice-Hall's sociology editor recommended a second edition. I welcomed this on several counts. First, though the first edition was still being used in college courses, many parts of it were becoming seriously outdated. Furthermore, I had developed some second thoughts about the first edition, and some new thoughts about the interplay between economic and social forces in the meantime. Revision offered me the opportunity to correct, refine, expand, and modernize the book.

In revising I did not find it necessary to alter the basic framework for presenting economic sociology; thus the chapter titles and many of the main headings within the chapters are the same as before. Under most of these headings, however, little of the original content survives. In particular, chapters 3 and 4 have been greatly expanded and reoriented in the light of accumulated research. Chapter 5 has been recast substantially as well. Finally, I have attempted to update and remove blemishes from the first two chapters, though their revision has not been as extensive as that in the other chapters. I hope that in this second edition I have recorded the advances in our knowledge of the workings of economy and society, while at the same time indicating the many remaining areas of ignorance and uncertainty.

Early in the revision several colleagues directed me to lines of relevant research in economics and anthropology. These were Professors Frederick Balderston of the University of California, Berkeley; George Dalton of Northwestern University; Frederic Pryor of Swarthmore College; and Benjamin Ward of the University of California, Berkeley. I thank them for their advice. Jacques Brissy, a graduate student at the

University of California, Berkeley, directed me to literature on managers and stockholders which I might not otherwise have located. I should also like to record my gratitude to staffs of the libraries of the University of California, Berkeley; the London School of Economics and Political Science; and the British Museum; who supplied, efficiently and without complaint, the innumerable books and journals I wished to consult.

THE SOCIOLOGY OF ECONOMIC LIFE

INTRODUCTION

THE AIM OF THIS BOOK

To understand and predict any aspect of social life, we cannot ignore economic forces. Consider only one timely example of this principle: the energy crisis of 1973 and 1974 that was occasioned in part by the price increases and temporary export restrictions by many of the oil-producing nations. The economic threat posed to industrialized nations by these measures encompassed a shortage of oil products, inflation, unemployment, and a slowdown if not a reversal of economic growth. These economic effects, moreover, threatened to penetrate the entire social and political order. They threatened to exacerbate group conflicts, as groups such as workers and pensioners found their economic position deteriorating while they witnessed record profits for large oil companies. They threatened to undermine the use of many items requiring energy consumption—cars, boats, distant summer homes—that occupy a central place as status symbols. They occasioned a set-back for efforts to preserve the environment, as clean-air requirements were postponed, and environmental objections to offshore drilling and to opening new areas like Alaska gave way to a heightened interest in exploiting reserves. They posed a threat to those parts of child socialization that are dependent on private transportation, such as carting children to school, music lessons, and friends' houses. Nothing was untouched, and we were forcefully reminded, if reminding was necessary, how dependent is our entire way of life on the economic forces built into industrial society.

In turn the noneconomic aspects of social life affect the economic. The crisis in the supply of oil, an economic fact, could not be understood without knowing the relations between the Arab states and Israel—relations dependent on political and religious factors as well as economic—and America's history of political and economic support of Israel. America's support, moreover, could not be understood without reference to the political role of the Jewish minority in the United States. And the resumption of oil exports by the producing nations, while dependent in part on market forces, was also the result of international negotiation and political compromise.

Even something so intimate as friendship may condition economic processes. If a clique of workmen in a factory do not accept management's goals of production, they often deliberately slow their output. Moreover, they use the lever of friendship and loyalty to enforce these restrictive practices. Members often "go along" with the group norms because they wish to remain in good standing in the clique.

It is essential to regard the social world as made up of many aspects—economic, political, religious, familial, educational, and others—all of which can be defined independently of one another, but all of which influence one another. Corresponding to these aspects are various branches of the social sciences. Economics and political science, for instance, concentrate more or less exclusively on the range of problems that arise in the economic and political areas, respectively. Sociology covers a number of social aspects, as indicated by its subfields—sociology of religion, sociology of education, and so on.

This book concerns the economic aspect of life, but it is not a book on economics, as the term is generally employed. Rather, it is concerned with the relations between the economic and noneconomic aspects of social life—how they overlap, how they influence one another. It is also concerned with the sociological analysis of economic activity itself. We refer to this subject as "economic sociology."

Economic sociology has grown in shreds and patches. Its contributors go under many labels—economists, labor relations experts, industrial sociologists and psychologists, demographers, economic sociologists, and those who study in areas known as the sociology of work, the sociology of leisure, the sociology of occupations, the sociology of formal organizations, and the sociology of economic development.

In pulling together some of these strands of thought and research, we shall be guided by three kinds of questions:

1. What do we need to know in the field of economic sociology? What are the main issues in the field?
2. What do we actually know? What are the major findings of economic sociology? What confidence can we have in these findings?

3. What remains to be known? Do the findings of economic sociology have any genuine bearing on what we need to know in the field? What are the major "unknowns" in theory and empirical research?

The Program of This Book

We shall examine these questions from a number of different angles:

1. From the standpoint of the *history of thought*. In part, the history of *economic* thought is a procession of major figures who have made advances in discerning the workings of the economic system. In developing their economic ideas, however, these thinkers have made certain assertions about the noneconomic aspects of life. Sometimes these assertions play a significant role in their economic theories. In chapter 1 we shall examine some of the noneconomic assumptions of Adam Smith, Karl Marx, John Maynard Keynes, and others. We shall also glance at the history of *sociological* thought, represented by figures such as Emile Durkheim and Max Weber, who inquired specifically into the relations among the economic and noneconomic features of society. Finally, to locate the viable issues in modern economic sociology, we shall examine a few recent trends in anthropology, economics, and sociology.

2. From a *theoretical* standpoint. In chapter 2 we shall inspect economics and sociology as disciplines. We shall ask what kinds of scientific problem are posed in each field, what kinds of concept are used in each to attack these problems, and what kinds of explanation are generated in each. Then we shall be in a position to give a formal account of the distinctive character of economic sociology, and to set it off from related lines of inquiry.

3. From a *systemic* standpoint. Having examined economic sociology from the historical and methodological angles, we shall turn to the substance of the field in chapter 3. Initially we shall consider the economy as one of many structures in society; then we shall ask how it is related to other structures—the cultural (for example, values and ideologies), the political, and the like.

4. From the standpoint of *economic processes*. If we concern ourselves only with major social structures and their relations, we remain at a very general level. To get a closer view of the relations between economic and noneconomic variables, we shall study the central economic processes in chapter 4. We shall examine the production of goods and services, then distribution and exchange, and finally consumption.

5. From the standpoint of *economic and social change*. It is one thing to examine the findings of economic sociology with reference to production, distribution, and consumption *within* given economic and social structures, as if these structures were not changing. It is quite another to study the relations among economic and social variables when the major structures in society are *changing*. We shall devote chapter 5 to the relations between economic and social change, emphasizing the experiences of the new nations of the world.

CHAPTER 1
HISTORICAL DEVELOPMENTS IN ECONOMIC SOCIOLOGY

In the past two centuries many eminent thinkers have sought to cope with the major issues of economic sociology. To focus our attention on these issues, we shall consider the history of economic thought, then the history of sociological thought, and finally some recent developments in several social-science disciplines.

SOCIOLOGICAL ASPECTS OF ECONOMIC LIFE AS REVEALED IN THE HISTORY OF ECONOMIC THOUGHT

So rich is the history of economic thought, even in the past two hundred years, that a full coverage would require volumes. With only a few pages available, we shall simplify our task in three ways. First, we shall consider only a few major thinkers. Second, we shall ignore the major economic significance of their thought and concentrate on the noneconomic byways. Third, among these byways, we shall restrict ourselves mainly to one dimension—the political. This restriction is not altogether unrealistic, for economics was called "political economy" through much of the nineteenth century and still retains a preoccupation with policy issues.

Mercantilism: The State's Economy

The concept of mercantilism refers to a heterogeneous body of ideas that dominated European economic thought during the seventeenth and eighteenth centuries. These ideas do not form a coherent economic theory, but a conglomeration of value judgments, policy recommendations, and assertions about the nature of economic life. The heterogeneity of mercantilism traces in part to the diversity of persons who espoused it—philosophers, heads of state, legislators, merchants, and pamphleteers From this array, we may extract a few central themes.

The first concerns the mercantilists' view of wealth. The wealth of a country was held to be equal to the amount of money possessed by that country. Moreover, mercantilists identified money with the precious metals, gold and silver. Since they conceived the total stock of wealth in the world as more or less stationary, they felt that whatever one country gained in wealth, another country lost. (This contrasts with the view of modern economists that foreign trade often benefits both countries, even though one may run a deficit for a time.) Hence the mercantilists stressed either accumulating precious metals outright or maintaining a balance of exports over imports so that precious metals would flow to the home country.

The second theme concerns the mercantilists' view of power and its relation to wealth. One way to increase national power, many felt, was to increase national wealth. As Taylor observed,

> In [the mercantilist epoch] . . . the main over-all purpose of each country's government, in its efforts to stimulate and direct or guide the country's commerce and handicraft industries, was to foster growth of national wealth *mainly for the sake of* national diplomatic and military power and security. The main concern of each nation's policy was for growth of the relative wealth-and-power of the nation-state as such and as compared with rival, foreign nation-states. . . .[1]

Mercantilists assumed that wealth works in the service of power, and that the objectives of increasing wealth and increasing power are in essential harmony, indeed almost indistinguishable from one another.

With respect to practical policy as well, mercantilists saw an intimate association between power and wealth. The state is the locus of power. To stimulate economic growth and the increase of wealth, the state should use this power to regulate industry and trade. It should give political and economic support—by establishing state monopolies, for instance—to industries that manufacture goods for export; it should restrict imports by taxation or prohibition; it should colonize in order both to acquire supplies of gold and silver and to secure raw materials to be worked

1. O.H. Taylor, *A History of Economic Thought* (New York: McGraw-Hill, 1960), p. 82. Emphasis in original.

up for export.[2] By increasing its wealth, the state was also increasing its power.

From the standpoint of the status of economic and political variables, the mercantilists had an undifferentiated theory. By increasing wealth a state increases its power; moreover, it uses its power to increase wealth. If properly controlled, the economic and political systems cannot work at cross-purposes; they are complementary to one another.

Adam Smith: The Weakening of the State's Economic Control

Adam Smith (1723–1790) was the foremost critic of the mercantilist doctrines. From the multi-sided polemic contained in his famous *Wealth of Nations*,[3] we may extract the following attacks on and reformulations of the basic themes of mercantilism.

With respect to wealth, Smith rejected the mercantilists' emphasis on money or treasure. The wealth of a nation, he argued, is found in its productive base, or its power to produce "the necessaries, comforts and conveniences of life." Money is a medium of exchange that facilitates the allocation of these goods. The level of production depends in turn on the division of labor. The more highly specialized is labor, the more productive it is. The level of specialization of labor depends in its turn on the size of the markets for the products of labor and on the availability of capital.

Consistent with this emphasis, Smith denied the importance of accumulating a treasure of precious metals. Rather, to increase wealth it is necessary to develop the widest possible markets for distributing products. This reasoning lies behind his argument for maximum international trade to be attained by freeing it from tariffs and other restrictions.

Smith also revised the mercantilists' ideas regarding the relations between wealth and power. While not denying that a nation's power depends in part on its wealth, he attacked the notion that the best way to increase wealth is through direct political action. Governments should not establish monopolies, fix tariffs, or show favoritism to certain industries. They should instead allow the power to make economic decisions to *reside in the hands of the economic agents themselves.* In terms of power, the famous doctrine of *laissez faire* meant that the state should not regulate but should give business and commercial agents the power

2. For an extensive review of the mercantilist economic theories and policies, see Joseph J. Spengler, "Mercantilist and Physiocratic Growth Theory," in Bert F. Hoselitz et al., *Theories of Economic Growth* (Glencoe, Ill.: Free Press, 1960), pp. 3–64.

3. First published in 1776. A widely used edition is Adam Smith, *Inquiry into the Nature and Causes of the Wealth of Nations* (New York: Modern Library, 1937).

to regulate themselves. Strictly speaking, laissez faire called for a reallocation of power in society, not simply an absence of power.

Such decentralization does not, however, solve all the political problems of a society. What guarantees that individual economic agents will not misuse their power, gain control of the market, and fix prices? Smith handled this problem by two devices:

1. He built into his theory an assumption that is a core element of the notion of the perfectly competitive market—the assumption that no individual firm has (or should have) the power to influence price or total output of an industry. No economic agent can at the same time be a political agent. Smith realized that in practice businessmen and others deliberately regulate prices and output; persons "in the same trade seldom meet together," he said, "but the conversation ends in a conspiracy against the public." But he felt these agreements were unnatural and illegitimate. If the economy were free, businessmen would devote their capital to the most productive enterprises, and the shares of income would find their natural level in the market. The economy would regulate itself.
2. He assumed that some general political constraints are necessary to prevent businessmen from pursuing their self-interest in an unbridled way. For instance, the state should provide laws to guarantee that sales and contracts are honored; the state should not grant favors to special groups in the economy. Thus even under laissez-faire assumptions, the state is not completely passive. It provides a moral, legal, and institutional setting that encourages business in general but not particular business enterprises.

Karl Marx: The State as Captive of the Bourgeoisie

The thought of Marx (1818–1884) is extremely complex, in part because he attempted to synthesize so many lines of intellectual influence that converged on him. Here we can give only the barest sketch of his view of economics and society, with special reference to his assertions about political forces.

According to Marx, every society, whatever its stage of historical development, rests on an economic foundation. Marx called this the "mode of production" of commodities. The mode of production in turn has two components. The first is "the forces of production," or the physical and technological arrangement of economic activity. The second is "the social relations of production," or the indispensable human attachments that people must form with one another in carrying on this economic activity.

But society is composed of more than its economic structure. Resting on it is what Marx called the "superstructure," or that complex of legal, political, religious, aesthetic, and other institutions.

The totality of [the] relations of production constitutes the economic struc-

> ture of society—the real foundation, on which legal and political superstructures arise. . . . The mode of production . . . determines the general character of the social, political, and spiritual processes of life.[4]

This determination might work out in the following way: The most fundamental set of social relations that emerge from the process of production is a class structure, or the division of society into a ruling wealthy class and an exploited poor class. Under the capitalist mode of production—Marx analyzed capitalism in greatest detail—the two classes are the bourgeoisie and the proletarians. The bourgeoisie own the means of production, direct the productive process, and reap the profits from it; the proletarians are wage-workers who provide the actual labor but who do not receive full rewards for it. Given these relations of production, we would expect the state, the church, the community—in short, the superstructure—to operate in the service of the bourgeoisie and help keep the workers subordinated. For instance, politicians and the police would repress worker discontent, and religious leaders would preach ideologies to the masses to convince them either that they are not oppressed or that they will find salvation in a future life.

Let us now examine the relations between economic and political forces. Marx assumed that the capitalist has access to power because of his position in the economic structure; he owns the means of production, and he buys the laborers' services. The worker, on the other hand, has only his labor to sell and only wages received in return. Because of his position of superiority, the capitalist is able to exploit the worker by lengthening the work day, forcing his wife and children to work, speeding up machinery, and displacing the worker by installing more productive machinery. The capitalist's power is buttressed, furthermore, by political authorities who pass laws detrimental to the workers and put down any attempts to protest. Under these circumstances, the political forces in society work in the service of the economic forces.

Marx maintained, however, that such a relationship between economic and political forces is not an enduring one. In fact, each type of economic system contains what he called "the seeds of its own destruction." Under capitalism, for instance, the bourgeoisie, driven by competition to maintain or increase their profits, gradually drive the workers into greater misery and desperation. These conditions are exaggerated by the occurrence of increasingly severe economic crises. How do the workers respond? At first they remain isolated, in competition with one another, and disorganized; they are capable of only scattered forays against the

4. Karl Marx, *Contribution to the Critique of Political Economy* (New York: International Library, 1904), p. 11.

means of production (for example, machine-breaking) and misguided attacks against the remnants of the feudal order. As workers are gathered into greater proximity to one another in factories, and as the march of industry obliterates the differences among them, they become more mobilizable into collective action groups, such as trade unions. They are now able to force their own recognition and to attain some legislative victories, such as laws limiting the length of the working day. And finally, at the height of their maturity, they form into a revolutionary party, which rises to destroy the capitalist system and usher in a socialist one.

Marx had a complex view of the relations between economic and political forces. In the vital phases of the development of an economic system, the political arrangements consolidate the economic ones; in the degenerative phases, the economic and political forces come into conflict, and this conflict leads ultimately to the destruction of the political and then the economic system. At any given time the exact functional relations between the economic and political forces depend on the stage of development of the society in question.

Adam Smith Revised: The Study of Imperfect Competition

In reviewing Adam Smith's assumptions about power, we noted that he established a model of the perfectly competitive market—the market in which no individual firm has the power to control price or output. Under such conditions, firms that price too high, produce too much, or operate inefficiently are forced either to come into line with the existing conditions of production or go out of business. This model has occupied a prominent place in the history of economic thought. By the early twentieth century, theory based on its assumptions had reached a high point of development.

Clearly, few market conditions approximate the model of perfect competition. For one reason or another, a few agents become sufficiently powerful to influence conditions of output or price. If one or two sellers control all the supply of a given product—sulfur, for instance—they can determine prices because buyers cannot turn to alternate sources. If the product—again, sulfur might be an example—has no substitutes, the sellers possess an advantage, again because buyers have limited alternatives. Finally, if a government establishes a public utility and sets prices, this means an agent is interfering with the conditions of price and output that would exist if competitive forces were allowed to work.

During the early decades of the twentieth century, economists and others became increasingly aware of such deviations from the perfectly competitive market. The year 1933 is a landmark in that growth of awareness, since two pioneering works—one by Robinson and the other by Chamberlain—appeared in that year.[5] Their work stimulated a number of other theoretical developments and many empirical studies of imperfect competition. This interest in imperfection also fed into public concern with antitrust policy.

Most economists who deal with imperfect competition study the influence of these market conditions on price and output; some are also concerned about resources wasted because of the inefficiency of production under imperfect competition. As economic sociologists, however, we may note that theorists of imperfect competition make new assumptions about the political forces affecting the economy. Under perfect competition no firm has power. Under imperfect competition, by contrast, firms and other agents sometimes behave as *political agents.* Consider the following examples: First, the very desire of a firm to control prices implies an interest in using political means to make the firm's market condition more predictable and comfortable. Second, firms sometimes set prices *not* directly on the basis of their own conditions of cost, but on the basis of political agreements with other firms. Third, firms sometimes *refuse* to merge because they fear legal action on the part of a government interested in trust-busting. Analysis of imperfect competition clearly requires assumptions about power relations in the economy; in fact, the study of imperfect competition marks a formal wedding between economic and political analysis.

John Maynard Keynes: The State as Equilibrator

In considering the work of Keynes (1883–1946) we shall stick to our political theme by sketching his ideas on the role of government in stabilizing the economy. Before doing so, however, we must mention a few more general features of his work.

Keynes's work can be understood as an attempt to challenge and modify two features of classical economics. The first feature concerns the conceptual level of economic analysis. In the classical tradition the focus of economics had been on the conditions of output and price for the *individual* firm. The condition of the economy as a whole—or, as economists would say, the behavior of *aggregates*—was less problematical. Keynes insisted that aggregate economic conditions constitute an impor-

5. Joan Robinson, *The Economics of Imperfect Competition* (London: Macmillan, 1933); Edward H. Chamberlain, *The Theory of Monopolistic Competition* (Cambridge: Harvard University Press, 1933). For a series of efforts to assess the subsequent impact of monopolistic competition theory, and to apply it to a variety of market situations, see Robert E. Kuenne, ed., *Monopolistic Competition Theory: Studies in Impact* (New York: John Wiley, 1967).

tant focus for analysis. The second feature of classical economics that Keynes challenged was the assumption that in self-regulating economies resources are more or less fully and stably employed. Certain automatic adjustment mechanisms guarantee that changes in the level of capital and production will be absorbed smoothly, aside from minor periods of adjustment. Keynes maintained that in capitalist economies serious imbalances can develop, and long periods of unemployment and depression can be expected.

Keynes made his case by assembling a number of economic and noneconomic variables. At the outset he maintained that an economy's level of income and employment can be viewed in two ways. First, from the standpoint of returns to individuals, a society's income is made up of that portion of returns that people spend for *consumption* plus that portion they put aside as *savings*. Second, from the standpoint of production, income is made up of those goods destined for direct *consumption* and those goods destined to be used in *investment*—that is, in producing other goods and services. Looking at income in this double way, Keynes obtained the following equation: Consumption + Savings = Consumption + Investment.

Keynes then made several assumptions about each of the ingredients—consumption, savings, and investment.[6] With regard to *consumption* and *savings,* Keynes maintained that consumers' tastes are fairly stable, and that in general consumers are not initiators in the economy. In addition, he assumed that as a consumer's income rises he lays aside an increasing proportion of his total income as savings. In the aggregate, this means that a growth in a society's income is not accompanied by an equally great relative increase in consumption.

With regard to *investment,* Keynes assumed that it is a function of the rate of interest and the "marginal efficiency of capital." The latter reflects businessmen's attitudes—in particular, estimates they make concerning the profits to be expected from new investment. In attempting to characterize these attitudes, Keynes assumed simply that businessmen predict that future returns will be approximately the same as present returns. The rate of interest is a function of the total stock of money (fixed by the monetary authority), and what Keynes called "liquidity preference," which reflects certain attitudes of speculators and determines how they prefer to hold assets—as cash or securities.

Keynes next showed that under certain conditions the economy experiences unemployment, inflation, or other kinds of instability. Notice

6. The original statement is in J.M. Keynes, *General Theory of Employment, Interest, and Money* (New York: Harcourt, Brace, 1936). A clear secondary treatment is found in Alvin H. Hansen, *A Guide to Keynes* (New York: McGraw-Hill, 1953).

that his reasoning rests on certain psychological and social as well as economic assumptions. As Hansen summarized it:

> Back of the consumption schedules is the psychological propensity to consume; back of the marginal efficiency schedule is the psychological expectation of future yields from capital assets; and back of the liquidity schedule is the psychological attitude to liquidity (expectations with respect to future interest rates). In addition to these . . . variables, rooted in behavior patterns and expectations, there is the quantity of money determined by the action of the Central Bank—an institutional behavior pattern.[7]

Finally, what place did Keynes give the political dimension in his theory? His concern appears primarily in his discussion of public policy. It is possible, Keynes argued, for the government to influence the level of national income and employment by manipulating its ingredients—consumption, savings, investment—and their determinants. Thus, in the role of *monetary policy,* the government varies the interest rate and the stock of money, influencing those variables that impinge on the marginal efficiency of capital and investment. By *fiscal policy* the government itself spends and invests (by building highways, public works, etc.), influencing both total consumption and investment. A related set of policies affects the *distribution of income*—taxation, welfare measures, subsidies, and the like. If such policies make for a more nearly equal distribution of income (as graduated tax schedules do), this will increase consumption, because of the principle that those with less absolute income spend larger proportions of it.

Such governmental practices show that according to Keynes, the strictly economic aspects of the system (income, price, consumption, investment) are intricately tied to political variables (taxation policy, defense policy, welfare policy). We cannot, especially in these days of big government, understand the workings of the economy without simultaneously knowing much about public policy.

Conclusion

For the economic thinkers just examined, we may observe a kind of back-and-forth movement with respect to the relations between the economic and political dimensions. For the mercantilists the purposes of the economy and the polity are nearly indistinguishable; an increase in wealth means an increase in power, and power is to be used directly to increase wealth. Smith scrapped this notion of an undifferentiated economy and the polity. The state and the economy should pursue their respective purposes as independently from one another as possible. For the

7. Hansen, *A Guide to Keynes*, p. 166.

economy, at least, its maximum growth will occur under conditions of free competition unfettered by political intervention.

Marx, while incorporating many features of classical economic thought, revised the classical notions on the relations between the economic and political dimensions. Insofar as he saw the purposes of the economy and polity as intimately associated, he looked back toward the mercantilists. He differed from them, however, insofar as he regarded the polity as *subordinated* to economic considerations; furthermore, he limited the role of the state to buttressing the class relations that arose from the conditions of production. Keynes, again, saw more autonomy than Marx in the relations between polity and economy. For him the political authority can influence the economy. But he saw this influence operating not so much through the *direct* exercise of political power as through the manipulation of key economic variables and the unfolding of the economic consequences of this manipulation.

SOCIOLOGICAL ASPECTS OF ECONOMIC LIFE AS REVEALED IN THE HISTORY OF SOCIOLOGICAL THOUGHT

In considering the historical development of sociology, we again have to select only a few figures from a vast interplay of schools of social thought. In addition, we focus on a dimension that is political in part—the dimension concerning the *integration* of economic activities. Any division of labor—which leads people to pursue diverse and possibly conflicting lines of economic activity—may generate conditions of social dislocation and inequity. What social arrangements are geared to establishing peaceful, cooperative, and equitable interchange among economic agents? How—and how effectively—does a society control economic conflict? In treating the theme of integration we shall examine the thought of three men—Spencer, Durkheim, and Weber.

Herbert Spencer: Harmony of Industrial Society

For a number of decades in the late nineteenth and early twentieth centuries, Spencer (1820–1903) was perhaps the most influential figure in sociology. One reason for his great stature at that time is that his thought marked a confluence of two great traditions—evolution and classical economics—both of which reached their apex in the last half of the nineteenth century.

From the evolutionary tradition Spencer incorporated two notions—the society as an organism and progressive social development. He saw many similarities between biological and social organisms. Both are capable of growth; both increase in complexity of structure as they grow in size; for both, this increasing complexity results in the growth of highly specialized activities; both display a close interdependence of parts; for both, the life of the organism is longer than the life of its parts.

Spencer viewed social evolution as similar to biological evolution. The social organism first undergoes an increase in integration (by "integration" he meant something like "expansion"). A simple example of increased integration would be the unification of two formerly separate city-states into a single political entity. This increase in integration results in the growth of increasingly differentiated (specialized) social structures. The unification of the city-states, for instance, called for more complex political activities to govern the new entity. Evolution as such proceeds as an alternation between the forces of integration and the forces of differentiation; the result is a process of growth *from* societies that are homogeneous in structure *toward* those that are heterogeneous.

To give further meaning to his general evolutionary scheme, Spencer introduced a distinction between two types of society—the militant and the industrial. The former is integrated by force. The military chief is its political head; industrial activity is subordinated to military needs; the individual is subjugated to the state. The principle of integration (and here the meaning of the word "integration" changes to something like "regulation") in a military society is *compulsory cooperation*; all integration, including the regulation of economic activities, stems from the actions of a politico-military authority.

The industrial society contrasts with the militant on many counts. Its political machinery is no longer subordinated to the single military principle; democratic structures, such as parliaments and cabinets, arise. Industrial activities thrive, independent of direct political control. The individual is freed from the domination of the state. The principle of integration of industrial society is *voluntary cooperation*; people enter into relations with one another freely and contractually.

The two types of society are opposed in principle; "[by] as much as cooperation ceases to be compulsory, by so much does it become voluntary; for if men act together they must do it either willingly or unwillingly."[8] In the industrial society the principle of integration is the principle of freedom; men interact by forming contractual arrangements. Political intervention should be minimized, for it upsets the voluntarily coordinated activities of free individuals. Thus in the end Spencer viewed industrial society much as Smith did the competitive economy. Power is so differentiated and dispersed—and free men so motivated—that integration is effected by balancing individual interests in a vast system of vol-

8. Herbert Spencer, *The Principles of Sociology, 3 vols.* (London: Williams and Norgate, 1897), 3:484.

untary interchanges. Active social integration of the industrial society thus became as unnecessary for Spencer as active political regulation was for Smith.

Elsewhere, however, Spencer developed a contrary line of reasoning. In summarizing his theory, he reaffirmed that social evolution involves both integration (this time, meaning increase in mass again) and differentiation (the change from homogeneity to heterogeneity). Continuing the summary, he introduced the concept of *coherence*, which is a sort of integration that is different from a simple increase in mass:

> With progressing integration and heterogeneity goes increasing *coherence*. We see the wandering group dispersing, dividing, held together by no bonds; the tribe with parts made more coherent by subordination to a dominant man; the cluster of tribes united in a political plexus under a chief with subchiefs; and so on up to the civilized nation, consolidated enough to hold together for a thousand years or more.[9]

He also maintained that the increasing complexity of society gives rise to a "dominant [political] centre and subordinate centres" and "increasing size and complexity of the dominant centre."[10] Spencer was evidently arguing that differentiation brings an increased internal regulation of parts.

Such statements, however, raise a confusion. On the one hand, we would expect to find a proliferation of political and regulatory agencies in modern industrial society, since it has such a complex division of labor. On the other hand, Spencer's characterization of industrial society indicates that political regulation is almost unnecessary in such a society, since social coordination is guaranteed by voluntary cooperation among individuals. Spencer's arguments seem to have produced a double, contradictory result for complex industrial societies. Whether actually contradictory or not, however, his observations point directly to the contribution of Durkheim to the study of social integration.

Emile Durkheim: Solidarity as an Active Force in Economic Life

Most of the insights of Durkheim (1858–1917) concerning economic integration are found in his book *The Division of Labor in Society*.[11] Durkheim was primarily interested in the ways in which social life is in-

9. Ibid., 1:596.

10. Ibid., 1:528.

11. First published in 1893. The English edition, translated by George Simpson, was published in 1933. The most recent edition is that published by The Free Press (New York, 1969).

tegrated and regulated. To conceptualize his argument, he set up a dichotomy between two types of society—the segmental and the complex. What are the characteristics of these types, and how are they integrated?

The segmental society is a homogeneous society. The social division of labor is limited to that between the sexes and among persons of different ages. Durkheim compared his segmental society to the earthworm. It is composed of structurally identical kinship units, which resemble the worm's rings; if some of these units are removed, they can be replaced immediately by new and identical parts. In this way the segmental society differs from the complex society with specialized roles—removal of some of which would leave the society without certain vital functions.

How are segmental societies integrated? Durkheim described this by the term *mechanical solidarity*. Any disruptive act is met by a passionate and cruel reaction of vengeance by society against the offending party. This punishment reflects the collective values of the segmental society. These values, moreover, are more or less identical for all members; this identity follows from the basic homogeneity of segmental societies. The most striking instance of mechanical solidarity is found in repressive law (for example, laws against rape, kidnapping, and murder, even in complex societies). Mechanical solidarity, then, consists of the subordination of the individual to the undifferentiated collective conscience of the society. Thus there are certain resemblances between Durkheim's concept of mechanical solidarity and Spencer's concept of compulsory cooperation, though the latter is rooted in the military exigencies of society and the former is rooted in its collective values.

Durkheim's view of the differentiated society also bears some resemblances to Spencer's notion of the industrial society. Both possess specialized role structures. Both encourage the emergence of individual differences, freed from the total domination of homogeneous segmental societies. The differences between their concepts of complex societies involve the issue of how such societies are integrated.

Durkheim maintained that the only viable principle permitted in Spencer's industrial society is that of free exchange. No independent integrative action, above and beyond negative controls to prevent persons from hurting one another, is necessary. (We noted, however, that Spencer's thought is not so simple—indeed, it is confused—on this score.) Durkheim doubted the possibility of stability in a society that is based on momentary contacts among individuals. He maintained, instead, that powerful forms of integration operate in differentiated societies. Durkheim found such integration—which he termed "organic solidarity"—primarily in restitutive laws, which govern the conditions under which contractual relations are valid. Other forms of organic solidarity are customs, trade conventions, and implicit understandings among economic agents. Durkheim's difference with Spencer, then, is that he stressed the increased salience of integration in complex societies, rather than tending to regard it as a by-product of individual interactions.

Max Weber: The Origins and Sustaining Conditions for Capitalism

In assessing the relations among types of societies and types of integration, both Spencer and Durkheim relied on simplified, abstract concepts—militant society, segmental society, compulsory cooperation, and organic solidarity. In the complexity of the empirical world, such concepts are never sustained in pure form; each historical case is a mixture, showing relative dominance of one or more such characteristics. The value in using such abstract constructs is to allow us to depict relations among different social forces in a precise, analytic manner.

Max Weber (1864–1920) refined this use of abstract concepts in his comparative analysis of societies. In particular, he developed and used widely the notion of *ideal type*. By this term he referred to a deliberate simplification of the complexities of the empirical world—a "one-sided accentuation . . . by the synthesis of a great many diffuse, discrete, more or less present and occasionally absent *concrete* individual phenomena, which are arranged [by the investigator] into a unified *analytical* construct. In its conceptual purity, this mental construct cannot be found anywhere in reality."[12] The investigator uses such ideal constructs to unravel and explain a variety of concrete historical situations. Weber mentioned explicitly two kinds of ideal-type constructs—"historically unique configurations," such as "rational bourgeois capitalism"; and statements concerning historical evolution, such as the Marxist laws of capitalist development.[13]

One of Weber's preoccupations was with the conditions under which industrial capitalism of the modern Western type arose and flourished. Initially he was careful to distinguish the ideal type of industrial capitalism from other forms, such as finance capitalism and colonial capitalism. The former—sometimes called high capitalism or rational bourgeois capitalism—refers to the systematic and rational organization of *production* itself. The essential features of this kind of capitalism, according to Gerth and Mills's summary of Weber, are as follows:

> [The production establishment] is based on the organization of formally free labor and the fixed plant. The owner of the plant operates at his own risk and produces commodities for anonymous and competitive markets. His

12. Max Weber, *The Methodology of the Social Sciences*, trans. and ed. Edward A. Shils and Henry A. Finch (Glencoe, Ill.: Free Press, 1949), pp. 90, 93. Emphasis in original.

13. Ibid., pp. 93, 101–3.

operations are usually controlled rationally by a constant balancing of costs and returns. All elements, including his own entrepreneurial services, are brought to book as items in the balance of his accounts.[14]

Having defined industrial capitalism, Weber sought to identify the historical conditions that gave rise to it and that are most conducive to its continuing existence. On the one side, he rejected explanations that the rise of capitalism could be explained by, for example, the increase of population or the influx of precious metals into Western Europe, pointing out that other parts of the world had experienced these phenomena without developing capitalism.[15] On the more positive side, one of his well-known arguments is that the rise of ascetic Protestantism, especially Calvinism, established social and psychological conditions conducive to this form of capitalism. Another argument is that bureaucracy provides the most rational form of social organization for perpetuating industrial capitalism. We shall return to both these arguments later.[16] At present we shall stay with the general theme of integration. What institutional structures are most permissive for industrial capitalism but at the same time regulate it?

Weber found many of these structures in the political-legal complex. Several property arrangements, for instance, are particularly advantageous for the existence of industrial capitalism: (a) Workers should not own their jobs, as they did (or almost did) under certain guild systems. This makes for sluggish labor turnover and for popular resistance to innovation. (b) Managers should not own their workers. Under conditions of slavery, for instance, managers are forced to support—however minimally—slaves' families, and they are unable to lay off slaves during slack seasons. From the standpoint of capitalist production, this is "irrational." (c) Workers should not own the means of production—tools, raw materials, and the like. This inhibits managers' ability to reallocate them as the occasion demands and restricts their ability to discipline the workers. All ownership of the means of production should be in the hands of those who decide production matters. (d) Capitalists should not own or control opportunities for profit in the market. This introduces monopolistic rigidities into the exchange system.[17] What did Weber mean by such ob-

14. H.H. Gerth and C. Wright Mills, trans. and eds., *From Max Weber* (New York: Oxford University Press, 1958), pp. 67–68.

15. Max Weber, *General Economic History*, trans. Frank H. Knight (Glencoe, Ill.: Free Press, 1950), pp. 352–57.

16. Below, pp. 46–51, 111–12.

17. For a full development of these themes, see Max Weber, *Economy and Society*, eds. Guenther Roth and Claus Wittich, 3 vols. (New York: Bedminster Press, 1968), 1:107–65.

servations? Economists have long insisted on the importance of the mobility of resources in a capitalist economy. Weber was specifying some of the institutional conditions under which maximum mobility is both permitted and regulated.

Weber also stressed the political-legal regulation of money and exchange. Above all, rational capitalism cannot flourish unless the political authority guarantees a money supply with relatively stable values. As to the *type* of medium of exchange, Weber saw the advantage of a generalized money currency (as opposed to payments in kind, which are limited to specific transactions), since currency allows for expansion of the market and creation of credit. Finally, Weber, like Durkheim, stressed the importance of a legal framework to guarantee the validity of contracts, and a functioning administrative and judicial system to enforce legal regulations.

Weber never developed his economic sociology into a full theoretical system. He instead remained at the level of generating insights about the pattern of institutional conditions that surround important historical phenomena. Even so, it is possible to see his distinctive contribution to economic sociology. Unlike traditional economists, he was not interested in the regularities produced *within* the capitalist system of production (regularities such as the business cycle), but in establishing the important background institutional conditions under which the capitalist system itself—and its regularities—could exist.

SOCIOLOGICAL ASPECTS OF ECONOMIC LIFE AS REVEALED IN ANTHROPOLOGICAL THOUGHT

The figures we have so far treated focused on economic activity in complicated civilizations (though Spencer and Durkheim referred to homogeneous societies). In such civilizations we can observe structurally distinct economic forms (such as firms, banks, and markets) and records of distinct transactions (such as books of accounts, bank deposits, and price payments). The separate study of economic activities—and their relations to other activities—is facilitated in complex societies because these activities are highly visible. The anthropologist studying simple societies lacks that advantage. Any activity he observes is likely to be simultaneously and indistinguishably economic, religious, political, and familial. This creates serious problems for the analytically separate study of economic life in such societies. Or, as Firth has put the problem,

> The principles of economics which are truly general or universal in their application are few. Most of those which purport to be general have been

> constructed primarily within the framework of ideas of an industrial, capitalist system. This means a machine technology, a monetary medium of exchange, an elaborate credit system using stocks and shares and banking institutions, developed private enterprise, and a social structure of an individualistic, Western kind. The anthropologist struggles with a diversity of types. Many are peasant systems, with money used for a limited range of transactions, a simple technology with hardly any machinery, and methods of enterprise, cooperation, credit, and income-getting very different from those in a Western economy. Some are truly primitive, with no monetary medium at all to facilitate the processes of exchange, distribution, and storage of wealth. . . . Without money there is no simple means of reckoning prices. Even where money is used, its limited range inhibits easy measurement of economic relations.[18]

In the past half-century a number of anthropological investigations have revealed that economic activities in simple societies are embedded in and guided by principles of chieftainship, clanship, and kinship. Let us review a few.

In 1922 Bronislaw Malinowski (1884–1942) published a path-breaking study of economic activity among the native tribes of the Melanesian New Guinea archipelagoes.[19] In both production and exchange he saw kinship and chieftainship as critical in inducing individuals to undertake specific kinds of economic activity. In the production of a canoe, for instance, he discovered a distinctive division of labor among chief, experts, and helpers. But these individuals did not donate labor for specific and proportional wage payments; rather, the aim of economic activity was "providing the chief or head man with the title of ownership of a canoe, and his whole community with its use."[20] In other spheres of production,

> Communal labour is . . . based upon the duties of . . . relatives-in-law. That is, a man's relatives-in-law have to assist him, whenever he needs their cooperation. In the case of a chief, there is an assistance on a grand scale, and whole villages will turn out. In the case of a commoner, only a few people will help. There is always a distribution of food after the work has been done, but this can hardly be considered as payment, for it is not proportional to the work each individual does.[21]

On the basis of these observations, Malinowski developed a criticism of traditional Western views concerning economic motivation.

18. Raymond Firth, *Elements of Social Organization*, 3rd ed. (London: Tavistock Publications, 1971), pp. 122–23.

19. Bronislaw Malinowski, *Argonauts of the Western Pacific* (London: Routledge & Kegan Paul, 1922).

20. Ibid., p. 158.

21. Ibid., p. 160.

Malinowski also stressed the integrative significance of magic for economic activities. The construction of a canoe, again, is accompanied at every stage by magical rituals. Malinowski interpreted this magic as a kind of supplementary force to well-exercised craftsmanship, supplying "the psychological influence, which keeps people confident about the success of the labour, and provides them with a sort of natural leader."[22]

The impingement of noneconomic variables appears even more clearly in the realm of exchange. Malinowski identified forms such as the pure gift, which usually involves presents (without expectation of return) between husband and wife, and between parents and children. Even forms of exchange that involve payment for services rendered are strictly regulated by custom. In still other cases individuals traded material goods for noneconomic items such as privileges and titles.[23] As Malinowski repeatedly pointed out, conventional supply and demand theory cannot account for such patterns of exchange.

A few years after the appearance of Malinowski's monograph, Marcel Mauss (1872–1950), Durkheim's student and collaborator, produced a small volume entitled *The Gift,* in which he surveyed a vast anthropological literature on ceremonial exchange patterns.[24] In such exchange Mauss observed binding obligations—on the giver to give, on the receiver to receive, and on the receiver to reciprocate (though the timing and exact amount of the return gift was open to variation). Mauss, like Malinowski, found it impossible to interpret these traditional exchanges in purely rational economic terms. Instead he emphasized the gift as a symbolic binding-together of a kinship unit or tribe.[25] Moreover, Mauss stressed the "total" character of these primitive phenomena:

> These phenomena are at once legal, economic, religious, aesthetic . . . and so on. They are legal in that they concern individual and collective rights, organized and diffuse morality. . . . They are at once political and domestic, being of interest both to classes and to clans and families. They are religious; they concern true religion, animism, magic, and diffuse religious mentality. They are economic, for the notions of value, utility, interest, luxury, wealth, acquisition, accumulation, consumption and liberal and sumptuous expenditure are all present. . . . Moreover, these institutions have an important aesthetic side. . . . Nothing in our opinion is more urgent or promising than research into "total" social phenomena.[26]

22. Ibid., p. 116.

23. Ibid., pp. 177–86.

24. Marcel Mauss, *The Gift*, trans. Ian Cunnison (Glencoe, Ill.: Free Press, 1954).

25. Ibid., pp. 70–71.

26. Ibid., pp. 76–78.

In his monographs on the Maori of New Zealand and the Tikopia,[27] Firth organized his discussion around traditional economic categories of division of labor, income, capital, distribution, and rational calculation; but he also showed how these activities were conditioned by the dynamics of chieftainship, kinship, magic, and prestige systems. In a more recent work on the economic structure of the Malay fishing industry,[28] he demonstrated how certain spheres of economic activity, especially marketing and credit, lend themselves to technical economic analysis, whereas other spheres, such as production and labor supply, are strongly influenced by familial, religious, and other noneconomic variables.

In the past decade or two, some economic anthropologists have continued their interest in analyzing patterns of production and exchange in preindustrial, even premonetary societies.[29] The horizons of others have expanded, however, in two ways, both involving a more dynamic mode of analysis. First, researchers have focused attention on the impact of colonial domination on indigenous social structures. Geertz's studies of Indonesia, for example, trace several centuries of Dutch colonial practices of discouraging native commerce and industry and simultaneously superimposing large-scale commercial agriculture—directed by and profiting the Dutch. He showed how these practices pushed the native population into a pattern of fragmented, labor-intensive subsistence farming that absorbed the increasing population rather than freeing it for employment in an indigenous, developing commercial and industrial sector.[30] Second, researchers have devoted attention to patterns of social change associated with economic development—especially at microscopic levels—in postcolonial societies. Epstein, for example, studied the different impact of irrigation on the economic and social organization of two villages in South India. In one it consolidated traditional farming patterns and initiated little sociocultural change, while in the other it diversified its occupational structure, bringing it into a larger regional economic and political network, undermining many of the ritual patterns of caste inter-

27. Raymond Firth, *Economics of the New Zealand Maori*, rev. ed (Wellington, New Zealand: Owen, 1959); *Primitive Polynesian Economy*, 2nd ed. (London: Routledge & Kegan Paul, 1965).

28. Raymond Firth, *Malay Fishermen: Their Peasant Economy*, 3rd ed., rev. and enlarged (London: Routledge & Kegan Paul, 1966).

29. Among the most notable of these contributions are Marshall Sahlins, *Stone Age Economics* (Chicago: Aldine, 1972), pp. 185–275, and Andrew Strathern, *The Rope of Moka: Big-men and Ceremonial Exchange in Mount Hagen, New Guinea* (Cambridge: Cambridge University Press, 1971).

30. Clifford Geertz, *Agricultural Involution: The Process of Ecological Change in Indonesia* (Berkeley: University of California Press, 1963).

action, and weakening its extended kinship system.[31] These new types of research in economic anthropology resemble the research conducted by other social scientists—sociologists and agricultural economists, for example—on the developing societies.[32]

A FEW RECENT TRENDS IN ECONOMICS AND SOCIOLOGY

Economics

1. Welfare economics. The life sciences (biology, bacteriology, and so on) concern the functioning of the organism, not as it "ought to be" but as it "is." Medicine, on the other hand, is concerned with the "ought" of preserving and improving the health of the organism by applying the laws generated by the life sciences. Similarly, economics can be considered as a relatively "value-free" study of the production, distribution, and exchange of scarce goods and services. But welfare economics—which has been a subject of increasing interest in recent decades—concerns the application of economic principles at the policy level to optimize the welfare of the individual and the community. It is the "theory of how and by what criteria economists and policy-makers make or ought to make their choices between alternative policies and between good and bad institutions."[33] Presumably, welfare economists should advise on tax policy and other public issues on the basis of economic principles.

In principle, this program for welfare economics leads directly into the complex interaction of economic, political, religious, and other variables that arise in connection with practical social policy. In practice, however, welfare economists have seldom raised questions relating to this interaction. Many have taken an interest only in the effects on an individual's welfare that result from changes in his economic environment alone.[34] Many have been preoccupied with *potentially* relevant sociologi-

31. T. Scarlett Epstein, *Economic Development and Social Change in South India* (Manchester: Manchester University Press, 1962).

32. For an extended discussion of issues in contemporary economic anthropology, see George Dalton, "Theoretical Issues in Economic Anthropology," in his *Economic Anthropology and Development: Essays in Tribal and Peasant Economies* (New York: Basic Books, 1971), pp. 70–119.

33. Kenneth J. Arrow and Tibor Scitovsky, eds., *Readings in Welfare Economics* (London: Allen & Unwin, 1969), p. 1.

34. This assumption is central to the welfare theory of Abram Bergson. See Jerome Rothenberg, *The Measurement of Social Welfare* (Englewood Cliffs, N.J.: Prentice-Hall, 1961), pp. 9–10.

cal questions: How is it possible to measure economic welfare? How is it possible to compare one individual's satisfaction with that of another? By what principle can we generalize from individual welfare states to the welfare of the community?[35]

In the past, however, welfare economists seldom launched systematic empirical investigations of human preferences. Their policy principles were often remote from what we normally consider to be practical policy questions. In recent years, however, taking advantage of increasingly sophisticated logical and mathematical tools, they have generated a series of complex formal statements on the relations between public policy and the preferences of members of a society.[36] On the more empirical side, they have generated models for assessing, for example, different feudal and capitalist systems of ownership and production,[37] and they have made detailed assessments of medical and educational systems, patterns of taxation, military conscription, and other institutions and policies of public concern.[38] Finally, and with even more empirical emphasis, economists, sociologists, policy makers and administrators alike have attempted to generate better data on which policies might be based and assessed—efforts such as the system of planning-programming-budgeting, social experimentation, evaluation research, and social indicators of conditions relevant to the national welfare.[39]

2. *Organizational decision-making theory*. As we shall see in chapter 4, the neoclassical theory of the firm rests on several assumptions about goals, power, and knowledge. In analyzing a firm at any given time, one assumes that its goals are given and unchanging. The firm, moreover, neither controls its external environment (other firms, consumers) nor experiences internal political problems (such as conflict). Finally, classical theory is based on the assumption that the firm has full knowledge of its possible lines of behavior, and full knowledge of the consequences of each.

35. For a collection of articles on these and other issues, as well as early and modern contributions, see Arrow and Scitovsky, eds., *Readings in Welfare Economics*.

36. For a survey of these technical developments, see Armatya K. Sen, *Collective Choice and Social Welfare* (San Francisco: Holden-Day, 1970).

37. L.S. Shapley and Martin Shubik, "Ownership and the Production Function," in *Quarterly Journal of Economics* 81, no. 1 (Feb. 1967):88–111.

38. For a survey of such analyses, see James M. Buchanan and D. Tollison, eds., *Theory of Public Choice* (Ann Arbor: University of Michigan Press, 1972).

39. See Alice M. Rivlin, *Systematic Thinking for Social Action* (Washington: Brookings Institution, 1971), and Eleanor Sheldon and Wilbert E. Moore, eds., *Social Indicators* (New York: Russell Sage, 1968).

In any empirical situation these assumptions frequently break down. Businessmen in firms change their goals, they exercise power, and they lack knowledge. The theory of imperfect competition, as we saw, incorporated formally into economic theory those situations in which the firm controls output and prices. Modern organizational decision-making theorists have relaxed many of the remaining classical assumptions. They have identified situations in which firms (and other organizations) search for new information, change their goals, and experience internal conflict. Furthermore, these theorists have brought a powerful new technique—computer simulation—to bear on the understanding and prediction of a firm's behavior.[40]

3. Game theory. In another way, the mathematical theory of games also modifies classical economic assumptions regarding goals, power, and knowledge. The game theorist sees two or more persons in interaction, each wishing to maximize gains or minimize losses. Furthermore, neither actor can fully predict the way in which the other is going to behave, nor is he able to control the other's behavior. Using such assumptions, game theorists have created complicated models of behavior based on different strategies, different conditions of winning and losing, different conditions of competition and cooperation, and so on. The application of game theory to economics has been most evident in the fields of imperfect competition, labor relations, decision making and organizational theory, and international trade.[41]

4. Economists have turned to noneconomic variables in labor economics, the economics of consumption, and the economics of growth. We shall mention these developments later.

5. Grants economy. A small number of economists, headed by Boulding, have argued that the notion of two-way exchange in a market setting—a notion that has dominated economics since the time of Adam Smith—is insufficient for the study of economic life. It must be supplemented by the systematic study of grants, or one-way transfers, which take forms such as charity, redistribution through progressive taxation,

40. A summary of organizational decision-making theory and research may be found in Donald W. Taylor, "Decision-Making and Problem-Solving," and Julian Feldman and Herschel E. Kanter, "Organizational Decision-Making," both in James G. March, ed., *Handbook of Organizations* (Chicago: Rand McNally, 1965), pp. 48–86, 614–49.

41. For economic applications see Martin Shubik, ed., *Essays in Mathematical Economics in Honor of Oskar Morgenstern* (Princeton: Princeton University Press, 1967); for applications in political and social settings, see Martin Shubik, ed., *Game Theory and Related Approaches to Social Behavior* (New York: John Wiley, 1964); for a series of psychological experiments on economic behavior which make use of game theory, see Lawrence E. Fouraker and Sidney Siegel, *Bargaining Behavior* (New York: McGraw-Hill, 1963).

subsidy, and even redistribution within integrative groups like the family. Such processes, they have insisted, are as important as they are neglected in complex industrial societies. The study of grants, moreover, focuses attention on processes in noneconomic settings such as governments and stratification systems.[42]

6. Radical economics. While the 1960s was characterized mainly by the continued development of economics along positivistic and quantitatively oriented lines, a number of voices of protest were heard. The most vocal of these came from a somewhat heterogeneous group of economists who expressed profound concern with evident evils of the capitalist economy—evils such as maldistribution of wealth both within the society and among societies, militarism, and racism—and criticized conventional economists for their insensitivity to, indeed participation in, these evils. The movement for a radical economics has reinvigorated certain interests long associated with Marxist economics and has heightened attention to issues such as the international political dimensions of economic development, the costs of economic exploitation of resources in terms of the "quality of life," and the systemic features of polity, society, and economy that perpetuate patterns of inequality in income and resources.[43]

Sociology

1. Industrial sociology. In the mid-1920s investigators conducted a number of experiments on productivity at the Hawthorne Works of the Western Electric Company in Chicago. Initially these experiments concerned the effects of lighting, rest periods, and so on, on work performance. During the course of the experiments, however, it became apparent to the investigators that these physical factors were not nearly so important in fostering high morale and productivity as various "human factors" —such as receiving status and being allowed to express grievances to a patient and responsive authority.[44]

Soon a school of thought developed—associated originally with Elton

42. See Kenneth E. Boulding, Martin Pfaff, and Anita Pfaff, eds., *Transfers in an Urbanized Economy* (Belmont, Ca.: Wadsworth, 1973); Kenneth Boulding and Martin Pfaff, eds., *Redistribution to the Rich and Poor* (Belmont, Ca.: Wadsworth, 1972); Kenneth Boulding, *The Economy of Love and Fear* (Belmont, Ca.: Wadsworth, 1973).

43. For two assessments of radical economics, see Martin Bronfenbrenner, "Radical Economics in America, 1970," *Journal of Economic Literature* 8, no. 3 (Sept. 1970):747–66; and Assar Lindbeck, *The Political Economy of the New Left: An Outsider's View* (New York: Harper & Row, 1971).

44. A summary of the Western Electric researches may be found in F.J. Roethlisberger, *Management and Morale* (Cambridge, Mass.: Harvard University Press, 1950).

Mayo, T. North Whitehead, and Fritz J. Roethlisberger at Harvard. Known as the "human relations" approach because of its emphasis, this school came to be the core of the field of industrial sociology, which grew rapidly thereafter, with the establishment of centers at various universities around the country. In the past two decades industrial sociology has developed into a subfield of its own, no longer especially identified with the human relations approach from which it originally grew. We shall discuss much of the research of this branch of sociology later.

2. Various other subfields of sociology have contributed to the development of economic sociology in the recent decades—the sociology of occupations, formal organizations, leisure, stratification, and modernization. We shall also consider some of their findings in subsequent chapters.

3. *Radical sociology*. As in economics, one of the manifestations of the protest movements of the 1960s was a movement to radicalize sociology—that is, to change its mission to one of working toward radical social change of society's institutions. While probably less productive of theoretical and empirical research than their counterparts in economics,[45] radical sociologists nevertheless contributed to the sensitization of sociologists and others to the human costs of inequality, racial and sexual discrimination, poverty, and war.

45. Paul Samuelson remarked, for example, on the "serious research movement" among radical economists. ("Foreword" to Lindbeck, *Political Economy of the New Left*, p. xvii), whereas Howard S. Becker and Irving Louis Horowitz, in a sympathetic review, observed that "for all the stated need for a more radical sociology, we find mostly programmatic statements and little substantive work that could reasonably be so labeled." ("Radical Politics and Sociological Research: Observations on Methodology and Ideology," *American Journal of Sociology* 78, no. 1 [July 1972]:61.) For a collection of essays in radical sociology, see David Colfax and Jack L. Roach, eds., *Radical Sociology* (New York: Basic Books, 1971).

CHAPTER 2
ECONOMICS, SOCIOLOGY, AND ECONOMIC SOCIOLOGY

The simplest way to characterize a discipline is to depict its subject matter concretely. Thus, economists may be described as spending their time in the study of businessmen and organizations as they produce and market commodities, and consumers as they buy and use these commodities. Political scientists study legislatures and governmental bureaucracies, voters' behavior, parties' campaigning tactics, and the like. The subject matter of sociology is very diffuse, covering behavior in families, hospitals, educational institutions, street-corner gangs, experimental small groups, armies, and religious revivals, to name only a few. To describe a social science concretely, however, does not yield a very scientific account, since it usually ends up as a list of topics that, over a long period, have interested those who call themselves economists, sociologists, or whatever. Such a description is likely to change, moreover, as new problems make their appearance in society—problems such as imperfect competition, racial injustice, mental illness, and poverty.

A more *analytic* way of describing and comparing disciplines is to ask how knowledge is generated and organized in each. This, in turn, breaks down into a number of more specific criteria:

First, it is necessary to specify what aspect of the concrete subject matter preoccupies the investigators. Economists are not interested in every aspect of the behavior of businessmen; they wish to discover specifically why businessmen produce different quantities of commodities at different times, why they charge different prices at different times, and so on. Sociologists are not interested in every aspect of the family; they focus on patterns of rights and obligations of family members, changes in the rates of family formation and dissolution, differences in fathers' and sons' career patterns, and so on. By specifying these aspects, we identify the distinctive *things to be explained, scientific problems,* or *dependent variables* of a discipline.

Second, it is necessary to specify what each discipline treats as the distinctive *causes* (determinants, factors, conditions) of variation in the dependent variables. In determining how much of a given commodity will be produced at a given price, the economist asks how much of the commodity the consumers are demanding, how much the businessman has to pay for raw materials and labor to produce the commodity, and how his competitors are behaving. In accounting for variations in divorce rates, the sociologist turns to the society's level of urbanization and industrialization; its levels of interreligious, interethnic, and interclass marriage; and its laws affecting divorce. In this search for associated conditions, the social scientist attempts to identify distinctive *independent variables.*

The focus of a scientific discipline can be specified by listing the dependent and independent variables that preoccupy its investigators. But these lists of variables do not tell the whole story. It is necessary, third, to specify the ways in which a discipline imposes a *logical ordering* on its variables. Indeed, merely by distinguishing between dependent and independent variables, we elicit one instance of logical ordering—that is, specifying which variables are to be viewed as effects and which as causes. On the basis of such ordering, various *hypotheses*—statements of the conditions under which dependent variables may be expected to vary—can be formulated. A more complex kind of ordering occurs when a number of hypotheses are combined into an organized system (often called a *model*). Suppose, for example, the economist is equipped with three types of hypotheses: that private investment influences aggregate employment in specific ways, that government spending influences employment in other ways, and that foreign trade influences it in still other ways. A model is created when the economist states the interactions among these determinants, all in relation to employment, in a logically rigorous way (for example, in the form of simultaneous equations).

Logical ordering does not end with the building of models. These models are invariably embedded in a number of definitions, assumptions, postulates, and general images of persons and their environment. The hypothesis that investment creates a higher level of employment, for example, rests on the psychological assumption that laborers are motivated to respond positively to wage offers extended by employers. Such definitions, assumptions, postulates, and images constitute the *theoretical framework* of a scientific discipline. Within this framework the specific hypotheses and models "make sense." Or, to put it more strongly, the hypotheses and models should be *derived,* as rigorously as possible, from the theoretical framework.

To compare economics and sociology, we shall now proceed to characterize each according to these criteria. Although many distinctions between the two fields are fairly clear, some overlapping between them exists. Furthermore, the analytic distinctions we make are bound to be controversial. All who call themselves economists (econometricians, labor economists, institutional economists, economic historians) do not agree about the precise nature of economics; all who call themselves sociologists (demographers, historians of social thought, social psychologists, and radical sociologists) are even more divided about the character of their own field.

ECONOMICS AS A DISCIPLINE

A well-known text on the subject provides an introductory description of economics as

> the study of how men and society end up *choosing,* with or without the use of money, to employ scarce productive resources that could have alternative uses, to produce various commodities and distribute them for consumption, now or in the future, among various people and groups in society. It analyzes the costs and benefits of improving patterns of resource allocation.[1]

From this definition let us build a statement of dependent variables, independent variables, and relations among these variables in economics.

Dependent Variables

A first set of dependent variables is found in the term *commodities.* What is the level of the total production of goods and services in a society? What different kinds of commodities (shoes, guns, butter) are produced, by whom, and in what proportions? Economists thus attempt to account for variations in the level and composition of production.

A second set of dependent variables is found in the term *scarce productive resources.* Goods and services are produced by the application

1. Paul A. Samuelson, *Economics,* 9th ed. (New York: McGraw-Hill, 1973), p. 3. Emphasis in original. A more concise definition is given by Bronfenbrenner: "Economics is the systematic study of social adjustment to, and management of, the scarcity of goods and resources." Martin Bronfenbrenner, "A 'Middlebrow' introduction to Economic Methodology," in *The Structure of Economic Science: Essays on Methodology,* ed. Sherman Roy Krupp (Englewood Cliffs, N.J.: Prentice-Hall, 1966), p. 6.

of the following factors of production: (1) land, or the state of the natural resources, cultural values, and technical knowledge; (2) labor, or the level of motivation and skill of human beings; (3) capital, or the level of resources available for future production rather than immediate consumption; and (4) organization, or the principles of combination and recombination of the other factors. Organization involves the operation of institutions such as property and contract as well as the activity of entrepreneurs. Economists are thus interested in explaining the levels and relative proportions of these resources in productive use, and the techniques by which they are combined.

A third set of dependent variables is indicated by the term *distribute*. Which individuals and groups receive the goods and services generated in the productive process? Or, to put the question in terms of payments, what is the distribution of income generated in the economic process?

The basic dependent variables in economics are production, techniques of organizing resources, and distribution of income shares. In the Keynesian system, for example, the dependent variables are the volume of employment (or the proportion of available labor in productive use at any given time) and the national income (or the total level of production).[2] Even in some of the subfields of economics, the problems posed turn out to be instances of the basic dependent variables. In the study of labor economics, for instance, the focus is on "the markets in which labor as a distinguishable productive service is bought and sold."

> [Labor economics] attempts to distinguish the economic relations of substitutability and complementarity that hold between individual laborers, between labor groups, and between labor and other factors of production in order to understand and to explain how these economic influences affect the operation of labor markets.[3]

This boils down to a focus on the patterns of utilization, allocation, combination, and differential rewards of labor as a scarce resource.

Independent Variables

How are the level and composition of production, the allocation of resources, and the distribution of income determined? In the broad comparative sweep these may be determined by religious decree, custom, politi-

2. J.M. Keynes, *The General Theory of Employment, Interest, and Money* (New York: Harcourt Brace, 1936), p. 245.

3. C. Glyn Williams, *Labor Economics* (New York: John Wiley, 1970), p. 8.

cal directive, or a variety of other sanctions. Formal economic analysis, however, has traditionally stressed the forces of supply and demand in the market as the immediate independent variables. For any given commodity a person will be willing to buy much if it costs little, little if it costs much. The producer of this commodity will be willing to supply much if the price is high, little if the price is low. The price of the commodity falls at that point where the demand curve and the supply curve intersect.

This supply-demand principle is used to account for the behavior of all the dependent variables. The level and composition of production depend on the existing supply and demand conditions for products; the level and composition of the factors of production depend on the same kinds of conditions for them; and finally, the proportions of income received by different individuals and groups depend on the supply and demand conditions governing the relations among economic agents.

Relations among Variables

One of the most famous models in economics concerns the prediction of the quantity of a given commodity that an individual firm will produce under conditions of perfect competition. Given a certain level of demand, the firm can expect to receive a given price (revenue) for each item it produces. But the firm itself has to pay for the factors it utilizes in production. These costs determine the conditions of supplying its commodity to consumers. By a series of constructions, economists have built a model that predicts that the firm will produce that quantity of a commodity at which the *cost* of producing the extra unit of the commodity (marginal cost) equals the *revenue* that it will receive for that extra unit (marginal revenue). Basically, this model says that the value of the dependent variable (quantity of the commodity produced by a firm) is a function of the value of two sets of independent variables (demand and supply).

Turning to the analysis of aggregates, the Keynesian model identifies the independent variables—in the first instance—as the propensity to consume, the schedule of the marginal efficiency of capital, and the rate of interest.[4] The propensity to consume is a demand category; the marginal efficiency of capital rests on expectations about profits to be returned for investments; and the rate of interest rests on the supply of money and the demand for liquidity. By manipulating the values of these independent variables, Keynes established a set of predictions leading to unemployment of a society's resources and reduction of its national product (dependent variables). This is the essence of the Keynesian equilibrium

4. Keynes, *The General Theory*, p. 245.

model. Other economic models, while differing in content and predicted outcomes, have the same formal characteristics.[5]

The Importance of "Givens" in Economic Analysis

In these illustrative economic models the behavior of various dependent variables—prices, level of production, etc.—rests on the operation of the economic forces of supply and demand. But in the real world things are not so simple. Many variables—economic, political, legal, religious—affect prices and production, and a complete picture of economic life would have to incorporate these variables into economic models. How do economists deal with this empirical complexity? A common method is to realize that while noneconomic variables affect supply and demand conditions, it is necessary *for purposes of analysis* to assume that these variables do not change. This is the meaning of the statement, frequently encountered in economists' writings, that economic analysis takes institutions and tastes as given. They constitute the "operating conditions of the . . . economic system,"[6] but economists regard these processes as transpiring *within* these given conditions.

To illustrate: In constructing his equilibrium system, Keynes considered several things as given: the existing skill of the labor force, the existing equipment, the existing technology, the existing degree of competition, the existing tastes of the consumer, the existing attitudes of people toward work, and the existing social structure.[7] All these, if they varied, would affect the independent variables (e.g., the propensity to consume and the marginal efficiency of capital) and through them the dependent variables (employment and national income); but they were assumed not to vary.

Similarly, in wage analysis, a whole array of economic and noneconomic variables affects wage differentials:

> Varying rates of population growth are an important factor in geographic differentials. Industrial differentials are to be explained, in large measure, by the nature of the industry . . . and by the policies and bargaining strength of the union or unions with jurisdiction in the industry. Inter-plant differentials locally for the same type and grade of labor seem to be the result mainly of four factors: industry differentials, differences in management and plant

5. William J. Baumol, "Economic Models and Mathematics," and Kenneth E. Boulding, "The Verifiability of Economic Images," in *Structure of Economic Science*, ed. Krupp, pp. 88–101, 129–41.

6. Wassily Leontief, "Mathematics in Economics," in *Essays in Economics: Theories and Theorizing* (New York: Oxford University Press, 1966), p. 23.

7. Keynes, *The General Theory*, p. 245.

efficiency, differences in employer wage policies, and the combination of company hiring policies and worker job behavior. Custom is also important.[8]

For any specific model of wage differentials, however, only a few of these factors are incorporated;[9] the others are considered to be either unimportant or unvarying.

With respect to the issue of givens, economic analysis faces a dilemma: whether to create theoretically advanced models while oversimplifying the noneconomic world or to take account of the complexity of the noneconomic world while sacrificing theoretical generality. Economists have most often chosen the first route and have generated more significant results than when they have chosen the second; occasionally, however, economists and others wonder whether, in so doing, they have systematically ignored many interesting and important features of social life. To choose the most recent example of such soul searching, Galbraith complained in his presidential address to the American Economic Association that neoclassical and neo-Keynsian economic frameworks are incapable of analyzing the concentration of planning and power in the modern American economy, primarily because they have focused too much on market processes and have made economics "a nonpolitical subject."[10]

One of the most important givens in traditional economic analysis is the postulate of economic rationality: If an individual is presented with a situation of choice in an economic setting, he will maximize his economic position; likewise, a firm will "choose the [input-output combination] which maximizes the difference between its total costs and revenue."[11] Such a postulate is clearly inadequate on many counts—peo-

8. Richard A. Lester, *Labor and Industrial Relations: A General Analysis* (New York: Macmillan, 1951), p. 68.

9. The noneconomic variable that is most often incorporated into models of wage determination is the political behavior of labor unions. See, for example, Allen M. Cartter and F. Ray Marshall, *Labor Economics*, rev. ed. (Homewood, Ill.: Irwin-Dorsey, 1972), chaps. 10, 12, 13.

10. John K. Galbraith, "Power and the Useful Economist," *American Economic Review* 63, no. 1 (March, 1973):1–12. See also Benjamin Ward, "Institutions and Economic Analysis," in *Structure of Economic Science*, ed. Krupp, pp. 187–92; and the exchange of views between Robert L. Heilbronner ("On the Limited 'Relevance' of Economics") and Robert M. Solow ("Science and Ideology in Economics") in Daniel Bell and Irving Kristol, eds., *Capitalism Today* (New York: New American Library, 1971), pp. 98–127. One of the major thrusts of the radical economists' critique is that traditional economic analysis has encouraged economists to ignore or gloss over many salient evils of capitalist society.

11. Leontief, "Mathematics in Economics," in *Essays in Economics*, p. 24. For a recent discussion of the utility function and "economic man," see Jerome Rothenberg, "Values and Value Theory in Economics," in *Structure of Economic Society*, ed. Krupp, pp. 227–33.

ple are ignorant of their environment, they make mistakes, and they sometimes live by habit and rule of thumb rather than calculation. Furthermore, because the social world is characterized by the *interplay* of so many noneconomic and economic variables, no one set of variables completely dominates in any social setting.

Should we then abandon the notion of economic rationality? Perhaps not; at least four meanings of economic rationality are current, and some are more acceptable than others.

1. The least acceptable meaning of economic rationality is the argument that, as a matter of psychological fact, material satisfactions are the sole motiviating factor in human existence, and that rational choices in relation to material satisfactions dominate all other considerations. This version has been discredited.

2. If it is argued that, although economic rationality may not be the *whole* of human psychology people do behave rationally when faced with situations of relative scarcity, the notion becomes less objectionable. Although people in all societies economize, the number and kinds of situations in which they economize are highly variable. For example, people in a simple society might display calculation in allocating resources to produce agricultural goods; but in exchanging these goods they might rely on highly traditionalized, "uneconomical" gift-giving to kinsmen and tribesmen. Regarded in this way, economic rationality itself is a dependent variable rather than a fixed postulate and may be expected to have a variety of manifestations. On the basis of his study of the behavior of African migrant laborers in the Rhodesias, Barber concluded that

> [The African's economic rationality] . . . is a rationality which can only be understood within the context of the dualistic economic structure within which he lives. If he is a wage-earner, he is well-advised—as long as the real wage obtainable from employment in the money economy remains at its traditional level—to keep a "foot in two camps" by moving between the money and the indigenous economies. He dare not risk a sacrifice in the output of the subsistence agricultural community which follow from his continuous absence. This situation recommends perpetuation of the migratory system—an arrangement which is both rational and economic, even though it may not appear so to the European employer or to an outside observer who expects rational economic behavior to take the same form in both the underdeveloped and the Western economies.[12]

Another advantage of treating rationality as a variable rather than a principle is that the investigator may inquire into the conditions under which it is likely to develop. Udy, in a comparative study of thirty-four nonindustrial societies, found his measure of rationality to be highly correlated with variables such as the specificity of organizational roles, the

12. William J. Barber, "Economic Rationality and Behavior Patterns in an Underdeveloped Area: A Case Study of African Economic Behavior in the Rhodesias," *Economic Development and Cultural Change* 8, no. 3 (April, 1960):251.

independence of an organization from its social setting, and the lack of traditional ascriptive demands.[13]

3. If an economist uses the notion of economic rationality explicitly as a device to aid investigation, he presents a strong argument in its favor. He advances no particular psychological theories or existential claims but uses the notion to come to terms with the enormous motivational variability of the empirical world, and to proceed *as if* the only independent variables were measurable changes in price and income. In so treating rationality, the analyst should also assume that his simplification is subject to revision or rejection if it seems unhelpful in analyzing the scientific problems he faces. In addition, he should be aware of knowledge accumulated in neighboring disciplines that throws light or doubt upon the particular version of rationality he has assumed.[14]

4. A final way of treating economic rationality is to consider it as an institutionalized value. Rationality now becomes something more than a psychological postulate; it is a standard of behavior to which people conform or from which they deviate. Thus in the American business firm it is not only the businessman's personal desire for profits but also the threat of negative social sanctions (for example, ridicule or loss of position) that makes him follow the criteria of efficiency and cost-reduction. The sociologist must insist on retaining this social meaning of economic rationality, for it lies at the heart of one of his central variables—social control.

SOCIOLOGY AS A DISCIPLINE

In sociology the task of specifying variables and relations is more difficult than in economics. Widespread disagreement among sociologists about the fundamental problems and concepts of their discipline has led to a mushrooming of variables and theories. Because of this superabundance, sociological analysts are less often able to present simple and coherent models; instead, analysis often focuses on categorizing social facts. Our analytic characterization of sociology must of necessity be approximate and oversimplified.

Dependent Variables

As we have just seen economics typically deals with behavior oriented toward the employment and allocation of scarce resources. This

13. Stanley Udy, "Administrative Rationality, Social Setting, and Organizational Development," *American Journal of Sociology* 68, no. 3 (Nov., 1962):299–308.

14. Thus it seems an overstatement for Duncan Black to argue that ". . . Economic Science itself does not . . . inquire by what events in the realm of fact . . . preference schedules have come to be what they are." "The Unity of Political and Economic Sciences," in *Game Theory and Related Approaches to Social Behavior*, ed. Martin Shubik (New York: John Wiley, 1964), p. 116. This may be an accurate characterization of economists' behavior, but if accepted as a normative statement, it would seem deliberately to encourage a posture of blindness toward knowledge in other fields that might influence the formulation of preference schedules.

behavior, furthermore, can be studied from the standpoint of the *individual* (for example, preferences and decision making on the part of a businessman) or in terms of the aggregated results of behavior (for example, the relations between an economy's level of savings and its rate of growth). Sociology deals with different types of behavior and a broader spectrum of behavior than economics. For that reason sociologists ask different kinds of questions. What is the scope of the sociologist's preoccupations? What does he wish to explain?

The feature of behavior that interests sociologists is its *social* aspect —that is, the fact that behavior is oriented toward other persons, groups, and institutions. This social aspect, furthermore, can be viewed from two angles: group and social structure. A group arises when numbers of individuals form as members of a collectivity with a more or less common and more or less purposive orientation or orientations. When studying groups, sociologists ask why individuals join groups, what influence group membership has on individual behavior, what interactive processes develops in groups, and so on. Groups may be studied at their own level, without reference to their individual members, as in the case of competition among political parties, conflict among racial groups, or status-striving among cliques. (This is analogous to the economists' studying relations among aggregated results of behavior, without reference to individuals.)

Social structure is a concept used to characterize recurrent and regularized interaction among two or more persons. The basic units of social structure are not persons as such, but selected aspects of interaction among persons, such as roles (husband-wife, politician-voter, employer-employee, businessman-consumer). The concept of person and role are analytically separate. The two concepts cut across one another. A person occupies many different roles; and a role cannot refer to a complete person, but only to selected aspects of his behavior. The concept of social structure refers to identifiable patterns of roles that are organized primarily around the fulfillment of some social function or activity—for example, religious structure, educational structure, economic structure.

Many central questions in sociology involve social structures and behavior related to them. Why are the elements of social structure patterned the way they are? Given some structure, when can conformity be expected? What are the consequences of conformity for the social structure? When can deviance from structured behavior be expected? What are the different forms of deviance, and why does one type rather than another arise?

The perspectives of group and social structure refer to different contexts of behavior, the one to organized collectivities, the other to relations among roles. Furthermore, the same behavioral phenomena can be legitimately characterized according to both perspectives. For example, a labor union can be characterized both as a group with individual members and as a system of interrelated roles—officers, shop stewards, representatives of locals, and the like—that give it structure. Whether emphasizing the group or social-structural aspect, however, sociologists are very often concerned with forces that operate, with varying degrees of effectiveness, as *social controls* over behavior. Three types of controls are particularly important:

1. *Values* legitimize the existence and importance of specific social structures and the kinds of behavior that transpire in a given social structure. The value of "free enterprise," for instance, endorses the existence of business firms organized around the institution of private property and engaged in the pursuit of private profit.
2. *Norms* are standards of conduct that regulate the interaction among individuals. The norms of contract and property law, for instance, set up obligations and prohibitions on the agents in economic transactions. As the examples show, at any given level of analysis norms are more specific than values in their control of interaction.
3. *Sanctions*—including both rewards and deprivations—involve the use of various social resources to control the behavior of personnel in social structures. Aspects of this control include the inducement of individuals to assume and perform the roles, and the control of deviance from expected role performance. Examples of sanction are coercion, ridicule, money payments, withdrawal of communication, and so on.

Finally, sociologists often focus on the individual's orientations to his social environment and on the ways these orientations affect behavior. These sociologists—referred to as social psychologists—regard people not as passive vessels through which social forces flow, but rather as more independent agents who endow their social environment with meaning, who develop attitudes and feeling about it, and who behave in terms of their own assessment of it.

To return to our original questions, the scope of the sociologist's preoccupations are several aspects of patterned, meaningful social behavior. He wishes to explain regularities and variations in individual orientations and behavior, group behavior, social structures, sanctions, norms, and values. How does he go about explaining them?

Independent Variables

By and large, sociologists find their explanatory variables by turning to those very phenomena they may, in other contexts, wish to explain. They frequently explain variations in voting behavior, for example, by reference to attitudes (whether a person is predisposed in a conservative or a liberal direction), by reference to group memberships (whether a person is a member of the American Legion), by reference to position in the social structure (whether a person is blue- or white-collar by occupation), or by reference to differential exposure to values (for instance, Catholicism). Similarly, sociologists frequently explain variations in attitudes by pointing to an individual's group memberships, to his positions in the social structure, or his cultural milieu. Some sociologists explain certain types of social structures (for example, the isolated nuclear family) by referring to other structural variables (for example, industrialization or urbanization). Others, who dispute such an explanation, point to the persistence of extended family systems in spite of industrialization (as in Japan)[15] and invoke distinctive cultural traditions to explain this persistence. And finally, sociologists often account for the content of cultural productions such as ideologies by referring to conditions in different parts of the social structure, for example to the social-class interests of those who invent or believe in those ideologies.

Relations among Variables

By comparison with sociology, economic analysis displays a paucity of explanatory variables. Furthermore, as we have seen, the typical vulnerability of economic analysis is not its inability to generate elegant, formal explanatory models, but rather the oversimplified and unrealistic character of such models as empirical explanations, given the complexity of forces impinging on the economy.

The typical point of vulnerability of sociological analysis is of a different order. For any given dependent variable in sociology, the number and kinds of conditions that potentially affect its variation are discouragingly great. An individual's ability to perform a simple task in a small-group setting is influenced most immediately by his intelligence, training, and motivation. These three immediate factors are further conditioned by his social-class background, his ordinal position in his family, the presence or absence of others in the same room when he is performing the task, the behavior of the person assigning him the task, and many other factors. When we turn to the search for conditions influencing social aggregates, such as changes in the divorce rate over the past century, the number and kinds of potential determinants are even more complex. The initial picture is one of a *multiplicity* of determinants, a *compounding* of their influences on the dependent variable, and an *indeterminacy* regarding the effect of any one determinant or several determinants in combination. The corresponding problems facing the sociologist are to *reduce* the number of determinants, to *isolate* one determinant from one another, and thereby to make precise the role of each determinant. How are these problems faced?

15. On the relations between economic structure and family structure, see below, pp. 79–87.

The general answer to this question is that the sociological investigator must impose some kind of organization on the various determinants. One of the simplest ways of organizing determinants is seen in the distinction between *independent* and *intervening* variables. A classic example will show the power of this distinction. Robert Michels, in his comparative study of political parties and trade unions,[16] was preoccupied with the problem of why large-scale organizations, even those with egalitarian ideologies, universally develop oligarchical authority systems. For Michels this problem constituted the dependent variable, or that which demanded explanation. According to Michels's account, three sets of independent variables produce oligarchy. The first is found in the technical and administrative characteristics of organizations themselves—the impossibility of direct communication and coordination of decisions by the many, with the consequence that responsibility falls into the hands of the few. The second is found in the psychological propensities of the masses to adulate and venerate leaders. The third is found in the superior oratorical, intellectual, and cultural skills of the leaders themselves.[17]

Oligarchy itself, once established, has consequences. In particular, Michels pointed out the tendency for leaders, once in power, to gain access to resources, to come to think of themselves as indispensable, and to regard their right to office as necessary and sacred. These by-products of oligarchical leadership, moreover, feed back and further consolidate the original tendencies for power to become centralized.[18] The several classes of variables identified by Michels thus constitute a set of independent, intervening, and dependent variables, as shown in Figure 1. The variables Michels chose are distinctively sociological (including social-psychological) ones. And the picture of the variables, as organized, is much simpler than a picture of the lengthy list of associations among every combined pair of variables.

The example from Michels also reveals that the distinction among independent, intervening, and dependent variables is a relative one; the status of any given variable may change according to the analytic purposes at hand. For example, the variable "oligarchical structure" is dependent with respect to "technical and administrative features"; it is independent with respect to "leaders' sense of indispensability"; and it is intervening with respect to the relation between "technical and administrative features" and "leaders' sense of indispensability." Furthermore,

16. *Political Parties: A Sociological Study of the Oligarchical Tendencies of Modern Democracy*, trans. Eden Paul and Cedar Paul (New York: Dover Publications, 1959).

17. Ibid., part 1.

18. Ibid., part 2, chap. 1, 2.

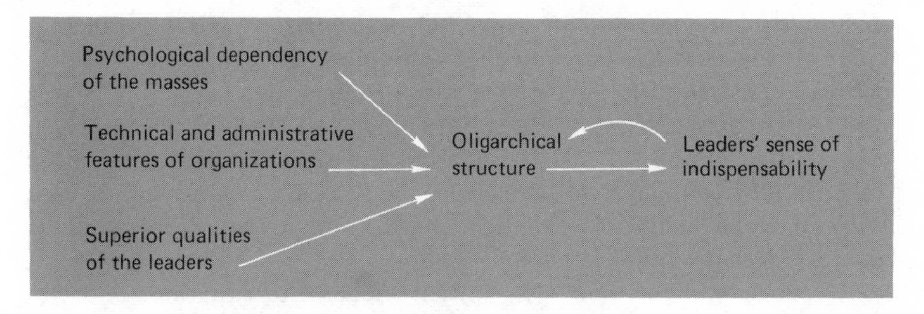

Figure 1 Variables in Michels's Theory of Oligarchy

"leaders' sense of indispensability" is both independent and dependent if we consider its feedback to the power structure. In sociological investigation, no given substantive variable can be considered as inherently independent, intervening, or dependent. Its status depends on its place in an explanatory model.

When sociologists proceed from more or less static accounts of variation to processes of adjustment and change, they bring to bear different sets of explanatory variables. Among the most important of these variables in sociology are the concepts of strain (or some similar term signifying a disequilibrium of some sort), reactions to strain, and attempts to control reactions to strain.

1. Strain. Social systems are never perfectly integrated. The sources of malintegration, moreover, may arise from outside or inside the system. Examples of externally imposed strain would be economic shortages arising from a blockade of shipping by a foreign power during a period of international hostility; or the dislocations of an underdeveloped economy occasioned by a colonial power's development of certain types of industry and not others.[19] An example of internally generated strain is the buildup of contradictions such as those envisioned by Marx in model of capital accumulation and its progressive intensification of conflict among classes. Whether generated externally or internally (or by some combination of both), strain imposes integrative problems on a social system and presses toward some form of adjustment, new forms of integration, or some sort of breakdown.

Among the many types of strain arising in social systems, the following are common: (a) Ambiguity in role expectations, in which information regarding expectations is unclear or lacking altogether. Many have cited the case of the modern American woman, whose traditional domestic duties have become uncertain, as a typical example of role ambiguity.

19. Above, p. 22.

(b) Conflict among roles, in which role expectations call for different kinds of behavior. A commonly cited example is the black doctor, whose occupational role calls for deference from others, but whose racial role traditionally has called for deference to others. (c) Discrepancies between expectations and actual social situations. An example of this would be an unemployment level of 15 percent in a society committed to high levels of employment. (d) Conflicts of values in a system, for example among different ethnic or religious groups.

2. *Reactions to strain.* The initial responses to situations of strain are expressions of dissatisfaction or discomfort on the part of those affected, responses that are frequently (but not always) further disruptive to the integration of the social system. Though the number and types of responses to strain have never been fully catalogued, they include various psychological manifestations such as addiction and mental disorders, group conflict, social movements directed at redressing imbalances and injustices, and so on.

3. *Attempts to control reactions to strain.* Given some strain and some expression of dissatisfaction, several general types of control are frequently employed to reduce the possibly disruptive consequences for the system. (a) Structuring the social situation so as to minimize strain. Examples are the institutionalization of priorities (so that conflicting expectations are ranked in a hierarchy of importance for the actor); scheduling activities (so that demands that would conflict if made simultaneously may be worked out serially); shielding evasive activity (so that illegitimate behavior is permitted so long as it does not openly disrupt the legitimately structured role-expectations); the growth of ideologies that justify certain types of deviance as "exceptions" while reaffirming dominant norms, perhaps by paying lip service to them. (b) Attempting to control reactions to strain once they have arisen. This involves the application of sanctions by various agencies of social control, such as the police and the courts.

Such is a brief and incomplete catalogue of the kinds of variables that sociologists incorporate into their explanatory models. Though the field still suffers from a shortage from theoretically adequate models, those that do exist may be classified into three types:

1. Static models, which organize one or more variables to account for some type of behavior or structural characteristic. The effort of Michels to account for the persistence of oligarchy is an example. We shall also discover numerous partially developed static sociological models to account for different types of economic behavior and economic structures as we review the empirical literature in chapters 3 and 4.

2. Process models, which refer to changes of variables *within* a social structure. Process models are used, for example, in analyzing rates of social mobility, voting rates, and certain types of social control (for in-

stance, psychotherapy, which often "rehabilitates" persons considered to be "disturbed"). In these examples the social structure is assumed to be unchanging.

3. Change models, which refer to changes of the social structure itself. For example, when attempts to contain responses to strain fail, the system may generate new structural arrangements. The movement to the new structure may be *controlled* (as when a new law is passed by the constituted authorities to meet a pressing social problem) or *uncontrolled* (as when a revolutionary party overthrows the authority and sets up a new constitution and government). The new structure, moreover, may be precarious; changes may generate pressure for even further changes. And repeated failure of social control and reform measures may result in the disintegration of the system. All these examples involve changes in the social structure.

The Problem of "Givens" in Sociological Analysis

Just as sociology—by comparison with economics—relies on a multiplicity and diversity of variables, as well as a certain looseness in organizing these variables theoretically, so also is it less precise in postulating what is given and what is variable in its explanatory models. Despite this vagueness, every sociological explanation necessarily rests on a number of unvarying assumptions, often of a psychological character. Formally these postulates resemble and serve the same purpose as postulates like economic rationality in economics. A convenient example of such a postulate in sociology is the analysis of strain and people's reactions to it. To assert that role-conflict is a source of strain is simultaneously to invoke the psychological principle that inconsistent demands are unsettling for an individual and call forth various efforts to cope with them. Such principles—like the psychological principle of the maximization of utility—no doubt have some validity but are certainly questionable on empirical grounds. In any case, in sociology as in economics, analysis must rest on some general assumptions if it is to generate manageable explanations with limited numbers of variables.

THE ANALYTIC FOCUS OF ECONOMIC SOCIOLOGY

Economic sociology is *the application of the general frame of reference, variables, and explanatory models of sociology to that complex of activities concerned with the production, distribution, exchange, and consumption of scarce goods and services.*

More concretely, this definition suggests two foci of analysis for economic sociology. The first is on economic activities alone. The economic sociologist asks how these activities are structured into roles and collectivities, by what values they are legitimized, and by what norms and sanctions they are regulated. And within economic organizations, such as the firm, he studies the status system, power and authority relations, deviance, cliques, and coalitions as these affect the economic activities of the firm. We will focus on this line of analysis in chapter 4.

The second focus is on the relations between sociological variables as they manifest themselves in economic contexts and sociological variables as they manifest themselves in noneconomic contexts. How, for example, does the structure of occupational roles articulate with the structure of family roles in an industrial society? What sorts of political conflict are generated by the economic arrangements in different societies? What kinds of class systems emerge in different kinds of economic systems? This relational focus leads to the larger issues of economic sociology—for example, public policy, labor-management conflict, and relations among economic classes—that lie in the tradition of Marxian and Weberian thought. We will focus on these issues in chapter 3.

CONCLUSION

In this chapter we have established what economic sociology is about. This required a preliminary excursion into the nature of economics and sociology. In the remainder of the volume we shall observe how the general variables of economic sociology work out in particular empirical settings. We begin with relations between the economic subsystem of society and its other major subsystems.

CHAPTER 3
THE ECONOMY AND ITS SOCIOCULTURAL ENVIRONMENT

In assessing research relevant to economic sociology, we shall proceed first on a grand scale, then on a small scale, then on a grand scale again. In this chapter we shall remain at the societal level and investigate the relations between the economy and four aspects of its sociocultural environment: (1) Cultural aspects. In particular, what is the economic significance of values and ideologies? (2) Political aspects. How is the economy related to many parts of its political environment—to labor organizations, stockholders, the government, and so on? (3) Integrative aspects. In particular, what is the economic significance of two types of solidary groupings—kinship and ethnic? (4) Aspects of social stratification. How does the structure of economic life affect—and how is it affected by—the differential ranking of individuals, positions, and classes in society?

In chapter 4 we shall continue to focus on the general variables of economic sociology, but as they manifest themselves in detailed *economic processes*—specifically, production, exchange, and consumption. Finally, in chapter 5 we shall return to the societal level and observe the interaction of economic and noneconomic forces in processes of *structural change* associated with economic development.

THE ECONOMY AND CULTURAL FACTORS

In considering cultural elements that affect and are affected by economic activity, we may ask two types of question about cultural beliefs: (1) Evaluational. Do economic activities occupy a major place in the cultural value system? Whether major or minor, are they positively or negatively valued? Are they valued as ends in themselves or viewed as subordinated to the pursuit of national power, the attainment of a religious end, or the consolidation of a lineage? (2) Existential. Are people defined as being economically motivated, or are these features of their existence underplayed? What is the nature of society? Does it provide opportunities for economic activity, or is this defined as being impossible in the good society? To ask such questions about any set of cultural beliefs is to set the stage for analyzing the relations between values and ideologies on the one hand and economic activities on the other.

What is the character of these relations? Unfortunately it is impossible to formulate final principles; we must be content with specifying several emphases that have been selected by those engaged in empirical research.

Religious Values as Variables that Facilitate or Inhibit Economic Activity

Weber, the outstanding analyst of the influence of religion on economic activity, argued that the themes of this-worldly asceticism developed in Protestantism (especially Calvinism) encouraged men to value highly the rational and methodical mastery of the social, cultural, and in particular the economic environment. The great classical Oriental religions—especially the Chinese and Indian—on the other hand, offered a much less encouraging cultural framework for the rational organization of economic activity.

Because Weber cited so many instances of Protestant spokesmen's exhortations to work, save, and accumulate,[1] it is tempting to interpret his thesis in a simple evaluational way—that Protestantism positively valued economic activities that are consistent with a capitalist spirit. Such an interpretation is in error. Weber rooted his interpretation in the cosmological (existential) features of Protestantism and other religions. Viewed in this way, his analysis is both more subtle and perhaps more generalizable than the simple evaluational version. Let me elaborate this point.

In his general sociology of religion Weber laid great stress on what he called "the problem of theodicy." This problem arises from the fact that every religious value system "has always required the notion of a god characterized by attributes that set him sublimely above the world"

1. Max Weber, *The Protestant Ethic and the Spirit of Capitalism*, trans. Talcott Parsons (New York: Scribner's 1958), chap. 5.

—a god perfect in some sense.[2] Invariably this notion ends in a dilemma: how to reconcile the perfection of a transcendental god with the imperfection and injustice of the world? This is the problem of theodicy. Weber considered it to be a crucial one; "[in] one form or another this factor belongs everywhere among the factors determining religious evolution and the need for salvation."[3] Weber regarded the religious conceptions of sin and salvation as man's efforts to cope with this dilemma by developing cosmologies, ideologies, and codes of conduct.

Weber noted a diversity of cosmological solutions to the problem of theodicy. In analyzing the codes of conduct that are believed to lead to salvation, he developed two dimensions: (1) whether salvation calls for a passive, contemplative mode (mysticism) or an active, mastering mode (asceticism); (2) whether salvation calls for a focus on this world, the other world, or the inner world.[4] Furthermore, he characterized the major religions of the world in terms of these dimensions. Oriental types of salvation contrast with Western ones in that "the former usually culminate in contemplation and the latter in asceticism."[5] And in the West, Weber singled out ascetic Protestantism, as the most extreme version of inner-worldly asceticism. In terms of its implications for a code of conduct, ascetic Protestantism preached active and methodical mastery of the world as the path to religious salvation:

> . . . an unbroken unity integrating in systematic fashion an ethic of vocation in the world was the unique creation of ascetic Protestantism alone. Furthermore, only in the Protestant ethic of vocation does the world, despite all its creaturely imperfections, possess unique and religious significance as the object through which one fulfills his duties by rational behavior according to the will of an absolutely transcendental god. When success crowns rational, sober, purposive behavior of the sort not oriented to worldly acquisition, such success is construed as a sign that god's blessing rests upon such behavior. The inner worldly asceticism had a number of distinctive consequences not found in any other religion. This religion demanded of the believer, not celibacy, as in the case of the monk, but the avoidance of all erotic pleasure; not poverty, but the elimination of all ideal and exploitative enjoyment of unearned wealth and income, and the avoidance of all feudalistic, sensuous ostentation of wealth; not the ascetic death-in-life of the cloister, but an alert, rationally controlled patterning of life, and the avoidance of all surrender to the beauty of the world, to art, or to one's own moods and emotions. The clear and uniform goal of this asceticism was the dis-

2. Max Weber, *Economy and Society: An Outline of Interpretive Sociology*, eds. Guenther Roth and Claus Wittich, 3 vols. (New York: Bedminster, 1968), 2:518.

3. Ibid., 2:519.

4. Ibid., 2:526–29, 541–51.

5. Ibid., 2:551.

> ciplining and methodical organization of conduct. Its typic representative was the "man of a vocation" or "professional", and its unique result was the rational organization of social relationships.[6]

In this reasoning lies the link between ascetic Protestantism and the spirit of capitalism. The ascetic Protestant, rationalizing his life in the interests of salvation in a predestined world, combined those attitudes and patterns of behavior that were particularly conducive to the methodical organization of resources and human relationships associated with rational bourgeois capitalism and other modern social institutions. The unique combination of this particular religious adaptation and other historical conditions gave rise to capitalism in the West, according to Weber's account.

The Weber thesis has a number of features not always recorded in interpretations of that thesis: (a) The emphasis on economic activities was not a direct positive valuation of such activities but rather was grounded in the ascetic Protestant's preoccupation with sin, worldly imperfection, and the threat of damnation; (b) The impact of this ideology on the development of capitalism was mediated through a complicated interaction with other historical forces; (c) The ascetic Protestant ideology called for the radical alteration of many kinds of social behavior and institutions, not only the economic.

Weber's analysis has exerted a profound effect on social scientists since the beginning of the twentieth century, when it was espoused. Some research on the origins of entrepreneurship shows his influence.[7] In addition, his work has stimulated analysis of the economic implications of religious systems other than those that he studied. Bellah noted similarities between certain nineteenth-century Japanese religious developments and those features of ascetic Protestantism stressed by Weber;[8] Ayal made similar observations about Japanese ethical movements and contrasted them with Buddhist values in Thailand, which focus on personal values, reincarnation, and ascetic withdrawal.[9] Other studies, more critical of the Weber thesis, have pointed out that many groups noted for their entrepreneurship have values quite different in content from ascetic Protestantism. Gerschenkron, for example, argued that the group of Old

6. Ibid., 2:556.

7. Below, pp. 126–29.

8. Robert N. Bellah, *Tokugawa Religion* (Glencoe, Ill.: Free Press and Falcon's Wing Press, 1957).

9. Eliezer B. Ayal, "Value Systems and Economic Development in Japan and Thailand," *Journal of Social Issues* 19, no. 1 (January, 1963):35–51. Bellah cited a number of studies of this sort in the same issue, p. 53.

Believers in nineteenth-century Russia "did reveal traits which Max Weber was willing to regard as the specific capitalist spirit" but held religious beliefs that were contrary to entrepreneurial motivations. Rather, Gerschenkron continued, the Old Believers began to engage in profitable economic activities as a means of overcoming their "social" condition of a penalized, persecuted group."[10]

Other scholars, while not directly critical of Weber, have pointed to the limitations of the indigenous model of economic development implied by his emphasis on a group's belief system. Bendix, for example, argued that cross-national influences have become more important as economic stimulants than indigenous factors in cases more recent than the British and French. He referred, for instance, to

> The influence of the French Revolution and of French culture on Russia and Germany during the eighteenth and nineteenth centuries; German borrowing of English technology and the prominence of English thought and institutions as a "reference group" of German intellectuals; the effect of the Napoleonic conquest in Germany; England and Prussia as "reference groups" for the modernization of Japan. . . .[11]

Both Rostow and Myrdal identified nationalism as an impetus to growth among latecomers, Rostow treating it as a reaction to advances by international competitors, and Myrdal regarding nationalism in the underdeveloped nations as arising from the vicious circle of impoverishment that develops in the relations between developed and underdeveloped nations.[12] And many have pointed out how elements of colonial domination—economic and political imbalances, exposure to Western education—stimulated the growth of nationalist beliefs in the colonial and recently independent countries of the world.[13]

Such nationalist beliefs, the argument continues, constitute a powerful stimulant for economic development. As Davis has put it,

10. Alexander Gerschenkron, *Europe in the Russian Mirror: Four Lectures in Economic History* (London: Cambridge University Press, 1970), pp. 30–46.

11. Reinhard Bendix, *Nation-Building and Citizenship: Studies of our Changing Social Order* (New York: John Wiley, 1964), p. 177.

12. W.W. Rostow, *The Stages of Economic Growth* (Cambridge: Clarendon Press, 1961), p. 34; Gunnar Myrdal, *Economic Theory and Underdeveloped Regions* (London: Duckworth, 1957), chaps. 5, 6. See also R.P. Dore, "Japan as a Model of Economic Development," *European Journal of Sociology* 5, no. 1 (May, 1964):138–54.

13. Gayl D. Ness, "Colonialism, Nationalism and Development," in *The Sociology of Economic Development*, ed. Ness (New York: Harper & Row, 1970), pp. 387–96; William H. Friedland, "Traditionalism and Modernization: Movements and Ideologies," *Journal of Social Issues* 24, no. 1 (January, 1968):9–24.

> nationalism is a *sine qua non* of industrialization, because it provides people with an overriding, easily acquired, secular motivation for making painful changes. National strength or prestige becomes the supreme goal, industrialization the chief means. The costs, inconveniences, sacrifices, and loss of traditional values can be justified in terms of this transcending, collective ambition. The new collective entity, the nation-state, that sponsors and grows from this aspiration is equal to the exigencies of industrial complexity; it draws directly the allegiance of every citizen, organizing the population as one community; it controls the passage of persons, goods, and news across the borders; it regulates economic and social life in detail. To the degree that the obstacles to industrialization are strong, nationalism must be intense to overcome them.[14]

In fact, nationalism seems in many cases to be the instrument designed to smash those traditional religious systems that Weber himself found antipathetic to rational economic activity. On the other hand, nationalism, like many traditionalistic religious systems, may hinder economic advancement by encouraging tariffs and other protectionist policies that inhibit economic activity, by reaffirming "traditionally honored ways of acting and thinking," and, more indirectly, by encouraging expectations of "ready-made prosperity."[15]

Where do these several lines of research and speculation leave us? The case for the importance of cultural values in stimulating economic development has surely been established by the work of Weber and those who have followed him. In addition, those cultural values—whether religious or secular—that seem to be most potent are not those that focus on economic activity alone, but those that envision a general transformation of many patterns of behavior and structures.[16] Furthermore, threatening historical situations appear to be conducive to the development of such

14. Kingsley Davis, "Social and Demographic Aspects of Economic Development in India," in *Economic Growth: Brazil, India, Japan*, eds. Simon Kuznets, Wilbert E. Moore, and Joseph J. Spengler (Durham: Duke University Press, 1955), p. 294. For an even more extensive catalogue of the aspects of ideology that are favorable to economic development, see Dennis M. Ray, "The Role of Ideology in Economic Development," *International Journal of Comparative Sociology* 11, no. 4 (December, 1970):306–16.

15. Arcadius Kahan, "Nineteenth-Century European Experience with Policies of Economic Nationalism," in *Economic Nationalism in Old and New States*, ed. Harry G. Johnson (Chicago: University of Chicago Press, 1967), pp. 17–30; Bert F. Hoselitz, "Non-economic Barriers to Economic Development," *Economic Development and Cultural Change* 1, no. 1 (March, 1952): 9; Hoselitz, "Nationalism, Economic Development, and Democracy," *Annals of the Academy of Political and Social Science* 305 (May 1956):1–11.

16. This argument has been developed by Robert N. Bellah in his "Reflections on the Protestant Ethic Analogy in Asia," *Journal of Social Issues* 19, no. 1 (January, 1963).

values, though the threat need not be rooted in a vision of the supernatural, as Weber stressed. It would seem that the appropriate research strategy for the future is not to continue the search for analogies to the Weber thesis interpreted narrowly—scoring a point for Weber when such an analogy is found, against him when it is not—but rather to direct comparative inquiry toward identifying the conditions under which transformational belief-systems arise and to the conditions under which they combine with other historical forces, both national and international, to move a society toward development.

Ideology as Moral Justification of Existing Arrangements

The term *ideology* refers to a set of asserted beliefs about the nature of persons and society—beliefs that also carry implications for how people ought to behave and how society ought to be organized.

Perhaps the most thorough study of the "control" aspects of ideology is Bendix's study of managerial ideologies in four industrializing countries—Great Britain, the United States, Russia, and East Germany.[17] Bendix was concerned with the justifications that managerial classes generate in the process of inducing workers to submit to their authority. He attempted to account for these ideologies in terms of the requirements of the industrial framework; thus he assigned to the "human relations" ideology the functions of proclaiming the legitimate rights of management as well as assisting managers to achieve coordination within their enterprises. Clearly the main function of ideology in Bendix's view is to legitimize growing or existing institutional arrangements.

It would be erroneous, however, to regard such ideologies as rigidly conservative or reactionary. Most ideologies have a certain flexibility; they are able to absorb and render intelligible new social situations. In a study of ideological statements made by business leaders, Heilbroner contrasted the arrogant, confident, and divine-right attitudes of businessmen of the late nineteenth and early twentieth centuries with the more self-effacing, pragmatic tone of more recent statements. The latter stressed the differences between the old "exploitative, harsh capitalism" and new "responsible, socially aware capitalism," emphasized professional responsibility, recognized the need for large-scale organization, stressed "human values," and accorded a new legitimacy to labor and government.[18] The new business ideology is no doubt as self-legitimizing as the old, but it

17. Reinhard Bendix, *Work and Authority in Industry* (New York: John Wiley, 1956).

18. Robert L. Heilbroner, "The View from the Top: Reflections on a Changing Business Ideology," in *The Business Establishment*, ed. Earl F. Cheit (New York: John Wiley, 1967), pp. 1–36.

also reveals the capacity of ideology to absorb past criticisms and new forces in the environment of business.

Ideology as Moral Attack on Existing Arrangements

In industrial disputes management typically defends its position with assertions concerning the principles of free enterprise and with assertions of management's interest in the welfare of the worker. On the side of the union, counter-ideologies develop, which also "represent self-justifications of union objectives":

> The [self-justification] of the largest scope is the contention that trade unions are instruments of social justice. The second moral justification underlying American unionism is that it protects the individual worker in his immediate work environment from exploitation and degradation.[19]

In situations of conflict and change, two opposing ideologies frequently develop, one defending and the other attacking existing arrangements—tsarist vs. revolutionary, colonial vs. colonized, for example. Furthermore, in the event of victory by those on the attack, *their* ideology then becomes one by which new institutional arrangements are legitimized and defended. In Russia in 1917 Bolshevism changed quickly from a rallying cry for destroying an old regime into a basis for legitimizing and mobilizing support for a new regime. Many nationalist, anticolonial ideologies experienced a similar shift as colonies gained their independence after World War II. Under these circumstances an ideology faces a severe test, and invariably the transition from attacking to defending produces a proliferation of new ideological material to give meaning to and justify the altered historical circumstances.

Ideology as a Device to Ease Situations of Strain

Many commentators have noted that ideologies flourish in situations of discrepancy between an ideal standard and an actual state of affairs, and that the main function of ideologies is to "rationalize" the discrepancy and help ease the strain in some way. Several studies of the American business ideologies lend support to this view. Sutton et al., in an analysis of the American business creed, attributed the tenacity of the free-enterprise myth among businessmen to various strains in their roles; for example, their own ambivalence toward the phenomenon of bigness in the American economy is smoothed over by a defiant reassertion of

19. Arthur Kornhauser, Robert Dubin, and Arthur M. Ross, "Problems and Viewpoints," in *Industrial Conflict* (New York: McGraw-Hill, 1954), pp. 18–19.

the values of free enterprise.[20] Rogers and Berg found considerable ideological differences among two kinds of automobile dealers: old-line dealers, often from blue-collar backgrounds, who started on a shoestring in the 1920s and 1930s, and who adhered to a business ideology containing many classical free-enterprise and populist ingredients; and new, large-volume dealers, of white collar origin, who went into business more recently, and who had an ideology emphasizing fair trade and protection less, risk and expansion more. Rogers and Berg traced these orientations to the different opportunity structures facing the two types of dealers; in particular, they regarded the reactionary ideology of the old line dealers as reflecting their precarious and declining market position.[21]

Such are some of the functions of ideology in economic life—to justify existing economic arrangements, to attack them, and to ease strains in them. These functions are not mutually exclusive, and their relative emphasis can shift quickly and subtly. Perhaps the most promising avenue for analyzing the changing vicissitudes of ideology—and their changing relations to economic life—is to link their study with that of the changing fortunes of social groups. Early in the development of a given ideology—e.g., laissez faire—its major significance may be to attack traditional economic arrangements and to provide a basis for legitimacy for rising business groups not yet well established in a society's status system. Then, as the groups espousing the ideology become more powerful and established, it turns to the defense of existing arrangements, the resistance of claims of striving, less-established groups, and the smoothing over of strains that arise in the roles institutionalized in the name of the ideology itself.

THE ECONOMY AND POLITICAL VARIABLES

We shall examine the political involvements of economic units through a series of expanding circles: (1) Political relations *within* the productive unit. We shall reserve this topic for chapter 4. (2) Political relations *among* productive units, which raises the subject of the concentration of wealth. (3) Political relations between productive units and the *immediate economic environment*. We shall mention firms' relations with consumers and stockholders and devote considerable attention to labor-management relations. (4) Political relations between productive units and *government*.

20. Francis X. Sutton et al., *The American Business Creed* (Cambridge, Mass.: Harvard University Press, 1956), pp. 58–64.

21. David Rogers and Ivar Berg, "Occupation and Ideology," *Human Organization* 20, no. 3 (Fall, 1961):103–11.

Political Relations among Firms

Much of the literature on the concentration of wealth and economic power is clouded on several counts. The subject itself is loaded ideologically. Given the historical legacy of faith in "free enterprise" and "individualism," the history of some business practices, and the history of antitrust sentiment, Americans have for generations been sensitive to bigness of business and the power that this connotes. In addition, many different measures of concentration are available, and the results produced by each are substantially different. Finally, the economic, social, and political implications of each set of results are far from self-evident.

Beyond doubt, giant corporations are a conspicuous feature of the American economy. Examining figures of employment, allocation of defense contracts, assets, and other measures, Kaysen concluded that "a few large corporations are of overwhelmingly disproportionate importance in our economy, and especially in certain key sectors of it. Whatever aspect of their economic activity we measure . . . we see the same situation."[22] In 1966 the fifty largest companies accounted for 25 percent of total manufacturing "value-added" (that is, the margin between purchase and sales price). When calculated on the basis of corporate assets, the result is that the hundred largest manufacturing corporations controlled half in 1968.[23]

These stark figures are tempered when read in the longer term and in the context of other measures. Changes in the shares of the 50, 100, or 200 largest manufacturing corporations have been modest during the past forty years.[24] And in terms of market concentration—the market share enjoyed by a few leading competitors—the picture is one of overall stability, with some ups and downs, since the beginning of the century.[25] This stability of market concentration in the manufacturing sector actually signifies a decline in overall concentration, since the manufacturing sector has declined relative to other sectors of the economy, which are

22. Carl Kaysen, "The Corporation: How Much Power? What Scope?" in *The Corporation in Modern Society*, ed. Edward S. Mason (Cambridge, Mass.: Harvard University Press, 1959), p. 88.

23. M.A. Adelman, "The Two Faces of Economic Concentration," in *Capitalism Today*, eds. Daniel Bell and Irving Kristol (New York: New American Library, 1971), p. 144.

24. Ibid.

25. Richard E. Low, *Modern Economic Organization* (Homewood, Ill.: Richard D. Irwin, 1970), pp. 99–103.

typically less concentrated than manufacturing. Viewed in international perspective, the United States has a lower market concentration ratio than the less-developed countries of the world, where a few companies dominate smaller markets. Among industrialized nations, the United States and Britain appear to have the lowest market concentration ratios, followed by Japan, France, Italy, Canada, India, and Sweden.[26] Companies are smaller in these countries, but the American market is so much larger than those of these other countries that the American market concentration ratio is generally lower.

On the other hand, the stable and low (relative to other countries) American market concentration ratios may obscure an effective centralization of decision making. On an absolute basis the giant corporations have grown enormously, and through merger and interlocking they have extended their influence.[27] Furthermore, many individuals sit on the boards of directors of more than one of the nation's largest corporations.[28] Finally, several enormous industries—petroleum, steel, and automobile, for example—on which the fate of the economy depends, are dominated by a few large and powerful organizations.

Some of the well-known economic consequences of the increasing concentration of wealth and power are the tendency for large firms to squeeze smaller enterprises out of the market (the small retail grocery store, which suffered greatly at the hands of the supermarket, is perhaps the most conspicuous recent victim); the ability of the large firms to accumulate large capital reserves and to finance costly investments and large-scale research; and the tendency for competition among very large firms to manifest itself in advertising, not pricing. In a historical survey of large, successful firms, Chandler uncovered a typical sequence of strategies adopted as the firm consolidated its position. The first phase was one of expansion and accumulation of resources; the second was to rationalize and systematize the operations of the firm to reduce unit costs and to make it responsive to market fluctuations; the third phase involved filling out its main line of products and expanding markets, but above all diversifying its products; and the final phase involved the creation of a multidivisional company structure to rationalize further the

26. Joe S. Bain, *International Differences in Industrial Structure: Eight Nations in the 1950's* (New Haven: Yale University Press, 1966), pp. 4, 6, 68, 119.

27. For a series of diagnoses of ownership and concentration, see Maurice Zeitlin, ed., *American Society, Inc.: Studies of the Social Structure and Political Economy of the United States* (Chicago: Markham, 1970), part 1.

28. Alfred S. Eichner, "Business Concentration and Its Significance," in *The Business of America*, ed. Ivar Berg (New York: Harcourt Brace Jovanovich, 1968), pp. 196–99.

firm's more complex production and marketing operations.[29] In the later, multidivisional phase the companies moved more into foreign operations, dominating the export markets, setting up overseas branches, and paving the way for the development of multinational corporations.[30]

Political Relations with the Immediate Economic Environment

Consumers. The political relations between business and consumers are manifested chiefly in the market. Under perfect competition, buyers and sellers have full knowledge of market conditions, and neither the individual buyer nor the individual seller can influence market conditions. Buyer and seller are thus politically equal because of their mutual omniscience and mutual impotence. Such conditions, however, have never existed in pure form. Moreover, modern industrial capitalism has skewed the market in favor of the seller. As more products and brands appeared, more knowledge was required of the consumer. As products came to rest on a complex technology, the consumer had to rely more on faith in the expertise and honesty of the seller and repairman. Simultaneously, with the advent of mass advertising, much of the knowledge available to the consumer is controlled by the seller. And finally, producers and sellers invariably become more concentrated—and better able to influence the market—than consumers.[31]

Whatever organized resistance to this asymmetrical situation consumers have been able to muster in modern complex economies has taken the following forms:

1. Direct political action against firms or products, mainly in the form of boycotts. These have been employed rarely and have been effective even more rarely.
2. The establishment of consumers' cooperatives to distribute goods and services. Although the consumers' cooperative movement has manifested itself in some form in almost every country, it has rarely been a significant force in an entire economy.
3. Agitation by consumers for regulating prices and products and for establishing standards of control of business behavior. This is typically not direct economic action on the part of consumers, but mainly political action through the government. In the past few decades governments have

29. Alfred D. Chandler, Jr., *Strategy and Structure: Chapters in the History of the Industrial Enterprise* (Cambridge, Mass.: M.I.T. Press, 1962), pp. 383–96.

30. Lawrence E. Fouraker and John M. Stopford, "Organizational Structure and the Multinational Strategy," *Administrative Science Quarterly* 13, no. 1 (June, 1968): 47–64.

31. E. Scott Maynes, "Consumerism: Origin and Research Implications" (Minneapolis: Center for Economic Research, University of Minnesota, 1972).

become increasingly sensitive to consumers as a pressure group, and when consumer groups organize—as in the case of the Ralph Nader organization—at least modest results have been obtained.[32] In addition, the growing consciousness of the ecological dangers of unregulated economic activity, plus the victimization of consumers by grave inflationary spirals, suggest that America and other industrial societies may witness consumer political activity on a larger scale in years to come.

Stockholders. Managers have consolidated their political power in relation to stockholders in recent times. In 1932 Berle and Means sketched the main lines of this consolidation.[33] Their main thesis was that ownership of corporate property had been increasingly separated from control of the firm's economic decisions. Before the mid-nineteenth century the control of the business enterprise lay in the hands of the individual or small group who owned all the property used as capital in the enterprise. With the rise of the corporate form, however, ownership was dispersed among stockholders remotely connected with day-to-day management. Control of decisions came to rest more in the hands of professional managers, whose actual ownership rights were minimal. Rostow recently summarized the position of the stockholders as follows:

> The . . . prototype, increasingly, is that of a corporation with stock widely scattered among individuals, investment trusts, or institutional investors, who faithfully vote for the incumbent management, and resolutely refuse to participate in its concerns. In such companies, the stockholders obey the management, not the management the stockholders. Most stockholders of this class are interested in their stock only as investments. The prevalence of this view makes it almost hopeless to expect that the electoral process can ever become anything more significant than an empty ritual.[34]

While the twentieth century might thus be referred to as "the age of the manager,"[35] such a diagnosis requires closer examination.

Some evidence points to a continuing evolution of the trends identified by Berle and Means. Larner consulted records for the 200 largest nonfinancial corporations for the year 1963—just as Berle and Means had

32. See David A. Aaker and George S. Day, eds., *Consumerism: Search for the Consumer Interest* (New York: Free Press, 1972); Ralph Nader, Peter J. Petkas, and Kate Blackwell, eds., *Whistle Blowing* (New York: Grossman, 1972).

33. A.A. Berle, Jr., and Gardiner Means, *The Modern Corporation and Private Property* (New York: Macmillan, 1932).

34. Eugene V. Rostow, "To Whom and for What Ends Is Corporate Management Responsible?" in *The Corporation*, ed. Mason, pp. 53–54.

35. Alfred H. Chandler, Jr., "The Role of Business in the United States: A Historical Survey," *Daedalus*, 98, no. 1 (Winter, 1969):32.

for 1929—and classified them as "privately owned" if an individual, family, corporation, or group of business associates owned between 50 and 80 percent of the voting stock and "privately controlled" if 10 percent of the voting stock was so owned. (Berle and Means had used a higher proportion, 20–50 percent, to signify private control.) Berle and Means had identified 12 corporations as privately owned; Larner found none. Berle and Means had identified 46½ corporations as under minority control; Larner found only 18, despite his use of a lower proportion of ownership to signify such control. Berle and Means had found 88½ corporations to be management controlled; Larner found 169.[36]

What remains obscure is the notion of "control." It is unclear, for example, why 10 percent of stock ownership should signify minority control. In fact, different investigators have used different percentages—ranging from 20 to 1 or 2—which naturally lead to different estimates of stockholder control.[37] In any event, such estimates are based on extrapolations from financial structures and do not refer to the processes by which control might be exercised. There is some doubt, moreover, whether the separation of ownership and management makes much difference in managers' behavior or firm performance. The results are conflicting on this score. Basing their analysis on the assumption that owners are primarily interested in profit-maximization and managers are primarily interested in maximizing their own incomes, Monsen, Chih, and Cooley estimated that owner-controlled firms outperform management-controlled firms.[38] Yet Kamerschen found type of control more or less unrelated to variations in profit rates among the 200 firms selected by Larner.[39] Add to this the observation that managers themselves are often substantial stockholders,[40] and that their personal fortunes (bonuses, promotions, etc.)

36. Robert J. Larner, "Ownership and Control in the 200 Largest Nonfinancial Corporations in 1929 and 1963," *American Economic Review* 56, no. 4 (September, 1966):777–87. The other categories were "majority ownership" and "legal device," both of which also declined between 1929 and 1963.

37. It is not surprising that those wishing to demonstrate the continuing importance of owner domination select lower percentages, those stressing manager domination higher. Theo. Nichols, *Ownership Control and Ideology* (London: Allen & Unwin, 1969), pp. 68–69.

38. R. Joseph Monsen, John S. Chih, and David E. Cooley, "The Effect of Separation of Ownership and Control on the Performance of the Large Firm," *Quarterly Journal of Economics* 82, no. 3 (August, 1968):435–51.

39. David R. Kamerschen, "The Influence of Ownership and Control on Profit Rates," *American Economic Review* 58, no. 3 (June, 1968):432–47.

40. Gabriel Kolko, *Wealth and Power in America* (London: Thames and Hudson, 1962), pp. 60–69; P. Sargant Florence, *Ownership, Control, and Success of Large Companies* (London: Routledge & Kegan Paul, 1961), p. 191.

often depend on the market performance of their companies. Such considerations suggest that the relations between owners and managers are not so much a matter of the degree of control or independence of managers as they are a matter of the degree of coincidence of interest of these two groups.

Labor. We begin by outlining a number of variations in labor-management relations. The key question is: In what *other* structures are the economic relations between labor and its employers embedded?

A common form of labor organization before the industrial revolution in England (about the mid-eighteenth century) was the "friendly society." These clubs of workingmen were interested in exercising influence over masters with regard to apprenticeship and the quality of goods produced, but they served a number of other functions as well. They were repositories for workers' savings; they were insurance societies against death, illness, and the like; they were convivial drinking clubs. And above all they often united with the masters with regard to the welfare of the industry as a whole. The friendly society, then, was a kind of multifunctional organization, standing in relative solidarity with the master manufacturers.

With the increasing separation of the worker from his capital and his product during the Industrial Revolution, the character of trade unionism also changed. During the first half of the nineteenth century, more specialized unions—unions interested in wages and working conditions and regarding themselves as opposed to the employing class—emerged. These came to dominate in both Great Britain and the United States in the nineteenth century.

Labor-management relations fuse with the larger political structure of society in a variety of ways. An extreme case is found in totalitarian countries—such as Nazi Germany or the Soviet Union in some of its historical periods—in which free collective bargaining was ruled out, and grievance procedures were carried out under a centralized political rubric. In some instances labor unions operated as an arm of government and management interests and assisted in educating and disciplining workers.[41] We find a less extreme pattern of government involvement in labor-management relations in many underdeveloped nations. In some African countries the early efforts on the part of colonial powers to impose

41. For a sample of labor relations in such countries, see Matthew A. Kelley, "Industrial Relations in National Socialist Germany," and Walter Galenson, "Soviet Russia," in *Industrial Conflict*, eds. Kornhauser, Dubin, and Ross, pp. 467–77 and 478–86. For an account of the liberalization of labor relations in the post-Stalin period, see Emily Clark Brown, *Soviet Trade Unions and Labor Relations* (Cambridge, Mass.: Harvard University Press, 1966), chap. 8. See also Charles Hoffmann, "Work Incentives in Communist China," *Industrial Relations* 3, no. 2 (February, 1964):81–97.

Western-type economically oriented unions on their colonies has failed. Instead, labor organizations have become intimately linked with—indeed subordinated to—the major political party in the society, lending it support and sometimes finding government in strict supervision of labor-management relations.[42] Still another variant is found in countries with nationalized industries (for example, modern Britain). While trade unions in such countries maintain autonomy, they deal with government boards as management.

Labor-management relations are sometimes influenced by a fusion with particular ethnic groupings. The bitter antagonism and the extraordinary degree of violence in the Pennsylvania mine disorders—known as the Molly Maguire riots—in the 1870s can be traced in part to the Irish origins and sentiments of the miners.[43] The peculiar character of labor-management relations in the California agricultural system of contract labor can also be traced in part to the domination of the labor force during different periods by the Chinese, the Japanese, and the Mexicans—each with distinctive traditions of social organization and attitudes toward authority.[44]

Finally, labor organizations are frequently fused with collective movements, such as anarchism, syndicalism, socialism, home rule, anticolonialism and nationalism. This fusion has always characterized continental Europe to a much greater degree than the Anglo-Saxon world, and in contemporary times many nationalist movements in the developing areas have been entangled with the labor movement of these countries.[45]

We turn next to a question closely related to the structure of labor-management relations: Why does one rather than another form of industrial conflict appear? It is closely related because the structure of industrial relations helps to shape the form of industrial conflict. Why is this so? Above all, to structure the relations among parties establishes a system of opportunities and restraints. Structure endorses some kinds of behavior, discourages others, and prohibits still others. Accord-

42. Stephan H. Goodman, "Trade Unions and Political Parties: The Case of East Africa," *Economic Development and Cultural Change* 17, no. 3 (April, 196):338–45; Jean Meynaud and Anisse Salah Bey, *Trade Unionism in Africa: A Study of Its Growth and Orientation*, trans. Angela Brench (London: Methuen, 1967), pp. 32–38, 93–101.

43. J. Walter Coleman, *The Molly Maguire Riots* (Richmond, Va.: Garrett and Massie, 1936), pp. 19–39.

44. Lloyd H. Fisher, *The Harvest Labor Market in California* (Cambridge, Mass.: Harvard University Press, 1953), especially pp. 24–37.

45. Meynaud and Bey, *Trade Unionism in Africa*, pp. 74–77.

ingly, the form of conflict behavior in industrial relations tends to follow the lines along which the political-economic structure "tilts" the opportunities for and constraints on the expression of conflict. Consider the following instances of this general principle:

1. In settings where central political control limits the range of conflict and where the political authorities appear to be capricious, informal channels for handling grievances often develop. Studying Soviet grievance procedures in the 1950s, Zawordny described such a situation:

> It seems clear that the workers hesitated to claim their admissible grievances. This was because formal agencies within a plant and the members of these bodies were repeatedly able to make an about-face on an issue whenever politically convenient and to attach an invidious political label to a worker's claim, the chosen manner of settlement, and the outcome. The members of the formal agencies could circumvent the law themselves in order to secure a satisfactory solution for the workers, particularly when such settlement could be used as an incentive. Conversely, the same type of grievance could receive the reverse treatment when a display of "socialistic vigilance" was deemed necessary for "educational purposes."[46]

Such an atmosphere discouraged the open presentation of grievances. What settlements did occur rested not on formal machinery, but on particularistic loyalties (friends, contacts); "workers used formal agencies as an official screen for the exchange of mutual assistance and the application of influence—these under the aegis of unwritten mutual amnesty."[47] After the 1950s, as channels for expressing grievances opened somewhat, more formal agencies such as the Central Council of Trade Unions and the central committees of the national unions increased their power, but not to the point of challenging policies of the party or securing the right to strike.[48] This change in the form of expressing conflict was a clear response to a change in the opportunity structure (through liberalization), which presumably reduced the need to rely on informal, secretive resolution of conflict.

2. In settings where the locus for expressing and resolving conflict is centralized *but* (unlike the previous example) other forms of conflict are not prohibited, unofficial protest may arise among those who not only feel grievances but also feel themselves remote from the center. Thus the "unofficial strike" and other informal forms of work stoppage seemed to come into prominence in Britain after the centralization of labor-man-

46. Janusz Zawodny, "Grievance Procedures in Soviet Factories," *Industrial and Labor Relations Review* 10, no. 4 (July, 1957):553.

47. Ibid.

48. Brown, *Soviet Trade Unions*, chap. 8.

agement relations associated with the nationalization of some industries.[49] Numerous work stoppages in Britain have also occurred when opposition groups rebel against settlements between union leaders and management.[50] A longitudinal study (1942–62) of four rayon plants in Britain—which experienced 118 wildcat strikes in this period—showed that "differences in the frequency of work stoppages were consistently associated with differences in fractional bargaining practices [bargaining by work groups and subsections of management]." More work stoppages occurred under centralized conditions—that is, in the absence of fractional bargaining. Furthermore, wildcat strikes frequently continued as long as management refused to bargain fractionally.[51] Such findings suggest that the wildcat strike often occurs when groups of workers feel they are isolated or receiving the "run-around" from big unions as they relate to big business or big government. Similarly, in the developing countries, as labor movements become enmeshed with a national party or with the government itself, they risk losing touch with and encountering unauthorized protest by the rank-and-file.[52] This series of examples shows the importance of the opportunity structure; if workers feel excluded from or helpless in the face of an official system of conflict settlement, they are likely to turn to unofficial forms.

3. Insofar as a labor movement is closely affiliated with a political party, this encourages the expression of conflicts in the larger society, especially in the form of electoral conflict, attempts to enact legislation favorable to one of the parties in conflict, and so on. The long historical affiliation of the British labor movement with the Labour party and the looser affiliation of the American labor movement with the Democratic party have constituted channels—or opportunity structures, if you will—for expression of interests via the constituted political process in each country.

49. For an account of the development of unofficial strikes after nationalization, see George B. Baldwin, *Beyond Nationalization: The Labor Problems of British Coal* (Cambridge, Mass.: Harvard University Press, 1955), pp. 63–69. For an indication that the unofficial type of work-stoppage is more common in Britain than in other countries—and possibly on the increase in Britain—see H.A. Clegg, *The System of Industrial Relations in Great Britain* (Oxford: Basil Blackwell, 1972), pp. 16–17.

50. Clegg, *The System of Industrial Relations*, pp. 332–36.

51. David R. Hampton, "Fractional Bargaining and Wildcat Strikes," *Human Organization* 26, no. 3 (Fall, 1967):100–109.

52. For an account of the occurrence of such an unauthorized strike in Ghana in 1961, see Lester N. Trachtman, "The Labor Movement of Ghana: A Study in Political Unionism," *Economic Development and Cultural Change* 10, no. 2 (January, 1962):183–200.

4. Insofar as a labor movement is an adjunct of a revolutionary political movement, the strike will be used less for economic gain (as it is in business unionism), and more for political attack. In the ideology of communism and syndicalism, for instance, the strike is avowedly a political weapon, and it has been used as such where groups adhering to these ideologies have been relatively strong—for example, in France and Italy.

5. Limited evidence suggests that in some cases different forms of conflict are inversely correlated with one another. In a study of strike activity in Great Britain between 1911 and 1947, Knowles reported that in the coal industry, "irrespective of the differences between years and the differences between districts, if strike losses are high absenteeism losses tend to be low and vice-versa." Two factors probably accounted for this: first, insofar as strikes cost laborers both wages and savings, they cannot afford to be absent from work during periods of collective strife; second, workers may come to the work place more frequently in order to be with other workers in periods of conflict. This negative correlation between different forms of conflict is, however, probably limited to certain types of situations; Knowles suggested that if labor unrest is very high, both strikes and absenteeism may be high.[53]

6. The forms of labor conflict have displayed change throughout the history of Anglo-American unionism, and these changes are associated with structural changes in unionism itself. It is possible to identify three broad phases. First, in the earliest stages of development of the labor force, conflict tended to take two forms—individual protest, in the form of high turnover, absenteeism, sabotage, irregular hours, and so on; and spontaneous collective protests, such as mob violence, destruction of machinery by raids, and quickly organized and chaotic strikes. The conflict rested in part on the severe strains that industrialization imposed on the working populace. Its particular form, however, reflected the relative lack of worker organization; conflict was not institutionalized and therefore apeared in the form of individual expression or spontaneous group outbursts.[54]

Second, in the middle period, conflict alternated between the use of strikes for economic gain and more dispersed forms of conflict. This alternation, moreover, followed the business cycle. During the nineteenth century, labor agitation in the United States followed a roughly cyclical pattern; "it . . . centered on economic or trade union prosperity only to

53. K.G.J.C. Knowles, *Strikes* (Oxford: Basil Blackwell, 1952), p. 225.

54. Clark Kerr, John T. Dunlop, Frederick H. Harbison, and Charles A. Myers, *Industrialism and Industrial Man* (Cambridge, Mass.: Harvard University Press, 1960), pp. 209–10.

change abruptly to 'panaceas' and politics with the descent of depression.[55] During prosperity, when labor was scarce, workers could use demands for wage increases and strikes effectively; furthermore, they could finance union organizations and periods of idleness more readily. During depressions these methods became less effective, and workers turned to demands for protective legislation from the government or to schemes such as cooperation to build a new economic structure.

Third, in more recent times, business unionism has become consolidated.[56] Unions have rationalized the conduct of the strike, reduced violence, disciplined the workers, localized strikes, reduced unnecessary damage to industry, and protected unions in the face of public opinion. Much of the heat has disappeared from strikes, and whatever revolutionary overtones strikes might once have had clearly diminished in mid-twentieth century. Peaceful collective bargaining has become the standard form of conflict. In America unions have become increasingly acceptable to the public, more willing to deal in partisan politics, and, indeed, more conservative politically than many other segments of the population.[57] And in the two decades of post–World War II prosperity in Western Europe, many European unions also appeared to drift from ideological to business unionism, while retaining some of their distinctive cultural and political traditions.[58]

It would be wrong, however, to regard the evolution of unionism as completed, and hazardous to predict stability and complacency on the part of organized labor for the future. Unions' overall influence in the society may decline. The movement has virtually ceased to grow among manual workers, as these categories of workers grow smaller in proportion to the total labor force. Furthermore, while some successes in organizing white-collar workers have been scored—notably among teachers and other public employees—resistances to organization remain among these

55. Selig Perlman, *A History of Trade Unionism in the United States* (New York: Macmillan, 1937), pp. 141–42.

56. Philip Taft has challenged the thesis—associated with the name of Selig Perlman—that business unionism is of recent vintage. He has argued that from the late eighteenth and early nineteenth centuries "unions primarily interested in improving wages and conditions of employment existed in every decade, and instead of being a development of the 1870's and 1880's, they have throughout the nineteenth and present centuries exercised a major influence upon the thinking and policies of organized workers." "On the Origins of Business Unionism," *Industrial and Labor Relations Review* 17, no. 1 (October, 1963):21.

57. Arthur M. Ross, "The Natural History of the Strike," in *Industrial Conflict*, eds., Kornhauser, Dubin, and Ross; Joseph Shister, "The Direction of Unionism 1947–1967: Thrust or Drift?" *Industrial and Labor Relations Review* 20, no. 4 (July, 1967):578–601.

58. Arthur M. Ross, "Prosperity and Labor Relations in Western Europe: Italy and France," *Industrial and Labor Relations Review* 16, no. 1 (October, 1962):84.

workers, and, even if widely organized, their interests and types of organization promise to be so diverse that integration between them and manual labor organizations will be difficult to attain.[59] Finally, the twin strategies of business unionism—to press for policies that sustain full employment, and to press through collective bargaining and the civilized strike for their share of the economic pie and for improved working conditions—may become increasingly archaic. Continued economic growth and full employment may not be on the agenda if population growth, shortages of raw materials, and a chronic crisis in the supply of energy create a long-term situation of economic stagnation marked by *both* unemployment *and* inflation. Surely the strategies of unions—which have been accustomed to fighting against one of these conditions at a time, but not both—cannot remain stable in the face of such gross changes in their environment.

Some studies have revealed a differential incidence of strikes over time and among industries. We have already noted that strikes appear to be positively correlated with business activity. The logic behind this is that unions strike in periods of prosperity because they wish to share in the increased profits and because they calculate that employers may be willing to settle favorably when profits are high. On the other hand, it could be argued that the strike would be used extensively in depressions, to protest against layoffs and deteriorating working conditions. What are the facts? In 1952 a study conducted by Rees indicated that by almost any measure—number of strikes, number of workers involved, or number of working days lost—strikes in America increased in prosperity and declined in depression. This relation held for 1915–38, but disappeared between 1938 and 1948, a period that included World War II and the postwar years in which Congress enacted the controversial Taft-Hartley legislation. In that decade, political considerations—such as appeals not to strike during the war—may have overshadowed economic determinants.[60]

In a subsequent study Weintraub, using the same time series as Rees, found that for the years 1949–61 the level of economic activity reemerged as a major correlate of strike activity.[61] Skeels distinguished

59. Shister, "The Direction of Unionism"; Everett M. Kassalow, "The Prospects for White-Collar Union Growth," *Industrial Relations* 5, no. 1 (October, 1965):37–47; George Strauss, "Professionalism and Occupational Associations," in *The Social Dimensions of Work*, ed. Clifton D. Daniel (Englewood Cliffs, N.J.: Prentice-Hall, 1972), pp. 236–53.

60. Albert Rees, "Industrial Conflict and Business Fluctuations," *Journal of Political Economy* 60, no. 5 (October, 1952):371–82; see also Knowles, *Strikes*, pp. 145–50.

61. Andrew R. Weintraub, "Prosperity vs. Strikes: An Empirical Approach," *Industrial and Labor Relations Review* 19, no. 2 (January, 1966):231–38.

among several measures of strike activity—number of strikes beginning in a quarter, percentage of workers in total labor force involved in strikes beginning in a quarter, and so on. He was able to show that one index—the number of strikes—was more responsive to variables such as level of output than other indices of strike activity (such as number of man-days lost in strikes). Skeels argued that the number of strikes reflected *decisions* to strike, which are more sensitive to economic conditions than are the by-products of those decisions.[62] Strikes also appear to display seasonal variation within a single year. In his study of strikes in Britain, Knowles found that strike rates peaked in May and August (months of highest economic activity, especially in building, when conditions of "prosperity" held). A slight decline was observable before holidays, a decline that presumably reflected the workers' increased need for cash in these times.[63]

Strike activity has also shown definite patterns in the longer run. Since the turn of the century, the average duration of the strike has decreased significantly, as collective bargaining methods have become consolidated and as the strike in some countries has come to signify a brief demonstration of political protest more often than an economic contest. With respect to numbers involved, however, the picture is more complicated; those countries having tight union organizations show increases, those with loose organizations or falling membership show decreases.[64] Basing his reasoning on such trends, Dubin predicted in 1953 that "measured by the length and intensity of strikes [industrial conflict] will show relative stability in the next several decades."[65] He based this prediction mainly on the assumptions that group behavior becomes stabilized through institutionalization (for example, of collective bargaining procedures), and that individuals develop an investment in continuing institutionalized behavior. In 1965 he argued that his "stability" prediction was confirmed by most measures.[66]

Later Ashenfelter and Pierce challenged Dubin, asserting that by

62. Jack W. Skeels, "Measures of U.S. Strike Activity," *Industrial and Labor Relations Review* 24, no. 4 (July, 1971):515–25.

63. Knowles, *Strikes*, pp. 157–60; Skeels, "Measures of U.S. Strike Activity."

64. Arthur M. Ross and Paul T. Hartman, *Changing Patterns of Industrial Conflict* (New York: John Wiley, 1960), pp. 22–24. Also Desmond W. Oxnam, "The Changing Pattern of Strike Settlements in Australia, 1913–1963," *Journal of Industrial Relations* 9, no. 1 (March, 1968):13–24.

65. Dubin, "Prospects of Industrial Conflict—A Prediction," in *Industrial Conflict*, eds. Kornhauser, Dubin, and Ross, p. 527.

66. Robert Dubin, "Industrial Conflict: The Power of Prediction," *Industrial and Labor Relations Review* 18, no. 3 (April, 1965):352–63.

his reasoning a further *decline* in strike activity should be expected, and produced figures that indicated such a decline in the late 1950s and 1960s.[67] Powerful as these long-term trends are, however, labor's position in the economy appears to be sufficiently uncertain[68] that it would be foolhardy to venture predictions about the permanent leveling or withering away of the strike or of labor protest in general.

Asking if certain industries are more strike-prone than others, Kerr and Siegel conducted research on strikes in eleven nations. They found a high propensity to strike in mining and maritime-longshore industries; medium high in lumber and textile industries; medium in chemical, printing, leather, general manufacturing, construction, and food industries; medium low in clothing, utilities, and services; and low in railroads, agriculture, and trade. Their first explanation of this differential distribution lay in the integration of the industrial workers among themselves and with the larger society. As the authors commented:

> (a) industries will be highly strike prone when the workers (i) form a relatively homogeneous group which (ii) is unusually isolated from the general community and which (iii) is capable of cohesion; and (b) industries will be comparatively strike free when their workers (i) are individually integrated into the larger society, (ii) are members of trade groups which are coerced by government or the market to avoid strikes, or (iii) are so individually isolated that strike action is impossible.[69]

Their second explanation was that isolated industries tend to draw tough, combative workers because of the unpleasant, unskilled, and seasonal character of these industries. These factors appear to account for gross variations but probably should be supplemented by reference to cultural and political factors. Rimlinger, for example, found differences in strike activity in coal mining (a strike-prone industry, according to Kerr and Siegel) in the United States, Britain, France, and Germany. He traced these differences to specific historical factors: German miners, for example, enjoyed almost a craft status, lived in farming communities and generally enjoyed a higher degree of social recognition, whereas in France —where strikes have been especially violent—miners were recruited from

67. Orley Ashenfelter and William S. Pierce, "Industrial Conflict: The Power of Prediction: Comment," *Industrial and Labor Relations Review* 20, no. 1 (October, 1966):92–95.

68. Above, pp. 64–65.

69. Clark Kerr and Abraham Siegel, "The Interindustry Propensity to Strike—an International Comparison," in *Industrial Conflict*, eds. Kornhauser, Dubin, and Ross, p. 195.

alienated former peasants and were sometimes subjected to government brutality.[70]

The clustering of industrial disputes over time and among industries leads to the question of the causes of strikes. By "causes" we do not refer to the issues over which strikes occur (wage disputes, arbitrary management action, inadequate union recognition) but rather to the underlying conditions that give rise to this form of conflict. What are these conditions?

We can divide fundamental causes of labor disputes into two broad categories: (1) permissive conditions, which refer both to the absence of obstacles to the right or ability to strike and to the availability of alternative channels to express grievances and interests; (2) sources of active unrest among workers. Among the first the presence of a strong labor organization encourages the use of the strike as a weapon; otherwise conflict is more likely to appear in individual or spontaneous group form. On the other hand, the longer an organization has been in existence, the more likely it is "to have completed [its] struggles for existence, recognition, and security, and to be integrated into [the] national [economy]"; with age, also, a union will likely have attained greater accommodation with employers and will rely less on the strike.[71] Furthermore, the financial strength of workers' organizations is a factor; one of the reasons, perhaps, why strikes occur more frequently in periods of prosperity is that workers feel they can better afford the temporary layoff occasioned by a strike. Finally, strikes are more frequent when a government allows them and less frequent when a government represses them, as in totalitarian states or in periods of national crisis. On the other hand, when unions are closely linked to a labor party, or when the government takes an active hand in settling disputes, this often constitutes an alternative channel for settling conflicts, and to a decline in strike activity.[72]

As to the general sources of unrest among workers, the picture is more confused, and scholars have been inclined to bunch into competing explanatory "schools." Among the approaches are the following:

1. The "economic advantage" school, which maintains that labor unions are "in business" and attempt to maximize the wage gains of their members.[73]

70. Gaston V. Rimlinger, "International Differences in the Strike Propensity of Coal Miners: Experience in Four Countries," *Industrial and Labor Relations Review* 12, no. 3 (April, 1959):389–406.

71. Ross and Hartman, *Changing Patterns of Industrial Conflict*, p. 65.

72. Ibid., pp. 68–69.

73. This position was argued by John T. Dunlop in *Wage Determination under Trade Unions* (New York: Augustus M. Kelley, 1950).

2. The "job security" school, which is a variant of the "economic advantage" school. It focuses on the desires of workmen to protect the conditions of their work rather than on short-term wage gains.[74]
3. The "class warfare" (or Marxist) school, which attributes unrest to the systematic exploitation of the working class by the capitalist class. This position has been modified by various historians of the labor movement.[75]
4. The "political" school, which emphasizes political conflict between unions and management over the recognition of unionism and collective bargaining, jurisdictional disputes among unions, internal leadership rivalries, and the influence of communism in unions.[76]
5. The "human relations" school, which traces basic dissatisfactions among laborers to the breakdown of primary groups among workers and the lack of communication and understanding between management and workers.[77]

Despite a great deal of spilled ink, no one of these schools has emerged triumphant, and economic sociologists are still to some degree at loggerheads over the relative merit of the different explanations of the basic causes of strikes. It may, indeed, be wrong to regard the various explanations as competitors; as our survey of findings shows, a *variety* of factors affect industrial conflict, and they differ in salience according to different historical situations. The various "permissive" variables—the institutionalization of collective bargaining, the availability of channels other than strikes to settle conflicts—are perhaps the most powerful in explaining the long-term trends toward decline of that form of conflict. The "economic advantage" explanation appears to have value in explaining labor's strategies as they are related to business ups and downs, but these economic factors may recede into the background during periods of national emergency or political conflict. And as we shall see, social integration at the workplace retains some power in explaining job dissatisfaction and its various manifestations.[78] Finally, different categories of working people are guided by different considerations. In a recent survey,

74. This school is associated with the name of Selig Perlman, who argued his case first in *A Theory of the Labor Movement* (New York: Macmillan, 1928).

75. See, for example, G.D.H. Cole, *A Short History of the British Working-Class Movement 1789–1947* (London: Allen & Unwin, 1952).

76. Ross and Hartman, *Changing Patterns of Industrial Conflict*, pp. 65–67; Ross argued this case at some length in *Trade Union Wage Policy* (Berkeley: University of California Press, 1948).

77. John T. Dunlop and William Foote Whyte, "Framework for the Analysis of Industrial Relations: Two Views," *Industrial and Labor Relations Review* 3, no. 3 (April, 1950):383–401; Louis Schneider and Sverre Lysgaard, " 'Deficiency' and 'Conflict' in Industrial Sociology," *American Journal of Economics and Sociology* 12, no. 1 (October, 1952):49–61.

78. Below, pp. 112–15.

for instance, Form posed questions relating to the purposes of unionism to automobile workers in the United States, Italy, Argentina, and India. Workers in all the countries stressed the "job" aspects of union activity—wages and working conditions—whereas union officers stressed more the political and ideological aspects of union activity.[79] In the light of such arguments and findings, the most appropriate strategy appears to be to abandon attempting to focus any one explanation, and to investigate the specific conditions under which each determinant—or combination of determinants—is likely to be salient in the genesis of conflict.

Finally, what have been the consequences of industrial conflict? Apparently, unions and their activities augment inflationary tendencies. Their emphasis on full employment has had an indirect inflationary effect. In addition, if wages increase more than workers' productivity—and if management compensates for this difference by raising prices—inflation results. Finally, insofar as unions are able to resist wage decreases, they augment the tendency toward high wage and price levels.[80] In many instances, however, labor is the follower in inflationary cycles—concentrating demands for wage increases only after prices and profits have risen in a business upswing; and certainly the primary impetus for the recent worldwide inflation lies in the increasing scarcity of fundamentals like foods and energy sources, with labor and other groups struggling to avoid a steady decline in standard of living.

How does union activity affect labor's share of the national income? When increased wages can be passed on in the form of higher prices, labor's gains are often negligible. When full-employment policies lead to a rising cost of living, labor suffers, for it engages in a "chasing" relationship with rising prices. On the other hand, labor can agitate for governmental tax and welfare measures that redistribute income in favor of the lower-income groups. With regard to wage differentials between unionized and nonunionized workers, union activity can raise the relative level of unionized workers' wages for a period, but over time the wage levels of others often rise as fast. Finally, organized labor can resist labor supply and keep wages high in some industries.

What has been the net effect of these diverse trends in the United States? The most recent studies show that labor's share of the national income has increased only very modestly since 1900.[81] With respect to the respective wages of organized and unorganized labor, Lewis concluded,

79. William H. Form, "Job vs. Political Unionism: A Cross-national Comparison," *Industrial Relations* 12, no. 2 (January, 1973):224–38.

80. Lloyd G. Reynolds, *Labor Economics and Labor Relations*, 5th ed. (Englewood Cliffs, N.J.: Prentice-Hall, 1970), pp. 667–69.

81. Ibid., pp. 215–19.

after a painstaking study of many industries, that "the effect of unionism on the average wage of all union workers relative to the average wage of all nonunion workers was at least ten per cent" in favor of the former between 1923 and 1960. This advantage was greatest in periods of recession or depression, when organized labor was better able than unorganized labor to resist reductions. The advantage all but disappeared in inflationary periods.[82]

With regard to the larger social consequences of industrial conflict, a *prima facie* assumption is that the less the conflict, the less the negative consequences for society. As long ago as the early 1950s, however—and not long after the era of bitter and divisive conflict surrounding the Taft-Hartley legislation—Kerr reminded:

> [Industrial conflict] assists in the solution of controversies; it may reduce intergroup tensions, and it may benefit the worker by balancing management power against union power. "Tactical" mediation can reduce aggressive industrial conflict by decreasing irrationality, by removing nonrationality, by aiding in the exploration of solutions, by abetting the parties in making graceful retreats, and by raising the cost of conflict, but its general contribution cannot be large; "strategical" mediation, or the structuring of the environment, on the other hand, can effect major changes. It involves the better integration of workers and employers into society, the increased stability, the development of ideological compatibility, the arrangement of secure and responsive relationships among leaders and members, the dispersion of grievances, and the establishment of effective rules of the game.[83]

Political Relations between Economic Units and Government

Among the complex relations between economic and political activity, one of the most firmly established is that the volume and complexity of economic activity are positively associated with the volume and complexity of political activity. This appears to hold both for nonindustrialized and industrialized societies. Ember undertook to demonstrate the relationship for the nonindustrialized by taking a sample of twenty-four societies from Murdock's World Ethnographic Sample. As indicators of economic specialization he used "upper limit of community size" and "relative importance of agriculture" (as contrasted, for example, with hunting and gathering). As indicators of political development he used "the degree to which political authority is differentiated" and "the level of integration in the society" as measured by the population of the

82. H.G. Lewis, *Unionism and Relative Wages in the United States: An Empirical Inquiry* (Chicago: University of Chicago Press, 1963), pp. 191–94.

83. Clark Kerr, "Industrial Conflict and its Mediation," *American Journal of Sociology* 60, no. 3 (November, 1954):230–54.

largest territorial group. He calculated rank-order correlations among all sets—except for size of community and political integration, which overlapped as measures—and observed strong positive associations on every count.[84] Serious reservations may be raised about the validity of Ember's indices, but the strength of the associations suggest that economic and political complexity are mutually reinforcing—that complexity of economic activity breeds conflict, inequity, and lack of coordination that call for political regulation, and perhaps that more complex political-legal arrangements provide an institutional setting in which a greater variety of economic activities may flourish.

This is certainly the relationship that Durkheim had in mind when he argued that an increasing differentiation of labor in society demands a multiplication of regulatory functions, increasingly centralized in a state.[85] It is verified, moreover, in the industrialized societies of the world, all of whom have developed political and administrative bureaucracies as their economies have developed. Using complexity and specialization of political structure as indices of political development, Cutright found them to be highly correlated with measures such as economic development, level of communications, and urbanization in a sample of seventy-seven nations.[86] In our own society, the classical laissez faire period of the nineteenth century is over. The government has capitalized on the possibilities of constitutional intervention. Its activities include assistance, promotion, management, regulation, manipulation of—to say nothing of engaging extensively in—economic behavior. These activities reach into many corners—agriculture, old age, labor-management relations, workman's compensation, commerce and business, natural resources, and defense. This growth of governmental power over the economy has been encouraged by the increasing need for coordination as the economy and social structure grow more complex, and by the thorny problems of securing justice and equality in the face of bigness. In addition, the past seventy-five years have been years of great crises—World War I, the Great Depression, World War II, and Cold War, the Vietnamese war—all of which have demanded a political mobilization of resources. Furthermore, the engagement of our massive economy in world trade and the insecurity of world markets threaten to continue the atmosphere of crisis and call for increased governmental regulation.

Some evidence suggests that the level of governmental activity ex-

84. Melvin Ember, "The Relationship between Economic and Political Development in Nonindustrialized Societies," *Ethnology* 2, no. 2 (June, 1963):228–48.

85. Above, pp. 16–17.

86. Phillips Cutright, "National Political Development: Measurement and Analysis," *American Sociological Review* 28, no. 2 (April, 1963):253–64.

pands regardless of political ideology or political system. In comparing various kinds of public expenditures cross-sectionally for 1956 and 1962, Pryor found that type of system (that is, communist or capitalist, decentralized or centralized) was *not* a statistically significant determinant of public expenditures for welfare and health. Rather, these are better explained by factors such as the level of economic development and how long a social insurance system has been in effect. By way of interpretation, Pryor suggested that

> the policy dilemmas facing decision makers of public consumption expenditures are quite similar in all nations, regardless of system. Such policy problems include: the desirability of financing a service through the public rather than the private sector; the proper relationship of different public consumption expenditures to the tax revenues, which must be raised; and balancing citizens' demand for particular services with the adjudged interests of the state. If the basic economic circumstances . . . are similar and if the policy dilemmas are similar, it should not be surprising that the decisions taken are also roughly similar.[87]

In a similar but less comprehensive study, Cutright found that the level of national social security programs is most powerfully correlated with level of economic development.[88] His results also cut across different types of political system.

Other relations between economy and polity are less clear and more controversial. One important topic concerns the implications of economic development for democracy and political stability. In 1960 Lipset developed a forceful statement of the familiar proposition that a high level of economic development encourages both. Defining democracy as "a political system which supplies regular constitutional opportunities for changing the governing officials, and a social mechanism which permits the largest possible part of the population to influence major decisions by choosing among contenders for office,"[89] Lipset classified some fifty societies as "European and English-speaking Stable Democracies," "European and English-speaking Unstable Democracies and Dictatorships," "Latin-American Democracies and Unstable Dictatorships," and "Latin-American Stable Dictatorships." He found these four groupings ranked, in the order listed, according to several indices of economic development—

87. Frederic L. Pryor, *Public Expenditures in Communist and Capitalist Nations* (London: Allen & Unwin, 1968), p. 285.

88. Phillips Cutright, "Political Structure, Economic Development, and National Social Security Programs," *American Journal of Sociology* 70, no. 5 (March, 1965): 537–50.

89. Seymour Martin Lipset, *Political Man* (Garden City, N.Y.: Doubleday, 1960), p. 45.

wealth, industrialization, urbanization, and education. To interpret these associations, Lipset relied on the following arguments: democracy is sustained best when there are few poor in a society and when citizens can afford to exercise self-restraint in politics; increased income, economic security, and widespread education permits the lower strata to develop longer time-perspectives and more gradualist views of politics; and increasing the wealth of the poor makes them more conservative, because they have an interest in holding on to what they have.[90]

Lipset's categorization of political types unfortunately did not separate democracy and stability, which may vary independently from one another. Research by political scientists and sociologists since has addressed each separately. Most studies support the contention that "there is a positive relationship between the level of economic development and stability," though cases like France continue to provide embarrassing exceptions to the rule; in addition, the association is stronger or weaker, according to the measures employed.[91] Likewise, most studies confirm the positive relationship between economic development and the development of democratic institutions, though these are subject to the same reservations.[92]

A second tradition, limited mainly to political conditions in the United States, has emerged with the opposite conclusion: that, as the United States has moved into its most advanced phase of capitalist economic development, democracy has experienced an effective decline. This tradition, associated closely with the work of C. Wright Mills and those who have succeeded him, rests on the arguments that political power has become increasingly concentrated in the United States, that the holders of power and makers of decisions are a small group of corporate executives and military officials, and that this group has consolidated itself as a governing elite.[93] This view has been challenged on methodological grounds.[94] In addition, opposing interpretations have been offered. Some

90. Ibid., pp. 48–66.

91. For a citation of studies relevant to this hypothesis, and a critical evaluation of it and other familiar hypotheses concerning the determinants of stability, see Leon Hurwitz, "Democratic Political Stability: Some Traditional Hypotheses Reexamined," *Comparative Political Studies* 4, no. 4 (January, 1971):476–90.

92. Philip Coulter, "National Socioeconomic Development and Democracy: A Note on the Political Role of the Police," *International Journal of Comparative Sociology* 13, no. 1 (March, 1973):55.

93. The most widely recognized statements of this position are C. Wright Mills, *The Power Elite* (New York: Oxford University Press, 1956); and G. William Domhoff, *Who Rules America?* (Englewood Cliffs, N.J.: Prentice-Hall, 1967).

94. Robert A. Dahl, "A Critique of the Ruling Elite Model," *American Political Science Review* 52, no. 2 (June, 1958):463–69.

social analysts have argued, for instance, that while it may be true that the federal government has increased in power, the sources of influence over the government have become more diversified than they were in the late nineteenth century, when the business and financial communities occupied their strongest position relative to the government.[95] Needless to say, this controversy between the "power elite" and "pluralist" positions has not been resolved. If anything, the respective positions were polarized during the political turmoil of the late 1960s, in which "the establishment" was such a sharp focus of attack and defense.[96]

In many respects the two opposing traditions just considered—that dealing with the positive relation between economic development and democracy and that dealing with the decline of democracy in the most economically advanced nation—are not comparable because they deal with different issues. The one is comparative, the other not; the one deals with democratic institutions (electoral systems, the existence of representative bodies), the other with positions of power and with political decisions; the one focuses on level of economic development in general, the other on economic institutions peculiar to capitalist development. In these ways the two traditions talk past one another. Both can be criticized, however, for their lack of regard for the *specific mechanisms* by which the economy and polity are linked. Assuming that the correlational studies are generally accurate, they say little about *why* economic development and stable political democracy might be associated. Is it the case, as Lipset argued, that wealth and education make for contentment on the part of the lower classes? Or does development create a state that is able, by virtue of its administrative machinery, span of control, and command of resources, to maintain stability despite significant discontent? And how seriously should democratic institutions be taken as measures of democracy? Do they indicate the extent of operative democracy? Or are they in part inventions to convince the citizenry that they are participating in the polity, whereas at a more fundamental level processes are at work that render this participation unimportant or irrelevant?

Similarly, those advancing the "power-elite" theory appear to be long on the characterization of general structures and short on the spe-

95. For different versions of this latter view, see John K. Galbraith, *American Capitalism: The System of Countervailing Power* (Boston: Houghton Mifflin, 1952); David Riesman, Nathan Glazer, and Reuel Denney, *The Lonely Crowd* (Garden City, N.Y.: Doubleday, 1954), pp. 246–58; Talcott Parsons, "The Distribution of Power in American Society" in *Structure and Process in Modern Societies* (Glencoe, Ill.: Free Press, 1960), pp. 199–25.

96. For an intelligent assessment of some of the literature, including a listing of salient issues and unanswered questions, see Clarence C. Walton, "Big Government, Big Business, and the Public Interest," in *The Business of America*, ed. Berg, pp. 83–113.

cifics of mechanisms and processes. The few empirical efforts to test structural connections—for example, the intimate link between corporate and military leaders—by examining policies relating to defense expenditures find the elitist theory wanting in explanatory power.[97] And surely the processes of influence and decision making differ significantly from one political issue to another. With respect to corporate taxes and military expenditures—or foreign economic policy in general—one would expect to find a disproportionate input from the military-industrial complex. On other issues, such as farm subsidies, civil rights legislation, or academic tenure, a different constellation of groups would emerge.[98]

Evidently these two traditions of analysis require supplementing in similar ways. The linkages between economy and polity are understood in part by outlining the economic conditions that are conducive to a democratic political apparatus and in part by mapping the official and unofficial positions of power in society. Yet to understand and explain the mechanisms by which economic forces influence political processes—and what implications this influence has for democracy—it is essential to engage in a careful study of the political processes themselves as they unfold, rather than infer the character of the processes from the broad economic and political contours of societies.

A related issue concerns the question of whether local communities are dominated by a business elite or whether community politics has a more pluralistic basis. In the 1950s a number of studies appeared—each concluding that decisions were guided by a small group of economically dominant individuals.[99] Subsequent studies challenged these conclusions and depicted a more diffused and shifting balance of political power in the community.[100] This debate—which parallels the elitist-pluralist controversy at the level of national power—has continued in the literature of sociology and political science. It has been enlightened to a degree by the

97. Stanley Lieberson, "An Empirical Study of Military-Industrial Linkages," *American Journal of Sociology* 76, no. 4 (January, 1971):562–84.

98. For a characterization of the ideologies, position, and activities of a variety of power groups in America, see R. Joseph Monsen and Mark W. Cannon, *The Makers of Public Policy: American Power Groups and their Ideologies* (New York: McGraw-Hill, 1965).

99. Floyd Hunter, *Community Power Structure* (Chapel Hill: University of North Carolina Press, 1953). See also Roland J. Pellegrin and Charles H. Coates, "Absentee-Owned Corporations in Community Power Structure," *American Journal of Sociology* 61, no. 5 (March, 1956):413–19.

100. Robert Dahl, *Who Governs?* (New Haven: Yale University Press, 1961); see also Nelson W. Polsby, *Community Power and Political Theory* (New Haven: Yale University Press, 1963).

injection of historical and comparative dimensions into the research on community power. In the study of a Midwestern community, Robert Schulze found that over a 100-year period there emerged a tendency for a "withdrawal of the economic dominants from active and overt participation in . . . public life." Schulze attributed this change in part to the increasing control of economic affairs of the community from outside the community, leaving the running of local social and political affairs to "a group of middle-class business and professional people, none of whom are in economically dominant positions."[101] In a follow-up study, Clelland and Form compared Schulze's findings (which applied to an independent city) with their research on a satellite city. Business withdrawal from local political affairs was observed in both cities as they became integrated into national markets, but it appeared to have gone further in the satellite city.[102]

The most ambitious comparative research on community power is Miller's study of Seattle (USA), Bristol (England), Córdoba (Argentina), and Lima (Peru). Miller painted a complicated picture of contrasts and similarities. Business and finance, for example, appeared to be the most influential institution in Seattle, but local government itself was the most influential institution in Bristol and Lima, and religion the most influential in Córdoba—at least according to the estimates of important citizens.[103] Business associations were most important in Seattle, but labor and political organizations overshadowed business associations in the other three cities. Businessmen and financiers represented about thirty percent of the top three dozen influentials in all four of the cities—considerably more than any other category of institutional identity—but among the dozen most influential, only in Seattle did more than half these persons have an institutional identity with business and finance. In Lima business was scarcely represented among the top dozen, seventy per cent coming from political parties, education, and government.[104]

Despite these differences, Miller emerged with one general conclusion: All four cities are industrial centers with heterogeneous economic interests and a salient institutional presence of labor, political party, and government interests. Because of this diversity and heterogeneity, the cities

101. Robert Schulze, "The Role of Economic Dominants in Community Power Structure," *American Sociological Review* 23, no. 1 (February, 1958):9–15.

102. Donald A. Clelland and William H. Form, "Economic Dominants and Community Power: A Comparative Analysis," *American Journal of Sociology* 69, no. 5 (March, 1964):511–21.

103. Delbert C. Miller, *International Community Power Structures: Comparative Studies of Four World Cities* (Bloomington: University of Indiana Press, 1970), p. 205.

104. Ibid., pp. 207–14.

give no evidence of a "single solidary elite structure and no hierarchical dominance based on one institutional structure." This statement, he continued,

> can be made for cities both with and without highly stratified social structures and high class consciousness, since all of these cities have democratic traditions which have allowed strong labor organizations to emerge. Also, suffrage has been extended to create strong opposition parties and independent governments . . . The economic sector is of course powerful in all the cities, and businessmen have a constant stake in most of the political contests in their cities, but no single hereditary economic structure exists in any city . . . in all the cities business, government, and labor are among the . . . most powerful institutions.[105]

THE ECONOMY AND SOLIDARY GROUPINGS

Kinship refers to that complex of social relations that are calculated on the basis of the biological fact of birth and the legal fact of marriage, as supplemented by various legal stipulations regarding adoption, guardianship, and the like. The family—and sometimes the extended kinship unit (including grandparents, grandchildren, uncles, aunts, and cousins) —is the focus of some of the individual's most cohesive social ties. We shall consider kinship as a first example of a solidary grouping.

A second example is the ethnic group. In the United States, according to one definition, "the ethnic group . . . is a loose agglomeration of individuals, aware of a common identity and organized in some degree in voluntary associations, which transmits a definable social and cultural heritage from generation to generation."[106] The ethnic group is closely related to kinship, since it is through the family that ethnic status is usually inherited and through the family that many ethnic influences are exercised. The distinguishing characteristics of ethnic groups are color, national or regional origin, religion, or some combination of these.

Kinship Groupings

In the broad comparative sweep there are rough congruences between type of family structure and type of economic activity. In an analysis of 549 cultures included in the World Ethnographic Sample, Nimkoff and Middleton found the following associations:

105. Ibid., pp. 223–24.

106. Oscar Handlin and Mary F. Handlin, "Ethnic Factors in Social Mobility," *Explorations in Entrepreneurial History* 9, no. 1 (October, 1956):1.

> The independent family system tends to predominate in hunting and gathering societies, the extended family where there is a more ample and secure food supply. The extended family system tends to be associated with social stratification [of property], even when subsistence patterns are held constant. . . . The modern industrial society, with its small independent family, is . . . like the simpler hunting and gathering society and, in part, apparently for some of the same reasons, namely, limited need for family labor and physical mobility.[107]

This general conclusion is consistent with the results obtained by Goode in his extensive comparative study of recent changes in family structure throughout the world. Goode's main proposition was that the social forces of industrialization and urbanization are working to produce a single type of family system—the conjugal system—which has fewer ties with distant relatives and greater emphasis on the nuclear family. Most of his research was designed to document this generalization; but he qualified this proposition in a number of ways. First, he noted that because family changes occur in different types of sociocultural milieux, they converge at different rates of speed. Second, he stressed that because traditional family systems in various regions differ so much from one another, the paths toward this common convergence might move in different directions. For example, one region with traditionally high divorce rates (Arab Islam) may be moving toward a rate that ultimately will be similar to that of another region (Western Europe) with traditionally low divorce rates, although for a long period the movement of their respective rates may be in opposite directions. Third, Goode noted different rates of change within any given society, with the consequence that social-class and other internal differences in family structure may persist for long periods. Finally, while emphasizing industrialization as the main causal factor, he also acknowledged the importance of other causal factors.[108]

More recently Blumberg and Winch have made an effort to consolidate these findings under the rubric of a "curvilinear hypothesis" relating social structure and family structure. They argued that when the structure of social life in general is relatively undifferentiated (as in hunting and gathering), the same will be true of the family; it will be constituted mainly of the independent nuclear family with little elaboration into extended forms. As social structure becomes more complicated, in agricultural or horticultural societies, the family structure likewise extends and becomes more complex. However, the complex economic and

107. M.F. Nimkoff and Russell Middleton, "Types of Family and Types of Economy," *American Journal of Sociology* 66, no. 3 (November, 1960):215–25.

108. William J. Goode, *World Revolution in Family Patterns* (New York: Free Press, 1963).

social structures of highly advanced agricultural and commercial-industrial societies reverse that trend, and the family structure recedes to simpler forms. To test this hypothesis, Blumberg and Winch classified 962 societies from the Ethnographic Atlas according to societal complexity (using technological level and several social-organizational measures as indices) and familial complexity (high or low). While the indices are admittedly crude, the authors found correlations in the expected direction for all the measures. To extend their analysis to industrializing societies, they took a sample of seventy-four modern nations, including countries as advanced as Israel and Japan, and found that the higher the level of socioeconomic development, the lower the level of familial complexity.[109]

Most sociological work on the contemporary family focuses on the impact of industrialization on the modern family. From the 1920s to around 1950, the dominant viewpoint was that the family was deteriorating. Scholars cited the decline of extended kin networks, the decline of parental authority, the increase in divorce rates, the deleterious effects of unemployment on family life, and the rise of juvenile delinquency. All these, it was commonly asserted, are signs of deterioration; this process, moreover, is intimately associated with the encroachments of the urban-industrial way of life, with its call for a small mobile family unit with members frequently in workplaces away from home.[110]

This viewpoint has not gone unchallenged. Parsons, for example, has argued that while it is true that the modern American family has undergone fundamental changes–changes associated with urbanization and industrialization–it is erroneous to regard these as signs of deterioration. Rather, the family has become a more specialized structure. It has lost some of its functions (such as producing economic goods and services as a cooperative unit, and educating its children); but it has become the more exclusive guardian of other functions (specifically, socializing the very young child and providing a setting for emotional tension-management for adults). In addition, the roles of the husband-father and wife-mother have become more specialized relative to one another. That is, the man has become the more exclusive performer of the "instrumental" (external, income-generating) functions of the family, the woman of the "expressive" (social-emotional) functions. These new features of the family, Parsons argued, signify the opposite of disintegration; they show a

109. Rae Lesser Blumberg and Robert F. Winch, "Societal Complexity and Familial Complexity: Evidence for the Curvilinear Hypothesis," *American Journal of Sociology* 77, no. 5 (March, 1972):898–920.

110. A representative statement of this position is found in William F. Ogburn and Meyer Nimkoff, *Technology and the Changing Family* (Boston: Houghton Mifflin, 1955).

nuclear family that is more effective than its predecessor in socializing children for adult roles in a modern urban-industrial complex.[111]

Another line of research that has developed in the past twenty-five years poses a challenge to both these interpretations by suggesting that the extended family has *not* undergone a serious decline. Litwak suggested that while the demands of the modern occupational structure make for high family mobility, this has not destroyed the extended family. In fact, Litwak asserted that "because technological improvements in communication systems have minimized the socially disruptive forces of geographical distance, and because an extended family can provide important aid to nuclear families without interfering with the occupational system," a sort of "modified extended family" has survived into the mid-twentieth century. Litwak attempted to buttress his assertions with studies of visiting patterns in large cities.[112] In addition, dozens of empirical studies in different industrialized societies have uncovered patterns of mutual aid (caring for children, extending credit, assisting in the search for employment), social interaction, and other signs of vitality of the extended kin unit.[113] Such evidence should not suggest, however, that economic changes are not disruptive to extended kin patterns, particularly in the short run. Marris, for example, traced the impact of the dispersion of a neighborhood in a slum clearance project in Lagos (Nigeria), which not only disrupted patterns of family interaction, such as visiting, but eroded the system of employment, credit, and mutual aid that was bolstered by the network of kinship loyalties.[114]

Such research on extended kinship suggests that family structures are not simply passive victims but have some capacity to "roll with the punches" occasioned by changes in their socioeconomic environment. Indeed, another line of research suggests that kinship structures are an important repository of *independent* variables that can inhibit or facilitate economic activity. What are some of the economic effects of kinship?

111. Talcott Parsons et al., *Family, Socialization and Interaction Process* (Glencoe, Ill.: Free Press, 1955), chap. 1.

112. "Occupational Mobility and Extended Family Cohesion," and "Geographic Mobility and Extended Family Cohesion," *American Sociological Review* 25, nos. 1, 3 (February and June, 1960):9–21, 385–94.

113. These studies are summarized in Marvin B. Sussman, "The Urban Kin Network in the formulation of Family Theory," in *Families in East and West: Socialization Process and Kinship Ties*, eds. Reubin Hill and René König (The Hague: Mouton, 1970), pp. 480–503.

114. Peter Marris, *Family and Social Change in an African City: A Study of Rehousing in Lagos* (London: Routledge & Kegan Paul, 1961). For a discussion of the public policy implications of this study, see Marris, "African Families in the Process of Change," in *Families in East and West*, eds. Hill and Konig, pp. 397–409.

Economic activities in all societies are conditioned by an individual's age, sex, and kinship roles. In tribal and peasant societies economic roles are often subordinated to kinship considerations; specific economic duties are assigned to children up to a certain age, others accrue to them at adolescence, and still other activities are taken away from men when their oldest son marries.[115] In modern society such age and sex regulation persists to a degree; we exclude very young children from work, we reserve certain classes of occupations for men and others for women, and we expel old persons from economic roles through retirement.

Kinship roles, moreover, often involve individuals in a network of loyalties that discourage them from taking an attitude of economic calculation, and thus dampen economic activity.[116] Several examples show this effect. Landes has argued that the peculiar structure of the French business family has kept the typical firm small and thus inhibited economic growth. The specific features of family life he stressed are the refusal to go outside the family circle for acquiring capital, a hesitation to separate family budgeting from business budgeting, and recruitment into the firm on grounds other than business ability.[117] Another instance is Fox's finding that in an Indian market town the size of business enterprises was limited by "the essentially familistic organization of business ventures, and the trader's fear of larger commercial organizations because of distrust of nonfamily members."[118] An interesting twist of the same principle was uncovered by Marris and Somerset in their study of African businessmen in Kenya. Unlike their Asian-Kenyan business counterparts, they were often *unwilling* to hire relatives, because of their feelings that relatives were more demanding and insubordinate and thus created jealousies among other workers and otherwise interfered with the conduct of the business.[119]

115. One of the best characterizations of the infusion of kin considerations into the pattern of productive activities is still Conrad M. Arensberg and Solon T. Kimball, *Family and Community in Ireland* (Cambridge, Mass.: Harvard University Press, 1940).

116. The general case for the power of ascriptive roles to weaken efforts to develop economically is stated in Bert F. Hoselitz, "The Power of Indirect Effects of Economic Development," in *Social and Economic Change*, eds. Baljit Singh and V.B. Singh (Bombay: Allied Publishers, 1967), pp. 277–95.

117. David Landes, "French Business and the Businessman: A Social and Cultural Analysis," in *Modern France*, ed. E.M. Earle (Princeton: Princeton University Press, 1951), pp. 334–53.

118. Richard G. Fox, "Family, Caste, and Commerce in a North Indian Market Town," *Economic Development and Cultural Change* 15, no. 3 (April, 1967):312–13.

119. Peter Marris and Anthony Somerset, *African Businessmen: A Study of Entrepreneurship* (London: Routledge & Kegan Paul, 1971), pp. 133–46.

On the other hand, kinship often proves to be an asset to economic undertakings. The Japanese rural family played a facilitative role in the development of an urban labor force in Japan. Through primogeniture it expelled noneldest sons from the land, placed them through intermediaries in jobs, and thus generated a steady supply of migrants to the towns. The resulting process was sufficiently controlled and gradual, moreover, that Japanese cities avoided some of the social disorganization associated with the mass migrations into European and American cities.[120] In quite another economic context—commercial shipping—Bernard Bailyn has argued that

> Kinship goes far in explaining the initiation of overseas trade in New England [during the seventeenth century] and the recruitment of the first New England merchants. Study of the family relations [especially intramarriage] in the second and third generations reveals the consolidation of these early mercantile families. And in the kinship ties secured between the established merchants and the post-Restoration commercial adventurers one may observe the final construction of the merchant group.[121]

In a recent study of ten large manufacturing family firms in Lebanon, Khalaf and Shwayri came to conclusions that at first appear directly opposed to the French case as presented by Landes. Their general argument was that interviewed businessmen found family members to be more competent, trustworthy, and more committed to the firm than outsiders—all qualities that are assets to the business. The authors observed that

> Lebanese firms have not yet reached such a size as to render the employment of outsiders in managerial positions a question of real meaning. . . . Furthermore, they do recognize that the process of dividing responsibilities among themselves cannot continue indefinitely, and that, as the firm grows beyond a certain point, the hiring of outsiders to fill managerial positions becomes a vital and inevitable requirement.[122]

This suggests not so much a contradiction of Landes's findings as a need to reformulate the issue of the effect of kinship on business activity. What may be resources at one stage of economic development (the

120. Ezra F. Vogel, "Kinship Structure, Migration to the City, and Modernization," in *Aspects of Social Change in Modern Japan*, ed. R.P. Dore (Princeton: Princeton University Press, 1967), pp. 91–111.

121. "Kinship and Trade in Seventeenth Century New England," *Explorations in Entrepreneurial History* 6, no. 4 (May, 1954):197–206.

122. Samir Khalaf and Emilie Shwayri, "Family Firms and Industrial Development: The Lebanese Case," *Economic Development and Cultural Change* 15, no. 1 (October, 1966):59–96.

availability of capital from kinsmen, the loyalty of relatives as employees) may become liabilities as credit needs expand beyond the family's capacities and as universalistic hiring practices become institutionalized. It also suggests the inappropriateness of attempting to arrive at a single judgment on the facilitative or obstructive character of the family, and the need to search for conditions under which different kinship structures produce these contrasting effects.

Finally, an analysis of family structure illuminates two important socioeconomic phenomena—female participation in the labor force and the status of the aged. In general, women display a higher turnover rate in employment than men (and, partly as a result, have a higher rate of unemployment); they enter casual and temporary employment more frequently; and they cluster disproportionately in occupations such as nursing, teaching, and clerical work. Furthermore, their level of participation is closely associated with age and marital status. A high participation rate is evident in the late teens and early twenties. A severe drop in participation characterizes the child-bearing years, but about age thirty the rate begins to climb rapidly again.[123]

These regularities rest in part on the general level of economic activity in the society, as well as males' resistances to relinquishing controls in occupations traditionally reserved for them.[124] They also result, however, from the heritage of sex-role norm that males are the primary breadwinners and females have primary responsibility in family matters. Because of the woman's responsibility for young children, her participation rate slumps in these years. Because she is subject to the demands of home, and because she is absent from the labor market for a number of years, she cannot pursue a straight career line as easily as can a man; hence the tendency to enter part-time, less-enduring employment. Finally, since women enter quasi-maternal and supportive occupations (nursing, teaching, social work, secretarial-clerical), a continuity exists between familial and occupational roles.[125]

The changes in female participation in the labor force during the

123. Evidence for these regularities is summarized in Beth Niemi, "The Female-Male Differential in Unemployment Rates," *Industrial and Labor Relations Review* 27, no. 3 (April, 1974):331–50; Gertrude Bancroft McNally, "Patterns of Female Labor Force Activity," *Industrial Relations* 7, no. 3 (May, 1968):204–18; Valerie Kincade Oppenheimer, "The Sex-Labeling of Jobs," *Industrial Relations* 7, no. 3 (May, 1968): 219–34; Hyman Rodman and Constantina Safilios-Rothschild, "Business and the American Family," in *The Business of America*, ed. Ivar Berg, pp. 324–25.

124. Harold L. Wilensky, "Women's Work: Economic Growth, Ideology, Structure," *Industrial Relations* 7, no. 3 (May, 1968):235–42.

125. Even in the medical profession, women doctors tend to specialize in pediatrics, obstetrics, child psychiatry, and the like.

past three decades have been astounding. Between 1948 and 1967 alone, female participation rose from 16.7 million to 28.4 million, a gain of seventy percent. The proportion of working women with children between six and seventeen years of age rose from 26.0 percent to 45 percent and those with children under six rose from 10.8 percent to 26.5 percent.[126] Demand during the prosperous years after World War II was an important determinant, as was the movement of women to break from traditional sex-role patterns;[127] but on the supply side family conditions shaped the pattern of the expansion. The level of husband's income, husband's employment status, and the presence of children all continue to affect the likelihood of a wife's working.[128] The growth of nursery schools, day-care centers, etc., that take responsibility for children at very young ages also free women to enter employment outside the home. In addition, women who had their mothers or other kin to take care of young children were more likely to work than those who did not.[129] The impact of the increase of women in the labor force on the family is not known, but a comparison of interview data from the United States and France indicated that in both countries a working wife increases the probability of her participation in the family's budget management, increases her exercise of authority in the family, decreases her household task performance, and decreases the expected and actual number of children in the family.[130] Families with working wives also appear to migrate over long distances less often than families in which the wife does not work.[131]

Despite the enormous increase in the proportion of women in the labor force, factors that skew their participation remain strong. Gross calculated an index of segregation for several hundred occupations and

126. McNally, "Patterns of Female Labor Force Activity," pp. 204–5.

127. Valerie K. Oppenheimer, "The Interaction of Demand and Supply and Its Effect on the Female Labour Force in the United States," *Population Studies* 21, no. 3 (November, 1967):239–59.

128. McNally, "Patterns of Female Labor Force Activity," pp. 209–10.

129. Barbara Thompson and Angela Finlayson, "Married Women who Work in Early Motherhood," *British Journal of Sociology* 14, no. 2 (June, 1963):165–66.

130. Andrée Michel, "Working Wives and Family Interaction in French and American Families," *International Journal of Comparative Sociology* 11, no. 2 (June, 1970):157–65; see also R. Ferber and F.M. Nicosia, "Newly-Married Couples and their Asset Accumulation Decisions," in *Human Behavior in Economic Affairs: Essays in Honor of George Katona* (Amsterdam: North Holland Publishing Co., 1972).

131. Larry H. Long, "Women's Labor Force Participation and the Residential Mobility of Families," *Social Forces* 52, no. 3 (March, 1974):342–48.

traced the behavior of this index between 1900 and 1960. Overall, the index changed scarcely at all. If anything, those occupations dominated by males early in the century maintained their level of segregation, and where diminution of segregation occurred was in occupations that were dominated by women early in the century and, over the course of the years, recruited more men. Most of the expansion of women in the labor force occurred in occupations already socially designated as "female" (clerical, lower professional such as teaching, etc.)[132]

A final word on the aged: three factors—one biological, one economic, and one social—have combined to make the problem of the unemployed aged increasingly pronounced in industrial societies. The biological factor is the increased life-expectancy associated with the improved standards of living and the development of modern medicine, which has increased the numbers of aged enormously. The economic factor is the difficulty that older yet preretirement workers have in securing reemployment. The social factor is the widespread institutionalization of retirement. All three have contributed to the widespread economic deprivation of the aged, as well as to their frequent isolation and loss of identity.[133] To the three factors must be added one more: the character of kinship organization in the modern Western world. Among the family's characteristics are its tendency to be mobile as a two-generation unit—parents and their children. Oldsters are frequently left behind; they no longer have a distinctive kinship role.[134] This contrasts with more traditional family structures, in which the aged continue to have a meaningful and sometimes highly venerated role. In such systems of kinship, social security and public medical care for the aged are less necessary because families perform some of their functions. The need for formalized, state welfare measures for the aged, then, reflects in part the relative absence

132. Edward Gross, "Plus Ça Change . . . ? The Sexual Structure of Occupations over Time," *Social Problems* 16, no. 2 (Fall, 1968):198–208. For two analyses of the kinds of obstacles—arising both because of occupational discrimination, however subtle, and because of familial considerations—see Rose Laub Coser and Gerald Rokoff, "Women in the Occupational World: Social Disruption and Conflict," *Social Problems* 18, no. 4 (Spring, 1971):535–54; Cynthia F. Epstein, "Encountering the Male Establishment: Sex-status Limits on Women's Careers in the Professions," *American Journal of Sociology* 75, no. 6 (May, 1970):965–82.

133. For a clear analysis of the role-changes in later life, see Irving Rosow, *Socialization to Old Age* (Berkeley: University of California Press, 1974).

134. We should not ignore that body of research, however, that reveals the considerable role of older women in caring for grandchildren, particularly in cases where the young wife works. Above, p. 85. In addition, many who appear on the surface to be isolated—for example, in old folks' homes—often maintain close kinship ties and, indeed, fashion a quasi-familial organization among themselves. For a case studying these integrative aspects, see Arlie Russell Hochschild, *The Unexpected Community* (Englewood Cliffs, N.J.: Prentice-Hall, 1973), chap. 5.

of significant membership in a kinship unit responsible for care and sustenance of its aged.

Ethnic Groupings

History provides many instances of the fusion between membership in an ethnic group and membership in an economic role. Perhaps the most familiar is that found in the pattern of American immigration. Roughly speaking, migrants throughout the past century and a half have filled the lowest economic rung upon arrival, only to be displaced "upward" by the new waves. Different groups, however, have moved upward economically at very different rates. Five factors determine the relative speed of ascent:

1. Economic conditions of demand. The changing economic circumstances of black labor—migration out of the south and entry into occupations other than predominantly farm labor—has resulted in large part from the increased economic opportunities generated by both World Wars and by the relatively continuous prosperity after World War II.
2. The internal resources of the ethnic group itself, both financial and sociocultural. Thus the Jews and Armenians, with a more highly developed commercial tradition than the Polish, Irish, or Italian peasant, possessed an initial advantage in terms of capital and commercial skills.
3. The continuing strength of particularistic ties. Once an inroad on a new, higher-level occupational rung is made by a given ethnic group, the successful few will allocate their new talent and resources to "bring in" people of their own kind to reap the advantages.
4. The degree to which the ethnic group is held back through discrimination. Every ethnic minority has experienced some discrimination; but for blacks this has been most extreme. The black population has been consigned to the ranks of manual labor and servant work and is underrepresented in professional occupations; its rate of unemployment is considerably higher than whites and grows faster than that of whites in periods of economic recession; furthermore, such patterned inequalities have remained quite stable over time.[135] Discrimination rests mainly on two bases—direct, in which employers and unions resist employment of blacks because they are black; and indirect, when employers refuse to hire them because they are less technically qualified for employment—which usually means they have experienced discrimination elsewhere in the system, especially in education.[136]

135. See, for example, E. Wilber Bock, "Farmer's Daughter Effect: The Case of the Negro Female Professionals," *Phylon* 30, no. 1 (Spring, 1969):17–26; Harry J. Gilman, "The White/Non-white Unemployment Differential," in *Human Resources in the Urban Economy*, ed. Mark Perlman (Washington: Resources for the Future, 1963), pp. 75–113.

136. For a summary of the factors influencing occupational opportunities of blacks, see Peter M. Blau and Otis Dudley Duncan (with the collaboration of Andrea Tyree),

5. The degree to which a minority group can improve its opportunities by pressing for political reforms that will remove obstacles to economic advance. Examples are pressures on businesses to adopt fair hiring practices; pressures on government for civil rights legislation; pressures on educational institutions to abandon quota restrictions or indeed to recruit disadvantaged groups preferentially. The precise effect of political pressures of this sort is difficult to calculate; they are probably most effective—that is, less likely to be undermined—when they coincide with other pressures, such as an expanding demand for labor.[137]

One final point is in order with respect to the economic influence of ethnic membership. Ethnic groups generally impose sanctions on their members to interact *within* the group with relatively greater frequency than they interact *outside* the group. There is pressure to vote for one's own kind, to marry one's own kind, and so on. We might suggest that the intensity of economic interaction within ethnic groups is directly related to the degree of knowledge of market conditions.[138] To illustrate: In an analysis of the spatial distribution of physicians in Chicago, Lieberson found that doctors of a certain ethnic background (e.g., Jewish or Irish) tended to concentrate and practice in the corresponding ethnic area of the city. Those ethnic groups that were overrepresented among physicians (Jews, Anglo-Saxons) tended to concentrate in the central Loop area and to concentrate in the medical specializations.[139] This ethnic association between occupational role and recipients of services is greater in medicine than it is in retail food distribution, pharmacies, and so on. The reason for this is that medical practice is, for many patients, both an "unknown" product (we cannot know its quality by trying it on or tasting it) *and* a product about which people have extremely deep emotional feelings. Because of these obstacles to economic calculation people tend to fall back on other criteria for choosing services; they go to people "of their own kind" whom they feel they can trust, and more often than not these people turn out to be members of their own ethnic group. The implications of this reasoning for the analysis of imperfect competition is that in the absence of knowledge or emotional neutrality about a prod-

---

The American Occupational Structure (New York: John Wiley, 1967), pp. 238–41; also F. Ray Marshall, "Racial Factors Influencing Entry into the Skilled Trades," in *Human Resources*, ed. Perlman, pp. 23–54.

137. For a case study, see Ray Marshall, "Some Factors Influencing the Upgrading of Negroes in the Southern Petroleum Refining Industry," *Social Forces* 42, no. 2 (December, 1963):186–97.

138. The model of perfect competition, it will be recalled, posited complete knowledge of market conditions for all actors.

139. Stanley Lieberson, "Ethnic Groups and the Practice of Medicine," *American Sociological Review* 23, no. 5 (October, 1958):542–49.

uct, people will rely on solidary groupings when purchasing goods and services. This criterion forms one of the bases on which markets deviate from the perfectly competitive model.

THE ECONOMY AND SOCIAL STRATIFICATION

Above we cited research that indicated a strain toward consistency between types of economic activity and types of political activity on the one hand, and between types of economic structure and types of family structure on the other. Such patterns of structural coherence are evident in the relations between economic arrangements and stratification systems. For example, Stinchcombe has found correlations between typical agricultural enterprises with typical patterns of stratification and styles of life.[140] Such structural coherence appears in industrial societies as well. Industrialization, while moving along diverse paths in different societies, nonetheless uniformly occasions a reduction in the proportion of agricultural workers, the creation of a large urban manual working population, an increase—over time—of the proportion of the population engaged in service occupations, and the creation of hundreds of new occupational specializations.[141] Such gross changes carry implications for stratification systems, since the economic organization of a society is invariably an important basis for the ranking of its roles. What are some of these implications?

One line of research is based on the argument that all industrializing countries create many similar occupations, such as engineer, factory worker, and salesman. Furthermore, because these occupations require approximately the same skill and responsibility everywhere, they are everywhere awarded the same prestige. As countries industrialize, they evolve systems of occupational prestige that resemble one another.

The first systematic comparative study of occupational prestige was published by Inkeles and Rossi in 1956. They located attitude surveys that had been conducted in the United States, Great Britain, New Zealand, Japan, Germany, and—by interviewing displaced persons—the Soviet Union. In these surveys respondents were asked to evaluate a large number of occupations. The results showed a similarity of occupational ranking in all six societies—an average correlation of .88. Occasional occupations showed a discrepancy—for example, a company director was rated higher in Japan than in the United States, a clergyman higher in the

140. Arthur Stinchcombe, "Agricultural Enterprise and Rural Class Relations," *American Journal of Sociology* 67, no. 2 (September, 1961):165–76.

141. Donald J. Treiman, "Industrialization and Social Stratification," *Sociological Inquiry* 40, no. 2 (Spring, 1970):215–17.

United States than in Great Britain or Japan, and in general occupations not inherently associated with industrialization (clergyman, military officer, doctor) differed more than occupations associated with industrial production. Nevertheless, Inkeles and Rossi argued that their findings indicated a relatively invariant system of occupational prestige in industrial societies.[142]

Later and more comprehensive studies, however, have suggested a more general interpretation. By 1966 enough additional survey data had accumulated to permit Hodge, Treiman, and Rossi to make a similar comparative analysis of surveys from twenty-four countries, many of which were non-Western and nonindustrialized (for example, Indonesia). The results were that the occupational-ranking systems of not only the industrialized societies but also the nonindustrialized ones greatly resemble one another. The average coefficients of all nonfarm occupations among all the nations were almost as high to those obtained by Inkeles and Rossi. From these and other findings, Hodge, Treiman, and Rossi argued that neither industrialization nor level of economic development apparently determines the similarity among occupational prestige systems, but that these similarities may rest on more general structural requirements shared by all complex societies.[143] Jakubowicz, in comparing twenty-six countries of differing levels of industrialization, found similarly high levels of correlation among all societies studied. His results led him to conclude that "there is considerable agreement in the occupational prestige hierarchies of different countries, regardless of their individual culture or level of industrialization," though he noted some differences among nations in their evaluation of blue-collar and white-collar groups.[144]

Research on comparative occupational prestige is weakened because most national surveys have employed different occupational categories, numbers of occupations in the survey, type of sample, and so on—all aggravating the problem of the comparability of results. Furthermore, even assuming the uniformity of results in industrialized and nonindustrialized nations, its interpretation is far from self-evident. Is it true, as Hodge, Treiman, and Rossi argue, that the exigencies of complex social organization induce all societies to evaluate roles similarly? Or might the uniformity be due to common socialization in the early education of students? That is to say, might not the uniformity be a product of cultural trans-

142. Alex Inkeles and Peter Rossi, "National Comparisons of Occupational Prestige," *American Journal of Sociology* 61, no. 4 (January, 1956):329–39.

143. R.W. Hodge, D.J. Treiman, and P.H. Rossi, "A Comparative Study of Occupational Prestige," in *Class, Status and Power*, 2nd ed., eds. Reinhard Bendix and Seymour M. Lipset (New York: Free Press, 1966), pp. 309–21.

144. Malgorzata Jakubowicz, "Comparative Studies of Occupational Hierarchies," *Co-existence* 5, no. 1 (January, 1968):81–83.

mission rather than of meeting structural exigencies? Despite such unanswered questions, the apparent uniformity of occupational ranking suggests the convergence of powerful social forces and encourages the continued search for the character of these forces.

Another structural congruence is between type of stratification and the type of social mobility. By mobility we here refer to the movement of persons through the stratification system. Mobility may take two forms: (1) The movement of *individuals* through a hierarchy of positions. The traditional American ideology stresses this type of mobility. (2) The movement of *groups* or *organizations* through a hierarchy of positions. The most common form of this type of mobility is the movement of family units, as when the head of the household advances through the occupational hierarchy, and the status of the family members moves accordingly. Another form of collective mobility is the movement of formal organizations, as when an academic department breaks into the ranks of the most prestigious departments in the nation.

One major determinant of the form of mobility—individual or collective—is found in the degree to which a stratification system is based on ascription or achievement. Societies vary in the degree to which roles (occupational, religious, political) follow from status ascribed at birth. The basis of ascription may be kinship, age, sex, race or ethnicity, or territorial location. Insofar as these criteria constitute the basis for entering roles, the society emphasizes ascription. Insofar as admission is independent of ascribed bases and rests on some sort of behavior or performance on the part of persons, the society emphasizes achievement.

The implications of the ascription-achievement dimension for the typical form of social mobility in a society are as follows: If ascriptive values are institutionalized, mobility tends to be collective; if achievement values are institutionalized, mobility tends to be individual.

To illustrate: A stratification system at the ascriptive extreme is to be found in classical India. Typically, the individual was born into a caste, and virtually every aspect of future life was determined by this membership—his marriage choice, his occupation, his associational memberships, his ritual behavior, his type of funeral. Choices were made for him from the instant of birth. Because role-memberships were settled in this way, individual mobility from caste to caste was impossible in the lifetime of one individual. The structure of the caste system did not permit it. What form did mobility take in such a system? According to Hutton's account, mobility manifested itself in the form of a *collective* splitting off of subcastes, or what he called the "fissiparous tendencies in Indian castes." He referred to a process whereby a caste was segregated into a subcaste, which for a time accepted wives from other subcastes but simultaneously refused to give daughters to these subcastes. This established a claim to superiority, which was fortified by some change in occupational duties. The final step was to adopt a new caste name and deny all connection with the caste of origin. Thus, in Hutton's language, "[B]y organization and propaganda a caste can change its name and in the course of time get a new one accepted, and by altering its canons of behavior in the matter of diet and marriage can increase the estimation in which it is held."[145] This multiplication of castes over the centuries is the clue to the distinctive form of mobility in classical India. Even after the considerable impact of Western individualistic values has opened the way for various kinds of individual mobility regardless of caste origins, caste mobility survives in modified form in contemporary society.[146]

A stratification system at the extreme of achievement is found by referring to the traditional American system of values. This system encourages the movement of individual persons away from ascribed positions (based on region, ethnic background, and even family of orientation) into new roles. In practice, ascribed characteristics—especially those based on race, sex, and age—have always prevented the operation of this system in pure form. Hence, side by side with an emphasis on individual mobility based on achievement are found a number of tendencies for collective mobility to develop. For example, when a person assumes an adult occupational role and reaches age thirty, for example, his mobility as an individual is more or less completed, except perhaps within the same occupational category. Thus adults holding the same occupational status are in certain respects in ascribed positions, though this ascription is not a matter of their position at birth. Under these circumstances mobility tends to become collective. Entire occupational groups (nurses, for instance) try to improve their position or to safeguard it from erosion. Or to take another example, the assignment of certain groups—notably the black minority and women—to occupational statuses has been based heavily on ascriptive criteria. As such this constitutes a block to individual mobility on the part of their members. Thus blocked from the form of dominantly institutionalized mobility, these groups have often turned to collective forms, usually manifested in a social movement directed at improving the general lot of the disadvantaged group. Both examples suggest a general conclusion: when the battle for individual mobility is effectively closed—or, to put it differently, when the individual is lodged in an ascribed group—efforts at mobility tend to become collectivized.

Thus the *form* of mobility is closely related to the structure of the stratification system. In addition, it has been argued that the *rate* of up-

145. J.H. Hutton, *Caste in India (London: Cambridge University Press*, 1946), pp. 41–61, 97–100.

146. M.N. Srinivas, "Some Expressions of Caste Mobility," in *Social Change in Modern India* (Berkeley: University of California Press, 1966), pp. 89–117.

ward mobility is closely related to the type of economic system. According to influential studies conducted by Lipset, Bendix, and Zetterberg, "the overall pattern [rates] of social mobility appears to be much the same in the industrial societies of various Western countries."[147] This conclusion ran counter to the common assumption that the United States is a relatively "open" society by contrast with many of the Western countries with a greater legacy of brittleness of class structures. Lipset and Bendix maintained that it is not the ideological and cultural differences among countries that influence rates of mobility most, but rather similarities and differences in their occupational structures. Thus industrial societies will present broad similarities in rates of mobility.

In addition to the fact that cross-national measures of mobility are fraught with methodological difficulties, we might observe that the only major type of mobility index utilized in the Lipset-Bendix-Zetterberg studies was the movement from manual to nonmanual occupations. This gross index, helpful for some purposes, conceals many sources of meaningful variation, such as the movement from business into professional occupations. Indeed, as scholars have conducted further research relevant to the hypothesis ventured by Lipset, Bendix, and Zetterberg, the comparative picture has become more complicated. This research on better data appears to confirm the gross similarities in manual-nonmanual shifts uncovered in the original study. In addition, however, rates of movement from nonmanual into manual strata, movement from manual strata into elite strata, and movement out of elite strata have shown considerable variations among industrial societies. In particular, movement from the manual strata into the elite strata (higher business and professional) appears to be higher in the United States than in other industrialized societies.[148]

Another topic discussed widely in the sociological literature concerns the American rate of mobility in comparison with its own past. In particular, there has been a preoccupation with whether the stratification system has become more rigid, less open to opportunity. In the 1940s and 1950s the predominant judgment among scholars and commentators was that the system was hardening. Among the reasons for inferring a decline

147. Seymour M. Lipset and Reinhard Bendix, *Social Mobility in Industrial Society* (Berkeley: University of California Press, 1959), p. 13.

148. Blau and Duncan, *The American Occupational Structure*; and S.M. Miller, "Comparative Social Mobility, A Trend Report and Bibliography," *Current Sociology* 9, no. 1 (1960):1–89. In another study Cutright found "occupational inheritance"—a negative measure of mobility—to be correlated negatively with such visions as level of technology, national structures facilitating mobility (e.g., provisions for occupational training) and family size. Phillips Cutright, "Occupational Inheritance: A Cross-National Analysis," *American Journal of Sociology* 73, no. 4 (January, 1968):400–416.

in upward mobility were the facts that foreign migration—which supplied a floor of unskilled labor—diminished as a result of the immigration laws of the 1920s; that the differential birth rates between classes had been diminishing gradually over many decades, leaving less room at the top; that many studies showing inflexibilities in mobility were conducted in local communities (where mobility to other communities was seldom measured); and that many of the studies of stratification in such communities were conducted in the depression period of the 1930s.[149] As better data have been generated through national samples, this judgment has been tempered. Several comprehensive surveys of the census and survey materials indicate that as of the middle 1960s, at least, there appeared to be no noticeable slackening of the rate of upward mobility—except perhaps for a dip in the depression of the 1930s—and that the continued opportunity for upward mobility in most recent decades has resulted from the rapid expansion of higher salaried positions.[150] Since, however, the rate of mobility appears to depend in large part on continued economic expansion and the occupational shifts that accompany it, it would be hazardous to posit a simple continuation of the recent trends into the 1970s and 1980s, given the uncertain prospects of the nation's and the world's continued economic growth.

Conclusion

The theme in this chapter has been the relations between economic and noneconomic variables at the level of society as a whole. Now we change lenses. We shall continue to focus on the relations between economic and noneconomic variables, but we shall do so at the more microscopic level of economic processes.

149. A sample of sources stressing this position are Elbridge Sibley, "Some Demographic Clues to Stratification," *American Sociological Review* 7, no. 3 (June, 1942):322–30; W. Lloyd Warner and J.O. Low, *The Social System of the Modern Factory* (New Haven: Yale University Press, 1947), p. 185; C. Wright Mills, *White Collar* (New York: Oxford University Press, 1951), p. 259; Vance Packard, *The Status Seekers* (New York: David McKay, 1959).

150. See, for example, Stuart Adams, "Origins of American Occupational Elites, 1900–1955," *American Journal of Sociology* 62, no. 4 (January, 1956):360–68; Elton F. Jackson and Harry J. Crockett, Jr., "Occupational Mobility in the United States: A Point Estimate and Trend Comparison," *American Sociological Review* 29, no. 1 (February, 1964):5–15; Blau and Duncan, *The American Occupational Structure* chap. 3.

CHAPTER 4 SOCIOLOGICAL ANALYSIS OF ECONOMIC PROCESSES

Economists commonly view the economic process as one of *production* and *consumption*. Production involves the assembling and applying of resources; consumption, the using up of the resultant product. The processes of production and consumption necessitate some technique for *distribution*—that is, channeling inputs (raw materials, capital, and labor) to the firm, and outputs to the consumers.

In this chapter we shall use this view of economic processes as an organizing principle. First, we shall observe the sociological variables that affect the productive process. Second, we shall investigate distribution and exchange, in particular the implications of different social-structural arrangements for the pattern of exchange itself, and the intervention of sociological variables in the markets for labor services, entrepreneurial services, and consumers' goods. Third, we shall turn to consumption, assembling some disparate results of research that have accumulated in economics and sociology.

THE PRODUCTION PROCESS

Technological and Related Determinants

Our effort to analyze the productive process will be in keeping with the general enterprise of economic sociology—to examine the impact of sociological variables on various kinds of economic pursuits.[1]

1. Above, pp. 43–44.

In the productive process, however, many of these variables cluster into patterns determined by the technological arrangements that govern production. The term *technological* refers, first, to the principles of knowledge (common sense, rules of thumb, scientific knowledge) on which production of goods and services is based, and, second, to the relations among tools, machines, energy sources, and people that arise from the application of this knowledge.

The immediate impacts of technology on human activities are the following:

1. The technical arrangements of work determine in large part the degree of physical exertion required from the human organism.
2. Technical features of the job influence the degree to which work is paced and human activities are structured. A highly integrated work flow (for example, serial assembly of a product on a line) calls for a corresponding tightness of control over the behavior of persons working at various points along the flow of work.[2]
3. Technical arrangements of production influence the level of skill required of workers. In a study of British firms, Woodward found the number of college graduates in "process" or "continuous flow" production—based on a highly complex technology—greater than in either "large batch and mass production" or "unit and mass production," and that mass production had a higher proportion of unskilled workers than either of the other two forms.[3]
4. Technical features determine in part the degree of specialization of the division of labor and the structuring of authority. Both clerical-administrative and management-supervisory categories of employees grow proportionately larger with greater technological complexity.[4] Furthermore, if the work flow is highly integrated, authority can be more decentralized, since control is exercised by the pace and organization of the work itself.[5]
5. Technological features of work influence the character of social interaction. The physical pattern of work calls for certain kinds of cooperation and communication on the job. This influence often extends to off-the-job interaction as well. A salient feature of modern family life is that for most of the daylight hours one or more family members are absent from the home in a workplace. Or, to choose a more striking example, the timing of work invades almost every aspect of the life of a railroader:

2. D.S. Pugh et al., "The Context of Organization Structures," in *Comparative Organizations*, ed. Wolf V. Heydebrand (Englewood Cliffs, N.J.: Prentice-Hall, 1973), p. 79.

3. Joan Woodward, *Industrial Organization: Theory and Practice* (London: Oxford University Press, 1965), pp. 57–58, 60.

4. Ibid., pp. 55–57, 59–60.

5. Pugh et al., "The Context of Organization Structures," in *Comparative Organizations*, ed. Heydebrand, p. 79.

> . . . the pattern of social relationships set by the occupation vitally affects the social life of the railroader. It prevents normal relationships between the wife and husband, father and child. While cutting him off from most other group behavior, thus intensifying their significance, these time relationships also interfere with normal family group activities such as eating, sleeping, and recreation. Time-dependency cuts the family off from other groups in the community as well as its members from each other. It interferes with community activity, preventing the assuption of civic responsibility, and denying status so gained.[6]

Technological forces may ramify even further into the social and natural order. To mention an apparently minor innovation, the introduction of the snowmobile (a technological advance over the dog and reindeer sled) into northern areas such as Alaska and Lapland revolutionized reindeer herding and hunting; shortened the workweek of hunter-trappers dramatically; increased their earnings; established a new basis of community ranking (who owns and who does not own a snowmobile); and generated a serious ecological imbalance as populations of snowbound game animals were wiped out.[7] In the larger picture the technological revolution of the past two centuries has greatly altered the distribution of the world's resources, productivity, and wealth. It has equipped humanity with the ability to destroy its civilization at a blow with nuclear weapons, and to destroy it gradually by ruining the environment or by exhausting the earth's resources.[8] And by developing extremely complex, technologically based societies, many Western countries have revolutionized their modes of recreation, social organization, and political control.[9]

Much research in economic sociology has attempted to assess the impact of technology on the working population. One of the most influ-

6. W. Fred Cottrell, *The Railroader* (Stanford, Ca.: Stanford University Press, 1940), pp. 76–77.

7. Pertti J. Pelto and Ludger Müller-Wille, "Snowmobiles: Technological Revolution in the Arctic," in *Technology and Social Change*, eds. H. Russell Bernard and Pertti J. Pelto (New York: Macmillan, 1972), pp. 188–99.

8. William O. Baker, "The Dynamism of Science and Technology," in *Technology and Social Change*, ed. Eli Ginsberg (New York: Columbia University Press, 1964), pp. 82–94; Kenneth Boulding, *The Meaning of the Twentieth Century: The Great Transition* (London: Allen & Unwin, 1965).

9. For a variety of diagnoses of the larger impact of technological forces, see Jacques Ellul, *The Technological Society, trans.* John Wilkinson (New York: Vintage Books, 1964); Jean Meynaud, *Technocracy*, trans. Paul Barnes (London: Faber & Faber, 1968); and Daniel Bell, *The Coming of Post-Industrial Society: A Venture in Social Forecasting* (New York: Basic Books, 1973).

ential studies is that of Blauner.[10] He identified worker alienation as his main dependent variable and specified several of its component parts—a feeling of powerlessness, which arises when the worker does not control his means of production or work situation; a feeling of meaninglessness, which arises when the worker contributes only in small measure to the final product; a feeling of isolation, which arises when a worker does not belong to an effective social unit on the job; and a feeling of self-estrangement, which arises when work becomes simply a means to make a living rather than a path toward individual self-fulfillment.

Blauner also assumed that factory conditions as such do not cause alienation, but rather that different types of industry give rise to different levels of dissatisfaction, because they have different technologies, different divisions of labor, different bureaucratic structures, and different positions in the economic structure. Accordingly, he decided to study worker alienation in four industries that differed from one another along these dimensions—automobile production, textile production, automated chemical production, and printing. He analyzed the structure of each industry, estimating which would be likely to produce an alienated work force. Then he checked these estimates against interviews of workers that yielded information on levels and kinds of dissatisfaction in each industry.

As expected, the auto workers were highest on alienation scores, and the printers lowest. On the assembly lines, the auto worker has little control over his conditions of work, little relief from monotony, little responsibility for the total final product, little personal interaction on the job, and little involvement in a cohesive occupational community. By contrast, the printer, a member of one of the surviving crafts, sets his own pace of work, sees the results of his labor, works in a more intimate social setting, and belongs to an occupational community.

The textile workers expressed an intermediate level of alienation. As loom tenders they are subject to the same constraints as the automobile workers; they are tightly supervised, their pace of work is set, and they have almost as little control over the final product. The particular setting of the workers studied, however, was a small Southern town with a traditional, homogeneous, and relatively stable social life, all of which counterbalanced the effects of the work situation.

The level of alienation among the operators in the chemical refinery was only slightly higher than among the printers. Though the operator does not determine the rate of production, he is responsible for monitoring it. He is often a member of a team, each of whose members makes a definite contribution to the total work process, and he has some

10. Robert Blauner, *Alienation and Freedom* (Chicago: University of Chicago Press, 1964).

freedom to vary his style of work. He is not likely to be closely supervised by managers.

In the past decade several lines of research have addressed the issues guiding Blauner's study. Some results are consistent with his work, others not so. The findings of Fullan's study of 1,491 Canadian manual workers from three industries–printing, automobile, and oil–mainly agree with Blauner's. The technologies of these three industries call for different degrees of worker integration with one another and with supervisors. Fullan found worker integration highest in oil, next in printing, and lowest in automobile manufacture; he also found measures of positive or negative attitudes toward the company and measures of labor turnover –both facets of alienation–to vary in the expected directions.[11] Also consistent with Blauner's line of argument is Kornhauser's study of the mental health of a sample of manual workers in Detroit's automotive manufacturing plants. Mental health was measured by an index constructed from interview data, supplemented by judgments by professional clinicians and workers' wives. Kornhauser concluded that large numbers of workers expressed feelings that demonstrated unsatisfactory life adjustments or mental health. More significantly, mental health indices were correlated with occupation; those in more skilled, more diverse, more responsible and higher-paid occupations showed fewer signs of inadequate personal adjustment. Furthermore, since prejob characteristics such as level of education did not appear to account for the observed differences, Kornhauser argued that the situational characteristics of the job were important in generating differences in mental health.[12]

Other research casts doubt on the alienative impact of factory work. In a study of British automobile workers, Goldthorpe found that assemblers were not satisfied with their jobs for the expected reasons: "the minute subdivision of tasks, repetitiveness, low skill requirements, predetermination of tools and techniques, and mechanically controlled rhythms and speeds of work." Overwhelmingly, also, the workers gave the level of pay as the main reason they remained in assembly work. But the majority of the sample had held jobs that were more skilled and more rewarding in terms of immediate work satisfactions. This led Goldthorpe to give a different reading to the alienation thesis:

> . . . the workers we studied had for the most part been impelled, by their desire for higher incomes, into taking work which was in fact better paid than most other forms of employment available to them largely to compensate

11. Michael Fullan, "Industrial Technology and Worker Integration in the Organization," *American Sociological Review* 35, no. 6 (December, 1970):1028–39.

12. Aruthur Kornhauser, with the collaboration of Otto M. Reid, *Mental Health of the Industrial Worker: A Detroit Study* (New York: John Wiley, 1965), pp. 260–62.

> for its inherent strains and deprivations. If, therefore, these workers are to be considered as 'alienated,' the roots of their alienation must be sought not merely in the technological character of the plants in which they are now employed but, more fundamentally, in those aspects of the wider society which generate their tremendous drive for economic advancement and their disregard for the costs of this through the impoverishment of their working lives.[13]

Goldthorpe suggested, in other words, that the workers were willing to endure monotony and other kinds of dreariness because of the money they made, rather than alienated by the job conditions.

Survey data from non-Western countries raises further doubts. Inkeles and his collaborators interviewed six thousand men from six developing countries in an effort to seek the determinants of "modern" outlooks in the populations of these countries. (By "modern" they referred to an outlook involving such attributes as an openness to new experience, independence from parental authority, and taking an active part in civic affairs.) Occupational experience in large-scale organizations, especially factories, appeared to contribute significantly to the development of modern attitudes. Yet, using a complex index of psychosomatic symptoms as a measure of mental stress, they could find no consistent relationship between exposure to the factory and stress.[14] Form surveyed workers in automobile plants—the exemplar of an alienating setting, according to other studies—in the United States, Italy, Argentina, and India. He found that in all these countries workers seemed relatively satisfied with their work life and routines; and he could find no relationship between technological complexity and "anomie" (a concept not unlike alienation). "Evidence mounts," he concluded, "that we should modify or abandon technological explanations of alienation and anomie."[15]

Equally conflicting evidence emerges from research that asks whether specialization of occupational performance is negatively related to level of worker dissatisfaction. A number of studies indicate that the more

13. John H. Goldthorpe, "Attitudes and Behavior of Car Assembly Workers: A Deviant Case and a Theoretical Critique," *British Journal of Sociology* 17, no. 3 (September, 1966):228–30.

14. Alex Inkeles, "Making Men Modern: On the Causes and Consequences of Individual Change in Six Developing Countries," *American Journal of Sociology* 75, no. 2 (September, 1969):208–25; Alex Inkeles and David H. Smith, "The Fate of Personal Adjustment in the Process of Modernization," *International Journal of Comparative Sociology* 11, no. 2 (June, 1970):101–3.

15. William H. Form, "Occupational and Social Integration of Automobile Workers in Four Countries," in *Comparative Perspectives on Industrial Society*, eds. William A. Faunce and William H. Form (Boston: Little, Brown, 1969), pp. 222–44; Form, "Technology and Social Behavior of Workers in Four Countries," *American Sociological Review* 37, no. 6 (December, 1972):727–38.

specialized the role, the more dissatisfied its incumbent.[16] On the basis of such a relationship, some firms have undertaken experiments of "job enrichment" or "job enlargement" as an antidote. Yet other empirical studies do not show the same association, and still others suggest that the association holds for workers who bring definite cultural expectations of autonomy and control to the job setting but not for workers who do not.[17] A recent study by Shepard underscores the importance of attempting to control extraneous variables if the confused findings are to be unscrambled. Defining functional specialization as high among machine operators, medium among monitors in an automated system, and low among craft jobs, he interviewed a sample of each kind of workers with respect to their sense of job satisfaction. But in addition he gathered data concerning the size of the workers' community and data concerning the workers' general orientation toward work, to see if these variables might account for differences in job satisfaction. According to his analysis, degree of job specialization remained a powerful predictor of level of dissatisfaction even after such intervening variables were introduced.[18]

A final line of research on the impact of technology concerns the effects of automation. Compared with the assembly line, automated production lessens the amount of physical labor required by workmen and reduces the close attention to detailed processes of production. Furthermore, the pacing of work is removed even further from the control of workmen than under assembly-line production. The general level of skill is upgraded. Whole ranges of unskilled and semiskilled positions (repairmen, clerks, typists) are eliminated or reduced in number. At the lower skill levels automation has reduced occupational specialization by removing highly specialized types of jobs. At the higher skill levels new specializations, demanding more detailed knowledge and training, have emerged.

The economic consequences of automation are only imperfectly understood. Initially the introduction of automated production raised the fear of large-scale unemployment. When the generally favorable postwar employment situation began to give way to higher levels of unemployment in the late 1950s, some attributed this to improved agricul-

16. For a review, see Jon M. Shepard, "Functional Specialization and Work Attitudes," *Industrial Relations* 8, no. 2 (February, 1969):185–89.

17. See A.C. MacKinney, P.F. Wernimont, and W.O. Galitz, "Has Specialization Reduced Job Satisfaction?" and Charles L. Hulin, "Individual Differences in Job Enrichment—The Case Against General Treatments," in *Organizational Issues in Industrial Society*, ed. Jon M. Shepard (Englewood Cliffs, N.J.: Prentice-Hall, 1972), pp. 378–410.

18. Jon M. Shepard, "Functional Specialization, Alienation, and Job Satisfaction," *Industrial and Labor Relations Review* 23, no. 2 (January, 1970):207–19.

tural technology and automation, which wiped out jobs at unskilled and semiskilled levels, leaving numbers of workers who could not move into upgraded positions—youth, minority group members, and displaced older workers.[19] Others countered that insufficient aggregate demand was primarily responsible for the rising unemployment, not structural rigidities in the labor market. The debate has not been finally resolved.[20]

Nor are the social and psychological effects of automation completely clear. In some cases workers are isolated more from one another; in others new patterns of interaction are generated by the different coordinative process.[21] In the short run any introduction of labor-saving devices raises anxieties about the security of employment.[22] As for the longer-run psychological effects, one line of research—consistent with Blauner's findings—suggests that workers in automated settings are more satisfied with their working conditions because they have a wider span of control over productive activities and pay less attention to matters of detail.[23] Such findings have been challenged, however; in a survey of twelve automating industries in Pennsylvania, Susman found that the technology of automation has introduced none of the presumably alienation-reducing features stressed by Blauner, with the possible exception that it generally elevated the status of jobs.[24]

Reviewing the work on the impact of technology, we are forced to conclude that it is uneven in quality and conflicting in results. Why should that be? For one thing, different investigators have employed such different measures of technology and its presumed effects that uniform

19. See, for example, Arnold Rose, "The New Problem of Large-Scale Unemployability," *The American Journal of Economics and Sociology* 23, no. 4 (October, 1964):337–50.

20. For a review of issues, see Arthur M. Ross, "Introduction: The Problem of Unemployment," in *Unemployment in the American Economy*, ed. Arthur M. Ross (New York: John Wiley, 1964); also V. Stoikov, "Increasing Structural Unemployment Re-examined," *Industrial and Labor Relations Review* 19, no. 3 (April, 1966): 368–76.

21. For a review of a number of studies, revealing the diversity of impacts, see Floyd C. Mann, "Psychological and Organizational Impacts," in *Automation and Technological Change*, ed. John T. Dunlop (Englewood Cliffs, N.J.: Prentice-Hall, 1962), pp. 43–65.

22. Dan J. Champion, "Some Impacts of Office Automation upon Status, Role Change, and Depersonalization," *Sociological Quarterly* 8, no. 1 (Winter, 1967):71–84.

23. See the references in footnotes 6 and 14 above. See also Jon M. Shepard, *Automation and Alienation: A Study of Office and Factory Workers* (Cambridge, Mass.: M.I.T. Press, 1971).

24. Gerald I. Susman, "Process Design, Automation, and Worker Alienation," *Industrial Relations* 11, no. 1 (February, 1972):34–45.

results can scarcely be expected to emerge. In addition, "technology" is not a single variable but a pattern of different variables such as required physical exertion, pacing, a mode of supervision, a level of specialization, and so on. In attempting to relate such a multi-variable phenomenon to level of worker satisfaction, for example, the investigator cannot know which aspect of the technological complex, if any, may be having the impact. The appropriate research strategy is to disaggregate the component aspects of technology into separate variables, and to attempt to relate them to less global variables than "satisfaction" or "alienation."

In this section we have considered the social and psychological aspects of work as they are affected by the technological features of the work situation. Now we shall treat these aspects as subjects in their own right. We shall apply the general variables of economic sociology to the social organization of production; and we shall observe how the social aspects feed back into and influence the productive process.

For purposes of analysis we shall consider two basic units of social structure—*occupational roles* and *organizations*. Roles and organizations overlap in two ways. First, sometimes an individual in a role (for instance, an individual medical practitioner) faces all the essential problems of production and distribution and is thus a sort of "one-person organization." Second, organizations consist of an interlocking set of roles (engineers, foremen, workmen, etc.).

Occupational Roles

Economists' versions of the attitudes and behavior of persons in occupational roles often follow the logic of supply and demand. They assume that the amount of work offered by an individual in the market is some function of the economic rewards available to him. The supply curve would be smooth and upward-sloping, as figure 2 shows.

At times economists have reconsidered this simple notion. Keynes's argument, illustrated by figure 3, is that while the general relation between

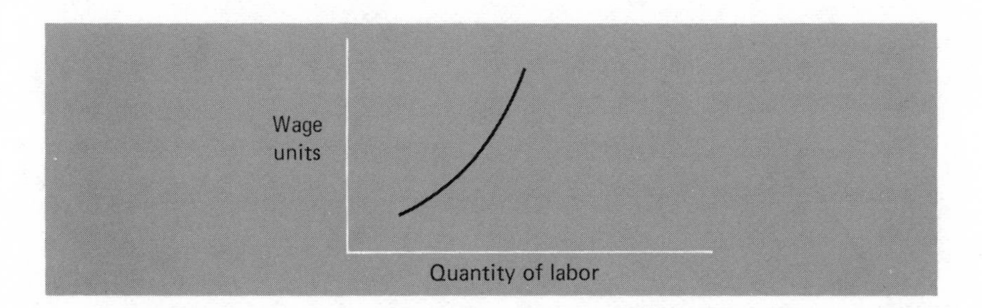

Figure 2

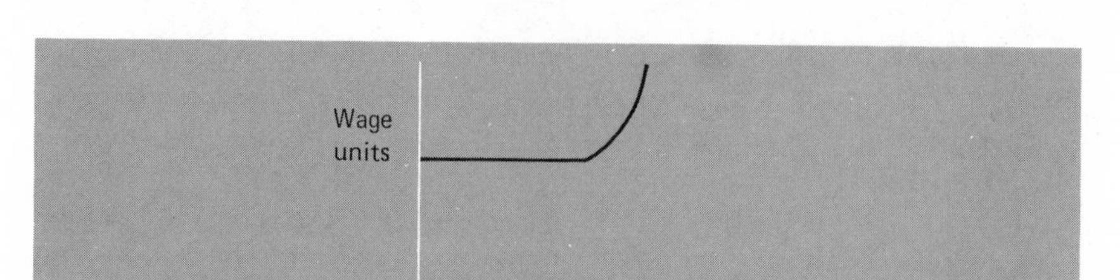

Figure 3

wages and labor is positive, the individual withdraws his labor altogether from the market rather than merely works less if money wages are cut beyond a certain level. Other economists have stressed that particularly in economically underdeveloped areas wage increases bring forth not more but less labor, because the individual prefers to spend his additional earnings on leisure activities rather than to work more. Figure 4 shows that this produces a backward-sloping supply curve. Finally, economists allow for the possibility that under certain conditions—for instance, changes in value systems, changes in technology—a labor supply curve may shift to the right or left.

From the standpoint of economic sociology, economists' notions on behavior in the labor role suffer from the following limitations:

1. Such views ignore the mutual interdependence among laborers. Hughes voiced this "human relations" objection as follows:

> [Many managers and social science investigators adhere to] the belief that an industrial organization is an aggregation of individuals, each seeking his own gain without reference to other persons, and consequently each capable of being induced to greater effort by devices focused upon this desire for

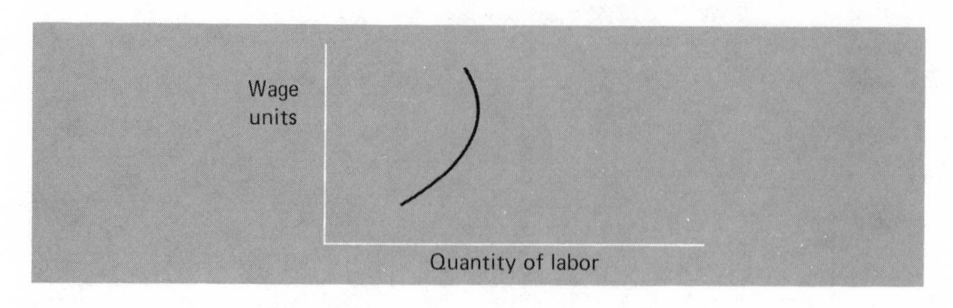

Figure 4

advantage. To this assumption [Elton] Mayo opposes the view that a working force normally consists of social groups, whose members are highly responsive to each other's social gestures and identify their fates with those of their fellows; social groups which, further, are related to others in the larger system of social relations in and about industry.[25]

This criticism is blunted, however, insofar as economists have systematically incorporated the role of labor unions into the determination of labor-supply curves or labor-management relations.[26]

2. In practice the positive relation between monetary reward and effort expended does not seem to work out, as seen in the ineffectiveness and even backfiring of incentive schemes such as piecework and merit plans.[27]

3. Even though economists acknowledge that additional psychological factors influence the motivation to work,[28] and that additional social factors (such as extended kinship obligations) influence a labor-supply curve, they typically assume such factors to be given. While permissible for purposes of formal economic analysis, this assumption is not sufficient for economic sociologists, who treat the additional factors as variable.

Thus the economic sociologist would insist that many more variables than wages determine the amount of work offered by a laborer. In addition, he asks about types of behavior other than the amount of labor offered; he focuses on workers' ideologies, their interaction among one another, their responses to authority, and so on. In short, the economic sociologist expands the number of dependent variables beyond the scope envisioned by the economist.

Let us now consider several occupational roles that have been analyzed in the sociological literature:

The executive role. As the business corporation has grown larger and more complex, executive or top managerial roles have taken on new dimensions. The political and integrative facts of those roles have become more salient. He must coordinate the input of information relevant to his decisions from a greater diversity of sources within the firm; and he must communicate his decisions to a vast array of departments and divisions of the firm so that they may be implemented. In addition, the

25. Everett Cherrington Hughes, "The Knitting of Racial Groups in Industry," *American Sociological Review* 11, no. 5 (October, 1946):512.

26. Above, pp. 70–71.

27. For an overview of a vast literature on this subject, see Robert L. Opsahl and Marvin D. Dunnett, "The Role of Financial Compensation in Industrial Motivation," in *Organizational Issues*, ed. Shepard, pp. 340–74.

28. For a convenient listing of various individual motives that influence the disposition to work, see Victor Vroom, *Work and Motivation* (New York: John Wiley, 1964).

executive is a coordinator—he must see that things get done on time, be a trouble-shooter, and listen to grievances and problems of heads of departments. With regard to the firm's external relations as well, many of his activities are coordinative—to balance off the demands of consumers, bankers, stockholders, directors, and union leaders.[29]

Sociologists have identified typical strains in the executive's role: (1) He is under cross-pressure from different individuals, groups, and agencies. (2) He is under pressure to make decisions in a relatively brief time, despite the fact that they must sometimes be made under conditions of ambiguity or uncertainty. (3) His role demands impersonality in human relations. Given the institutionalized emphases of his role—calculation, profit making, responsibility, and authority—the businessman must be practical and sometimes ruthless in dealing with human beings. He has to issue unpleasant orders; he is under pressure to fire subordinates he regards as incompetent, even though they might in other contexts be his friends.[30]

A widespread reaction to cross-pressure and uncertainty is the development of magical beliefs that reduce ambiguity and thus provide a standard for decision making and action.[31] Many self-images of the businessman serve this function. Consider the following stereotypes: (a) The businessman as a "man of action," the driving, aggressive, impulsive decision maker personified. He is pictured as irascible, impatient with assistants, and convinced of the rightness of "the decision" as such. (b) The "intuitionist," who, after sitting in contemplation for a moment, comes intuitively to a decision, which is correct because it "clicks." (c) The "man of common sense" or the "practical man." Such self-images provide a rationale for making decisions in ambiguous situations and, in addition, protect the executive against inroads on his authority by subordinates and by "experts." Sutton et al., suggested that one reason why businessmen scapegoat government lies in their effort to assign meaning

29. For a summary of empirical studies describing the various facets of the managerial role, see Leonard R. Sayles, *Managerial Behavior: Administration in Complex Organizations* (New York: McGraw-Hill, 1964), p. 44. Also Chester I. Barnard, *The Functions of the Executive* (Cambridge, Mass.: Harvard University Press, 1958); Thomas A. Mahoney, Thomas H. Jerdee, and Stephen J. Carroll, "The Job(s) of Management," *Industrial Relations* 4, no. 2 (February, 1965):97–110.

30. For discussion of these and other strains in the businessman's role, see Eugene V. Schneider, *Industrial Sociology, The Social Relations of Industry and the Community*, 2nd ed. (New York: McGraw-Hill, 1969), pp. 146–50; also Francis X. Sutton et al., *The American Business Creed* (Cambridge, Mass.: Harvard University Press, 1956), chap. 16.

31. The classic statement of the relation between uncertainty and magical beliefs is found in Bronislaw Malinowski, *Magic, Science and Religion and Other Essays* (Garden City, N.Y.: Doubleday, 1955).

to uncertain situations by blaming outside agents for the occurrence of unfortunate events.[32]

In this connection one finding from a comparative survey of managerial attitudes deserves mention. In a study of 3,641 managers from fourteen countries with different levels of economic development, Haire, Ghiselli, and Porter administered a questionnaire designed to determine what managers thought about the managerial role.[33] One finding that held across all the societies was that businessmen simultaneously believe that the average individual has little capacity for leadership and that the best method of leadership in business is the democratic-participant method.[34] On the face of it these beliefs stand in tension if not outright contradiction. If they are regarded, however, as reactions to strain in the businessman's situation, they make some sense. That is to say, to hold a low opinion of a subordinate's capacity for leadership is simultaneously to assure oneself of one's own capacities; and to treat democratic participation as a "method of leadership" is, in part, to assure oneself that he remains in control, and that participation of subordinates in decision making is an instrument of leadership rather than a threat to leadership.

A number of reactions to strain are related to the pressure to make decisions without regard for human considerations. The most common rationalization is the image of the "hard-headed" businessman who, in a very competitive business, cannot afford the luxury of taking human feelings into account without shirking his responsibilities. A number of business practices also cushion the "inhumanity" built into the executive role. An example is "kicking upstairs"—removing an incompetent executive from a position of real responsibility to a "higher position" of less responsibility; another is "lateral movement" that is in effect a disguise for demotion; another is the application of indirect pressure on subordinates to induce them to resign rather than be fired.[35]

The top executive, then, as a coordinator in a profit-making organization, is ensnarled in many strains, and many of his attitudinal and behavioral adaptations can be interpreted as attempts to relieve these strains. Persons in lower management levels (junior executive, production manager) are also under strain, but of different kinds. Their status

32. Sutton et al., *The American Business Creed*, pp. 332–36, 368–79.

33. Mason Haire, Edwin E. Ghiselli, Lyman W. Porter, *Managerial Thinking: An International Study* (New York: John Wiley, 1966).

34. Ibid., p. 26.

35. For a case study of ways in which organizations attempt to make demotion acceptable, see Fred H. Goldner, "Demotion in Industrial Management," *American Sociological Review* 30, no. 5 (October, 1965):714–24.

and authority are between the top executive and the lower echelons. Frequently their relations with both are ambiguous. In addition, the lower executive struggles continually with specialized staff officials—engineers, sales officials, personnel managers—over matters of company policy. His adaptations to such ambiguity and conflict frequently include excessive preoccupation with the external symbols of status (number of telephones, number of secretaries, size and position of desk), and a tendency to downgrade specialized staff officials on the grounds of their peripheral connection with the "real business" of the company—production.[36]

The professional role. The term "professional" implies that one "professes" or "believes." All professions, in varying degree, involve a commitment to standards of knowledge and excellence, and a commitment to practice in accord with these standards. At the same time the practitioner is "in business," in the sense that he must in some way be paid for his services. This tension between the service and commercial aspects of the professional role is reflected in the ways professionals charge their clients and advertise their services. Various mechanisms for regularizing the commercial aspect of professional services have been devised. Free-lance professional practitioners normally charge a fee, either a percentage of the sum involved (e.g., one-third of the settlement for lawyers) or a standard office-call fee. Some professionals (e.g., academics, clergymen) are removed from the market for their services altogether, charging their clients (students, parishioners) nothing directly, but receiving a salary from a superordinate organization, which may or may not impose a charge on the clients. Other ways of handling the tension between professional commitment and economic self-interest include the downgrading of the latter in the official ideologies of professional groups.

When professionals enter industrial bureaucracies, other problems arise. The conflict between their independent commitment to professional standards and their necessary involvement in the commercial interests of the bureaucracy often occasions tensions and conflicts within the organization. In addition, the ambiguous authority relations between the "experts" of the staff and the managers of the line, the differences in educational background between them, and their different expressive styles, aggravate these tensions and conflicts.[37] The longer professional scientists

36. See Robert L. Kahn et al., *Organizational Stress: Studies in Role Conflict and Ambiguity* (New York: John Wiley, 1964); Delbert C. Miller and William H. Form, *Industrial Sociology: The Sociology of Work Organizations*, 2nd ed. (New York: Harper & Row, 1964), pp. 480–86.

37. William H. Kornhauser, with the assistance of Warren O. Hagstrom, *Scientists in Industry: Conflict and Accommodation* (Berkeley: University of California Press, 1962); Melville Dalton, *Men Who Manage* (New York: John Wiley, 1959).

remain with an industrial organization, however, the less severe they regard the tension between themselves and the organization.[38]

Many professional roles provide the incumbent with unambiguously high status, as well as a cluster of interests around which their personal identification and style of life revolves.[39] Semiprofessional occupational roles, however, are likely to be the focus of ambiguity and relative deprivation. The role of engineering technicians, for example, as described by Evan, is "bounded by the engineer [a relatively established professional role] on one side, and by the craftsman or skilled worker on the other, and he himself may have ambivalent feelings with regard to either or both of these occupations."[40] He may be as skilled as an engineer but is usually less well paid, has less prestige, and has fewer opportunities for advancement. In a study of people in this occupation, Evan found evidence of reaction to relative deprivation–job-hopping to improve their financial setting, developing a preoccupation with the symbols–for example, office space, clerical help–of an engineer's role, forming close relationships with engineers, or attempting to secure an engineering degree.[41] We should also expect that incumbents of such semiprofessional roles would often mount collective efforts to "professionalize" the role in the public eye.[42]

The foreman. Another "man in the middle" of conflicting expectations is the foreman in the industrial plant. Such a role is intermediate between superordinate and subordinate in a hierarchy, and feelings of ambivalence inevitably develop toward both. In addition, industrial developments have diminished this once-important role in two ways: first, centralized management of control has made the foreman less an independent authority over production and more an implementor of decisions; second, the centralization of handling grievances in unions has

38. Mark Abrahamson, "The Integration of Industrial Scientists," *Administrative Science Quarterly* 9, no. 2 (September, 1964):208–18.

39. This contrasts greatly with industrial worker roles. See Louis H. Orzack, "Work as a 'Central Life Interest' of Professionals," in *The Social Dimensions of Work*, ed. Clifton D. Bryant (Englewood Cliffs, N.J.: Prentice-Hall, 1972), pp. 54–63; also Robert Dubin, "Industrial Workers' Worlds: A Study of the 'Central Life Interests' of Industrial Workers," *Social Problems* 3, no. 3 (January, 1956):131–42.

40. William M. Evan, "On the Margin—The Engineering Technician," in *The Human Shape of Work: Studies in the Sociology of Occupations*, ed. Peter L. Berger (New York: Macmillan, 1964), p. 88.

41. Ibid., pp. 100–102.

42. Harold L. Wilensky, "The Professionalization of Everyone?" *American Journal of Sociology* 70, no. 2 (September, 1964):137–58.

relieved him of certain "human relations" functions. The foreman, thus caught in a role that is simultaneously emptying and confusing, often flits among identification with management, identification with workers, and identification with other foremen.[43]

The low-skill worker. A recurring theme in the occupations we have examined is the *conflicting* role demands that are met by various attempts to resolve the accompanying strains.[44] For low-skill workers a different theme emerges. Strains in this role focus not on ambiguity so much as outright deprivation—remuneration may be inadequate; the worker often reaches the end of the career line in his twenties and may be discriminated against as he grows older; the opportunities to advance from low-level skill jobs to management within the plant appear to have diminished; the worker may be unemployed during recession; and the minimum skills required provide little challenge and little basis for personal identification. Most studies of reactions to such strains have focused on the resulting ideological orientations of workers—such as defensive rationalizations about failure; redefining "success" in more limited ways; focusing on out-of-plant goals such as consumption or children's opportunities; and developing feelings of alienation and class-consciousness.[45] Like the relationship between technology and worker satisfaction, however, the exact relations between the life situation of the worker and his outlook are still only imperfectly understood.

To sum up, the occupational structure of technologically advanced, specialized, organization-dominated societies has yielded a mixed record with respect to human gains and costs. It has reduced physical exertion by harnessing other energy sources and has raised the general level of material rewards to unprecedented levels. Yet that occupational structure —and the process of creating it—has occasioned serious dislocations as well. It first created vast numbers of unrewarding roles calling for little skill, then proceeded to erase many of these jobs by further technological

43. The analysis of the foreman's problems has a long history in industrial sociology. A good summary is found in Richard H. Hall, *Occupations and the Social Structure* (Englewood Cliffs, N.J.: Prentice-Hall, 1969), pp. 218–29. See also R.A. Hudson Rosen, "Foreman Role Conflict, An Expression of Contradictions in Organizational Goals," *Industrial and Labor Relations Review* 23, no. 4 (July, 1970):541–52.

44. In a national survey, Kahn et al., *Organizational Stress*, chaps. 4 and 5, found that fully one-third of the labor force experienced ambiguity in their occupational roles, tracing in large measure to various forms of role conflict.

45. See Ely Chinoy, "Manning the Machines—The Assembly-line Worker," in *The Human Shape of Work*, ed. Berger, pp. 51–81; above, p. 53; John C. Leggett, *Class, Race and Labor: Working-Class Consciousness in Detroit* (New York: Oxford University Press, 1968); for a summary of the vast literature, see Steven E. Deutsch, "The Sociology of the American Worker," *International Journal of Comparative Sociology* 10, nos. 1–2 (March and June, 1969):46–70.

advances, perhaps leaving their incumbents often unable to scramble for new places. It has created new occupations, leaving their incumbents with relative deprivation bred from status-anxiety. And by virtue of the specialization of roles, interdependence among roles, and combination of roles into complex organizations, it has created an abundance of opportunities for role-conflict and its attendant anxieties.

Formal Organizations

Economists have traditionally viewed the firm as an organization that is guided by the criterion of profit-maximization—securing the largest difference between revenue and cost. In analyzing the firm's behavior, certain demand conditions for its products and certain supply curves for the firm itself are posited. The firm's supply curve is a statement of the marginal cost for its distinctive product. Marginal cost depends in turn on the supply-demand relations between the firm and the suppliers of its factors of production. These factors presumably weigh most heavily in the firm's calculation of its course of action.

Having assembled these analytic tools, the economist then asks: How will (or should) a firm behave under different kinds of competition? How much should it produce in order to maximize its profits? At what point will it go out of business? What effects do external economies have on the firm? Since it is customary to assume institutional structure, technology, and tastes as given, the firm's behavior turns out to be a resultant of the interplay of a number of supply and demand relations, translated into statements of cost and revenue.

Since, for the economist, the firm's decisions depend so much on market conditions, internal analysis of the firm is often not problematical for him. It does not matter whether the manager has difficulty in enforcing his authority (the economist's model of the firm assumes that decisions are translated into action); it does not matter whether communication processes misfire or backfire in the firm (the economist's model of the firm assumes perfect knowledge in the firm); it does not matter whether the executive is effective in coordinating his enterprise.

Sociological writings on formal organizations—the firm is an example—have opened these internal dynamics to direct consideration. Weber was the sociological pioneer in this line of analysis. Concentrating on bureaucracy, he stressed that this form of organization, in contrast to traditional or spontaneously generated forms, is an *efficient* apparatus. (Common sense and popular folklore emphasize its sluggishness and red tape.) To maximize its efficiency, a bureaucracy develops a system of specialized jobs, a set of rules and procedures, a pyramid of authority, an emphasis on "the position" rather than "the person" as the important unit of organization, and the principle of distributing rewards according to position and performance. According to this view of bureaucracy, efficiency can be increased by rearranging jobs and altering rules, at the same time freeing administration from the potential inefficiencies of nepotism and personal loyalties and traditional rules of thumb.[46]

Research since Weber's time has established limitations to the generalizability of his model and has extended his analysis in new directions. His model of the efficiency of formal organization seems most applicable when organizational goals are unambiguous and its situations are routine; when the environment is more problematical, formalization may not be an efficient way of dealing with it.[47] Formal bureaucracy may develop features that impede efficiency. Specialization of roles itself reaches a point of diminishing economic returns; though such a point has never been established empirically, in principle it appears when overhead costs begin to exceed the contribution of overhead to the value of the product. Specialization of roles according to fixed rules may also go awry when workpeople, typically rewarded for living by the rules, begin to treat the rules as ends in themselves, thereby contributing to the development of red tape, ritualism, and rigidity of organizational functioning.[48] The work of scholars such as Gouldner and Selznick has shown how inadequate individual leadership may lead to conflict and ineffectiveness in organizations,[49] while other studies have revealed how inventive bureaucrats are in erecting defenses against and subverting orders from superiors and demands from clients.[50]

In the remainder of our discussion of the productive processes, we shall illustrate the areas into which sociological research on organizations has penetrated in the past several decades.

Formal and informal organization. The formal organization of a

46. Max Weber, "Bureaucracy," in *From Max Weber*, eds. Hans Gerth and C. Wright Mills (New York: Oxford University Press, 1958), pp. 196–216.

47. See Jerald Hage and Michael Aiken, "Routine Technology, Social Structure and Organizational Tools," *Administrative Science Quarterly* 14, no. 3 (September, 1969):366–77.

48. For an early statement, see Robert K. Merton, "Bureaucratic Structure and Personality," in *Social Theory and Social Structure*, rev. and enlarged ed. (New York: Free Press, 1963), pp. 195–206; also Michel Crozier, *The Bureaucratic Phenomenon* (Chicago: University of Chicago Press, 1964).

49. Alvin W. Gouldner, *Patterns of Industrial Bureaucracy* (Glencoe, Ill.: Free Press, 1954); Philip Selznick, *Leadership in Administration* (Evanston, Ill.: Row, Peterson, 1957).

50. R. Bar-Yosef and E.O. Schild, "Pressures and Defenses in Bureaucratic Roles," *American Journal of Sociology* 71, no. 6 (May, 1966):665–73.

bureaucracy can be and frequently is represented as an organization chart, complete with specialized positions and hierarchical arrangements. Formal organization is often explicit, impersonal, and functionally specific.

In actually carrying out the organization's work, however, people have proved to be ingenious in devising other, more informal, understandings as to how the work is to be done—understandings that themselves take the form of "rules" that are enforced in the network of friendships and cliques that arise in the workplace. Consider the routine of postal deliveries, for example. The official rules of the postal service prescribe the route to be followed by the postman, the amount of time he should spend in delivering, and so on. In practice, however, the letter carrier invents ways to deliver the mail differently than is prescribed—by altering the order in which he delivers mail, by using his own car, by walking across lawns (prohibited in the work manuals), and by delivering second and third class mail less often than every day—thereby making leisure time for himself. Moreover, substitute carriers are pressured not to "kill the route"—that is, to take substantially less or more time than the regular carrier—and various sanctions are applied to enforce this pressure.[51] In less solitary occupations, more visible codes of conduct and tighter methods of enforcement develop.[52]

Membership in informal groups is largely determined by occupational position in the formal organization. Cliques seldom extend very far across authority lines to include both workers and managers; staff and line also provide criteria for clique membership. Several other factors, however, influence which individuals will become members: ecological and temporal factors (cliques are most often composed of persons who work near one another on the same shift, with the same times for lunch hours and coffee breaks); sexual factors (cliques in bureaucracies tend to be one-sex groups); racial and ethnic factors (segregation between black and white cliques is especially pronounced).

Industrial sociologists have been primarily interested in the relations among formal organization, informal organization, morale, and productivity. Barnard argued that the relationship is basically positive: the major functions of informal organization are to facilitate communication that may be impeded by formal channels, to maintain cohesiveness in the organization as a whole, and to maintain the sense of personal in-

51. Dean Harper and Frederick Emmert, "Work Behavior in a Service Industry," *Social Forces* 42, no. 2 (December, 1963):216–25.

52. Numerous studies could be cited. As examples, see Donald Roy, "Efficiency and 'The Fix': Informal Intergroup Relations in a Piecework Machine Shop," and Ellwyn R. Stoddard, "The Informal 'Code' of Police Deviancy: A Group Approach to 'Blue-Coat Crime,' " in *Organizational Issues*, ed. Shepard, pp. 157–72, 527–48.

tegrity of the individual in the organization.[53] In performing these functions, informal groups engage in frequent interaction on the job (horseplay, joking, gambling) and off the job (golf, bowling, playing cards).

When such a positive relation can be maintained, informal organization emerges as a kind of complement for authority relations, rendering it less necessary to invoke the latter for the productive functioning of the enterprise. This is well demonstrated in a longitudinal study by Trist et al., of the impact of different types of work organization in the British coal industry.[54] The earliest, called the single-place system, consisted of self-selected teams of six workers, each performing the same range of tasks and sharing in a common paynote. Traditionally this system led to the development of harmonious group relations and cooperative work among teams. The second system, which displaced the first, was called the conventional longwall system. It entailed a more formal division of labor, with different-sized groups performing different tasks, and receiving different paynotes. Since this system segregated workers and provided no basis for spontaneous cooperation, "co-ordination and control [had] to be provided entirely from outside—by management."[55] A third type of work organization, the composite longwall system, removed some of the difficulties which had stemmed from overspecialized work roles, segregated task groups, and lack of cohesion in the longwall system team:

> There is a common paynote, based on a fixed rate, to which a bonus is added according to the amount of coal produced. All members of the team share equally. By this means they have a direct interest in the completion of the [coal-removal] cycle and arguments with management over amounts due are eliminated. The team undertakes full responsibility for allocating men to shifts and tasks and the methods devised to give rise to multi-skilled roles and a ready experience of the consequences for others of neglected work. The task groups . . . are not segregated from each other but are interchangeable in membership. As soon as the scheduled work of a shift is completed, men spontaneously carry on with whatever activity is next in sequence. . . . Such group regulation and continuity of face operations parallels the self-regulation and continuity characteristic of single-phase working.[56]

The composite longwall organization also tended to be more conducive

53. Barnard, *The Functions of the Executive*, p. 122.

54. E.L. Trist et al., *Organizational Choice Capabilities of Groups at the Coal Face under Changing Technologies: The Loss, Rediscovery and Transformation of a Work Tradition* (London: Tavistock, 1963).

55. Ibid., p. 290.

56. Ibid., p. 291.

than the conventional longwall system to "productive effectiveness, low cost, work satisfaction, good relations, and social health."[57]

Informal group organization can thus be regarded as a resource, contributing both to morale and to productivity. But this is not always the case. Most research on informal groups in industry has concentrated on their *restriction of output*; workers develop their own norms for an appropriate pace of work, often below the expectations of management, and develop sanctions to discourage "rate-busting"; these sanctions often prove stronger than incentives for higher production extended by management.[58]

Evidently, then, there is no simple relationship among informal work groups, morale, and productivity. If relations between management and workers are harmonious, informal groups may contribute to both morale and productivity. If these relations are conflict-ridden, informal groups may develop—and even have high morale—and subvert management's production-oriented strategies.[59] At least some studies have shown that even when worker morale is low, productivity can remain high.[60] And finally, when the pace of production is outside worker control altogether —as in some kinds of automation—informal groups and worker-morale might have very little to do with productivity.[61]

Informal structure is an extremely potent force in formal organizations, but its impact is variable and must be assessed in relation to the simultaneous impact of technology, labor-management relations, and other variables.

Authority. The variables of morale and output also dominate research on authority in industrial sociology. Specifically, the issue boils down to the relations between style of supervision and worker morale and its behavioral manifestations. Many studies have revealed that morale is higher under "employee-centered" leadership than under leader-

57. Ibid.

58. The classic study of work restriction by small groups of workmen is found in F.J. Roethlisberger and William J. Dickson, *Management and the Worker* (Cambridge, Mass.: Harvard University Press, 1947).

59. Abraham Zaleznik and David Moment, *The Dynamics of Interpersonal Behavior* (New York: John Wiley, 1964), pp. 354–69.

60. William J. Goode and Irving Fowler, "Incentive Factors in a Low Morale Plant," *American Sociological Review* 14, no. 5 (October, 1949):618–24.

61. Doctór found that in Polish factories engineering departments provided less opportunity for regulation of the pace of work than in departments where work was done by hand. Kazimierz Doctór, "Research on Behavior and Opinions of Workers in a Polish Factory," *Polish Sociological Bulletin* nos. 3–4 (July–December, 1962): 113–16.

ship oriented to technical standards of efficiency, and that high-morale workers cooperate better with one another and management and thus affect productivity positively.[62]

The matter is, however, more complex than this. In his survey of research on supervision and productivity, Dubin concluded that a variety of supervisory styles can be effective, depending on the type of organizational context.[63] For example, authoritarian leadership undoubtedly has different consequences in a military company, a business firm, and a university department, which differ in values and expectations. Cross-cultural differences in the effects of leadership styles are also evident. Most studies of supervision have been carried out in countries with democratic traditions—especially the United States and Great Britain. In a comparative study, however, Whyte and Williams found that for American workers, perceived closeness of supervision and perceived pressure on work by the supervisor were negatively correlated with work satisfaction, whereas the opposite relation held for Peruvian workers.[64] In Japanese factories, management-worker relations have traditionally been built on a high level of worker security and the exercise of paternalistic authority by managers. As Japanese values have become more democratic, however, increasing dissatisfaction with paternalistic leadership styles have appeared.[65]

The impact of expectations on the effectiveness of different leadership strategies is shown in studies of abrupt changes in leadership style as one manager succeeds another. In a study of a gypsum plant, Gouldner traced how the arrival of a new manager (with strict, disciplinary policies) shook up established patterns of interaction, created a hiatus in the chain of command, and led older officials in the company to oppose him and mobilize rank-and-file sentiment against him. One feature that exacerbated these reactions was that the new manager had been preceded by

62. For a sample of such studies, see Robert L. Hamblin, "Punitive and Non-Punitive Supervision," *Social Problems* 11, no. 4 (Spring, 1964):345–59; *Studies in Personnel and Industrial Psychology*, rev. ed., ed. Edwin A. Fleishman (Homewood, Ill.: The Dorsey Press, 1967), sections 4 and 5.

63. Robert Dubin et al., *Leadership and Productivity* (Scranton, Pa.: Chandler Publishing Co., 1965).

64. W.F. Whyte and L.K. Williams, "Supervisory Leadership: An International Comparison," *Proceedings of the Thirteenth International Management Congress* (1963), pp. 481–88.

65. See Robert E. Cole, *Japanese Blue Collar: The Changing Tradition* (Berkeley: University of California Press, 1971), pp. 81–87, 179–83; Kunio Odaka, "Traditionalism, Democracy in Japanese Industry," *Industrial Relations* 3, no. 1 (October, 1963):95–103.

a permissive worker-oriented managerial regime.[66] In a subsequent study Guest assessed the effects of the arrival of a new manager whose emphasis was not on role-enforcement but rather on worker participation in decisions. Accordingly, his arrival did not stir the conflict and loss of morale observed by Gouldner; indeed, it increased the effectiveness of authority.[67] And in a Japanese die-cast factory, Cole was able to observe a replication of the process identified by Gouldner—conflict and dissatisfaction generated when an indulgent manager was succeeded by a punishment-centered manager—even though expectations regarding the behavior of authorities are very different in the United States and Japan.[68] Some additional conditions may attenuate the impact of managerial succession; in a series of simulated experimental studies, Grusky showed that if the successor arrives with an "ally"—an assistant manager—to mediate with subordinates, the transition tends to be less formalistic and smoother than if he arrived unaccompanied.[69]

Status. Both occupational role and authority are important determinants of a person's general status in the organization; a person who wields authority (a manager, for instance) has higher status than a person lower down the line, and a person with a white-collar job is likely to have higher status than a manual worker. In addition, the level of remuneration (which is correlated with, but not identical to, occupation and authority) determines in part an individual's status in an organization. Several other determinants of status are "imported" from outside the workplace: age (older persons, up to a limit, occupy higher positions); sex (males occupy higher positions); and racial or ethnic background (blacks, especially, are relegated to lower positions).

Since so many criteria potentially affect an individual's status, a major focus of strain is ambiguity about one's *actual* status. One is never completely certain which criterion—authority, prestige, remuneration, seniority—is most important, or exactly where one stands according to each criterion. One consequence of this ambiguity is the tendency for persons to fixate on objective, identifiable *symbols* (such as number of secre-

66. Gouldner, *Patterns of Industrial Bureaucracy*, pp. 70–101.

67. Robert Guest, *Organizational Change: The Effect of Successful Leadership* (Homewood, Ill.: Dorsey, 1962). For a comparison of the studies by Gouldner and Guest, see Guest, "Managerial Succession in Complex Organizations," *American Journal of Sociology* 68, no. 1 (July, 1962):47–54, with a comment by Gouldner and rejoinder by Guest, pp. 54–56.

68. Cole, *Japanese Blue Collar*, pp. 214–20.

69. Oscar Grusky, "Succession with an Ally," *Administrative Science Quarterly* 14, no. 2 (June, 1969):155–70.

taries per office, size of desk) as evidence of status. Many conflicts in organizations focus on the distribution of symbols of status.[70]

A common characteristic of status systems in formal organizations is a certain "tension toward crystallization of several determinants of status, such as income, prestige, age, sex, and authority. This tension rests on the assumption that people are comfortable if they and their coworkers are *either* high or low on *all* features of status, uncomfortable if they are high on some and low on others. In a study of clerical workers, Homans concluded that filing clerks—whose jobs were repetitive, tiring, low paid, and closely supervised (in short, low on all aspects of status)—had little concern with status. "While the filing clerks did not like their job," he observed, "they felt, in effect, it was just and right they should have it." The ledger clerks on the other hand, whose job was better on some but not all counts than other positions, were more dissatisfied and continued to try to "bring all the status factors in line in their favor."[71] Such tension underlies many conflicts in industrial settings—disputes over bringing wage and skill differentials into line, opposition to promoting a young executive too rapidly for his age and experience, opposition to women in positions of authority, and opposition to elevating blacks to high-level positions.

Communication. A fundamental condition for effective operation in a bureaucracy is a flow of information and orders. If information is lacking altogether, too slow in arriving, distorted in passage, informed decision making and coordination are correspondingly undermined. Many studies of industrial bureaucracies have uncovered typical points of bottleneck and distortion in the passage of information. Too great centralization of information makes for decision making that is not understood by those subordinates who must implement the decisions; too great decentralization renders decision making unwieldy. Specialized departments in organizations frequently come to regard the exclusive possession of information as a resource to be protected against rivals. Up and down the line of an organizational hierarchy, the problems are omission and distortion at each level. Subordinates understand only those parts of instructions they wish to understand; foremen soften orders out of sympathy with workmen; subordinates sweeten information they pass on to their superiors, particularly if they have ambitions for advancement in the

70. Above, pp. 107–8. For a brief discussion of the importance of symbols, see Chester I. Barnard, "Functions and Pathologies of Status Systems in Formal Organizations," in *Industry and Society*, ed. William F. Whyte (New York: McGraw-Hill, 1946), pp. 50–52.

71. George Homans, "Status among Clerical Workers," *Human Organization* 12, no. 1 (Spring, 1953):9–10. This kind of strain is a special case of role-conflict and relative deprivation. Above, pp. 41–42.

organization.[72] Particularly disturbing to a bureaucracy is the practice of "jumping the line"—that is, sending information and grievances from low levels in the hierarchy directly to high levels, thus subverting the ability of the middle levels to censor or control this communication.[73]

DISTRIBUTION AND EXCHANGE

The Comparative Analysis of Exchange Systems

Our exposure to economic thought for two centuries has led us often to assume that the exchange of economic goods and services occurs in a market. Even in our own market-dominated society, however, we must contend with several other forms of exchange:

1. The gift for a bride or baby, the services of a friend's wife who prepares dinner, the "good turn"—all are exchanges of goods and services of potential market value. To offer to pay in such exchanges, however, is both inappropriate and insulting.
2. The redistribution of wealth through charity or progressive taxation is again an exchange of potentially marketable commodities outside the market.
3. The mobilization of economic resources for public goals—through eminent domain, taxation, direct appropriation, and selective service—involves the transfer of economic goods and services without the intrusion of an economic market.

On the other hand, we still observe the market in varying degrees of perfection, and we know the value of the economists' theoretical apparatus for explaining and perhaps predicting the course of market behavior. What, then, is the scope of economic analysis with respect to exchange?

In societies where the self-regulating price market is inconspicuous or absent, the categories of economic analysis grow correspondingly paler. What can we say about fluctuations of production and prices in the Soviet Union? Certainly the solutions for free-market economies have their limitations. Even more, what can we say about the traditionalized and reciprocal gift-giving among island peoples, which does not hint at economic calculation, prices, or gain? What can we say about the postharvest dis-

72. William H. Read, "Upward Communication in Industrial Hierarchies," *Human Relations* 15, no. 1 (February, 1962):3–14.

73. For an extensively illustrated discussion of sources of distortion, see Harold L. Wilensky, *Organizational Intelligence* (New York: Basic Books, 1967), chap. 3.

tribution of Indian villages in which the guiding principle is caste organization?

Anthropologists have been providing descriptions of nonmarket exchange systems for some time,[74] and economists have acknowledged other forms of income than economic—for example, "psychic" income—but have not analyzed them systematically. A number of recent developments in different disciplines, however, has generated a new concern with nonmarket mechanisms. Interest in comparative exchange was stirred by the appearance in the late 1950s of a volume edited by Polanyi, Arensberg, and Pearson.[75] Roaming through the records of Babylon, Mesopotamia, Greece, Mexico, Yucatan, the Guinea Coast, and village India, they depicted how trading practices are separated from the familiar practices of free-market exchange. In addition, the authors criticized traditional economic theory and suggested an alternative framework for a better comparative economics of exchange.

Polanyi and his associates identified three main patterns of exchange. The first, *reciprocative,* is illustrated by the ritualized gift-giving among families, clans, and tribes—as analyzed, for instance, by Malinowski and Mauss.[76] Another illustration is found among farmers of many civilizations, who frequently work for one another, especially at harvest times. Economic calculation, price payments, and wages are typically absent. Goods or services are given because it is traditional to do so; the only principle of calculation is the loose principle that giving and receiving should balance out among the exchanging parties in the long run.

The second pattern is *redistributive.* This brings economic goods and services to a central source—often governmental—and then redistributes them throughout the populace. Polanyi, Arensberg, and Pearson identified several instances of this exchange pattern in ancient Asian and African civilizations. Modern examples are organized charity and progressive taxation. As in reciprocative exchange, economic calculation and price payments are absent. Calculation seems to be based on justice or equity—what each class of recipients traditionally deserves.

The third pattern, more familiar in the modern West, is termed, simply, *exchange.* In this case economic goods and services are brought into a market context. Prices are not standardized on the basis of tradition but result from bargaining for economic advantage.

Sahlins extended and elaborated the model of reciprocative exchange by distinguishing among several types of reciprocity. The first is

74. Above, pp. 19–23.

75. Karl Polanyi, Conrad Arensberg, and Harry Pearson, *Trade and Market in the Early Empires* (Glencoe, Ill.: Free Press and Falcon's Wing Press, 1957).

76. Above, pp. 20–21.

"generalized" reciprocity, which is putatively altruistic, and for which any obligation for repayment is suppressed or left indefinite. The clearest example is food-sharing with members of a nuclear family. At most, receiving the food (say, by young children) "lays on a diffuse obligation to reciprocate when necessary to the donor and/or possible for the recipient."[77] The second is "balanced" reciprocity, in which repayment of an equivalent is made without delay, as in the case of marital settlements or peace agreements. This is more calculated, less personal than the first. The third is "negative" reciprocity, or "the attempt to get something for nothing with impunity, as in haggling, gambling, stealing, or plundering." Sahlins argued that the best way to predict which type of reciprocation will dominate is to trace the "kinship distance" between parties; and he pulled together ethnographic data on patterns of giving and taking to demonstrate his central hypothesis that "[reciprocity] is inclined toward the generalized pole by close kinship, toward the negative extreme in proportion to kinship distance."[78]

In a different kind of analysis, Titmuss investigated international differences in patterns of blood donation. This unusual form of gift—which is in one sense an act of generalized reciprocity in that nothing is expected in return, and in another sense an anonymous, impersonal act—has survived in large part as a voluntary, unrewarded act in a few societies, such as Great Britain, but in other societies blood has become a marketable and even a profitable commodity. In the United States and the Soviet Union, for example, fully half the donors are paid, and in Japan almost all donors receive money. Titmuss was not able to account for such differences, but he suggested that the best place to look is in the "fabric of values, social, economic, and political, within which acts of giving, rewarding, compelling or selling take place."[79]

A second line of interest in nonmarket transfers has been stimulated by scholars working on communist and socialist societies. These societies, characterized in ideal-typical terms, have a central authority that owns all the means of production, determines output and directs production administratively, determines consumption through rationing, and assigns labor at predetermined wages. Thus characterized, the "command economy" leaves little room for market exchange.[80] In practice, however,

77. Marshall Sahlins, "On the Sociology of Primitive Exchange," in *Stone Age Economics* (Chicago: Aldine-Atherton, 1972), p. 186.

78. Ibid., p. 196.

79. Richard Titmuss, *The Gift Relationship: From Human Blood to Social Policy* (London: Allen & Unwin, 1970), p. 179.

80. See Oleg Zinam, "The Economics of Command Economies," in *Comparative Economic Systems*, ed. Jan S. Prybyla (New York: Appleton-Century-Crofts, 1969), p. 16.

communist and socialist economies have not even approximated the ideal type, and many market mechanisms have developed, just as many market economies have supplemented market mechanisms with political and administrative controls.[81] While acknowledging that any given economy relies on several different mechanisms, Grossman nevertheless attempted to classify economies in terms of which kind of mechanisms are *dominant*: tradition, or "generally accepted, customary, and persistent specific patterns of relationship among economic units or agents"; market; and command.[82] This classification is not unlike that of Polanyi, Arensberg, and Pearson, though their notion of "redistributive" also contains many traditional elements. In terms of sanctions, the market economy relies mainly on economic sanctions, the command economy mainly on political sanctions, and the traditional economy on a residual group of social and political sanctions.

A third line of interest in nonmarket transfers is found in research on the grants economy. By "grants" is meant a "one-way economic relationship whereby party A conveys an exchangeable to party B without receiving in return an exchangeable of equal market value."[83] This contrasts with the two-way exchange characteristics of markets, in which both parties receive economic consideration. Examples of grants are redistribution through taxation, charity donations, public support of children, and intrafamilial transfers of goods and services. Boulding defined the grant in economic terms, and while he admitted that a transfer from A to B "may be accompanied by certain intangible transfers from B to A in the way of prestige, status, and so on," he added that "these things are not usually classified as exchangeables."[84] This exclusion is unfortunate, since so many economic grants are locked into a system of other kinds of rewards for the grantor—the politician who distributes benefits to the poor in return for votes and power, the philanthropist who secures prestige in the public eye for his good works, and the like. Despite this limitation, Boulding regarded grants as having primary significance not in the economic but rather in the "integrative structure of society"; fur-

81. For an introductory characterization of the "mixed" character of the Soviet economy, see William N. Loucks and William G. Whitney, *Comparative Economic Systems*, 8th ed. (New York: Harper & Row, 1969), pp. 392–532.

82. Gregory Grossman, *Economic Systems*, 2nd ed. (Englewood Cliffs, N.J.: Prentice-Hall, 1974), pp. 18–20.

83. Kenneth Boulding, "Urbanization and the Grants Economy: An Introduction," in *Transfers in an Urbanized Economy*, eds. Kenneth E. Boulding, Martin Pfaff, and Anita Pfaff (Belmont, Ca.: Wadsworth, 1973), p. 1.

84. Kenneth E. Boulding, "The Grants Economy," in *Collected Papers*, ed. Fred R. Glahe (Boulder: University of Colorado Press, 1971), p. 477.

thermore, they are reflective of relationships of community, legitimacy, loyalty, love, and trust.[85] He suggested that the great increase in public grants in recent decades might be an "integrative" compensation for declining private transfers in financing health, education, and welfare, and for declining extended family—a private, "granting" agency, *par excellence*.[86] Whatever the merits of this formulation, the focus on one-way exchanges is leading economists to ask new kinds of questions about exchange, such as whether suburban communities compensate central cities for the services they provide, whether transfer payments through welfare have a substantial impact on poverty, and the like.[87]

These lines of research interest constitute several new ways of discovering that economic exchange—like economic activity in general—is embedded in a network of noneconomic structures and sanctions. The identification of different systems of exchange—"grants," "reciprocative," "command," and the like—points to the different kinds of embeddedness. Each system of exchange presumably has its strengths and weaknesses, its implications for economic growth and stagnation, its rigidities, its cumulative imbalances and injustices. Systematic assessment of the strengths and weaknesses of each—as well as of various combinations—is clearly on the agenda for future research. So, too, is the need to establish improved measures for other kinds of exchangeables, such as political and integrative rewards.[88] With such tools it would be possible to build more sophisticated models of exchange, and to throw more light on the processes by which rewards are distributed into different patterns of equality and inequality.

Noneconomic Elements in Market Systems

Even in exchange systems dominated by the money complex, we can observe the intrusion of sociological variables. We shall remark on three types of markets: the market for labor services, the market for entrepreneurial services, and the market for consumers' goods.

85. Ibid., p. 478.

86. Boulding, "Urbanization and the Grants Economy," ibid., p. 3. The discussions of social security and public expenditures above, pp. 72–73 and 87–88, follow the same logic.

87. Ibid., chaps. 1–6.

88. For a preliminary effort to do this, and to account for the differential incidence of political corruption—an instance of the exchange between political and economic sanctions—see Neil J. Smelser, "Stability, Instability, and the Analysis of Political Corruption," in *Stability and Social Change*, eds. Bernard Barber and Alex Inkeles (Boston: Little, Brown, 1971), pp. 7–29.

The labor market. We have already covered the role of labor organizations and the role of the family and ethnic groups as they affect the labor market.[89] One more aspect of the labor market should be noted: the accent on security. This theme underlies workers' concerns with controlling the supply of jobs through closed shop and apprentice control, seniority, layoff rules, severance pay, guaranteed annual wages, and their broader concerns with maintaining full employment and compensating for unemployment. Unlike other markets, the labor market is dominated by a concern with security.[90]

Why should this be so? Labor emanates above all from the household or family unit.[91] The family, moreover, has as its central functions the socialization of the young and the expression of emotions and tensions of the family members. Loss of income or employment seriously threatens the performance of these delicate functions.[92] Most societies have institutionalized arrangements for "grants"—poor laws, minimum-wage laws, insurance, charity, compensation, welfare funds—that insure a family against "bankruptcy" in the usual business sense. A family may break up, but it is generally felt it should not do so for reasons of simple insolvency. The institutional arrangements guarantee a minimum "floor" of economic security for families and a minimum of stability of income and employment. These arrangements stem from the distinctive sociological—or integrative, following Boulding's usage—functions of the family.

Why should not the market for consumers' goods—which largely involves the household as well—be characterized by a similar preoccupation with security? The answer lies in the nature of occupational roles. The breadwinner typically has an all-or-none relation with his job; he is either employed or unemployed. If unemployed, his *total* flow of income stops.[93] In the market for consumers' goods, no single item dominates

89. Above, pp. 60–71 and 78–89.

90. Lloyd G. Reynolds, *Labor Economics and Labor Relations*, 5th ed. (Englewood Cliffs, N.J.: Prentice-Hall, 1970), pp. 10–12.

91. Talcott Parsons and Neil J. Smelser, *Economy and Society* (Glencoe, Ill.: Free Press, 1956), pp. 53–56.

92. Glen H. Elder, *Children of the Great Depression* (Chicago: University of Chicago Press, 1974).

93. These statements must be qualified by the facts that some unemployment compensation often awaits the unemployed, that an increasing number of families have more than one breadwinner, and that a significant minority of the labor force—probably around ten percent—holds more than one job. Above, pp. 84–86, and Harold L. Wilensky, "The Moonlighter: A Product of Relative Deprivation," *Industrial Relations* (October, 1963):105–24.

the budget in a way comparable to the work role of its breadwinners.[94]

Considerable research has been conducted on detailed aspects of allocation and performance within a labor market—especially on labor turnover and absenteeism. Several economic and social factors influence the rate of labor turnover. During times of prosperity the rate of voluntary labor movement from job to job rises; during depression this rate falls. Involuntary layoffs increase during depression and decrease during prosperity. Economic fluctuations constitute perhaps the most important single determinant of labor mobility. Other influences are occupation (the average turnover of teachers, for instance, is much lower than that of factory workers); age (older workers tend to change jobs less); sex (women move in and out of the labor force more than men, but probably do not move geographically and occupationally as much); and race (black men tend to show higher mobility rates than white men). Labor unions *directly* reduce rates of quitting by their pressure for seniority, their opposition to newcomers to plants, and their grievance procedures that help solve labor problems short of forcing the laborer to quit work. Insofar as unions agitate for full-employment programs (and prosperity), however, they *indirectly* increase voluntary rates of quitting and decrease involuntary layoffs.[95]

Some of the conditions that encourage absenteeism are high wages (which lead to the backward-sloping supply curve and a preference for leisure); distance of residence from a plant; size of firm (which is undoubtedly related to morale); occurrence of holidays (absenteeism drops just before holidays); age (young men display absenteeism more than old); marital status (single more than married men); and arduousness of work (which encourages absenteeism).[96] A study of a British iron and steel factory showed a strong positive association between the rate of industrial accidents and the rate of absences not sanctioned in advance (taking the day off without notifying anyone) and a negative association between rate of industrial accidents and sanctioned absences (requesting

94. In the markets for providing housing, health services, and education, however, all of which are intricately tied to the performance of the family's central functions, a similar concern with security appears.

95. Reynolds, *Labor Economics*, pp. 59–61; Herbert S. Parnes, *Research on Labor Mobility* (New York: Social Science Research Council, 1954), pp. 140–43; Hilde Behrend, "Normative Factors in the Supply of Labour," *The Manchester School of Economic and Social Studies* 23, no. 1 (January, 1955):62–76.

96. George B. Baldwin, *Beyond Nationalization: The Labor Problems of British Coal* (Cambridge, Mass.: Harvard University Press, 1955), pp. 208–25; John B. Knox, "Absenteeism and Turnover in an Argentine Factory," *American Sociological Review* 26, no. 2 (April, 1961):242–48; F.D.K. Liddell, "Attendance in the Coal-Mining Industry," *British Journal of Sociology* 5, no. 1 (March, 1954):78–86.

permission to be absent). To the authors these results implied that the less responsible type of employee was more likely to have accidents, and that taking unsanctioned leave and being involved in accidents "may be different forms of negative reaction implying a bad relationship" between individual and company.[97]

The market for entrepreneurial services. In one sense the market for entrepreneurship is a market for labor services. Unlike many laborers, however, the entrepreneur disrupts existing patterns of production and initiates new patterns, all under conditions of risk and uncertainty.

Like all markets, the market for entrepreneurial services has a demand and a supply side. On the demand side we ask: What is the economy's level of per capita income? What is its rate of growth and its anticipated rate of growth? What are likely future shifts in tastes? Are new foreign markets opening or likely to open? Market opportunities are clearly one necessary condition for the success of entrepreneurial undertakings; furthermore, economists have tended to lay greatest emphasis on the demand side.[98]

On the supply side we may ask two separate sets of questions: First, what makes people want to be entrepreneurs? Where is the drive? Second, given some drive, what are the opportunities and obstacles to undertaking successful entrepreneurial activities? With respect to the first, the Weber thesis on Protestantism becomes relevant. It might be argued that ascetic Protestantism inculcated in individuals a complex of motivations that encouraged the systematic exploitation of economic opportunities.[99] It might be argued, further, that this motivational complex is not restricted to religious beliefs such as Protestantism but might be encouraged by other aspirations as well. For example, Marris and Somerset found that many Kenyan entrepreneurs had been very active in the country's struggle for independence, and they envisioned their own entrepreneurial activity in distinctively nationalistic terms.[100]

Two major statements of a largely motivational theory of entrepreneurship are those of McClelland[101] and Hagen.[102] The former, building

97. J.M.M. Hill and E.L. Trist, *Industrial Accidents, Sickness and Other Absences* (London: Tavistock, 1962), p. 21.

98. Peter Kilby, "Hunting the Heffalump," in *Entrepreneurship and Economic Development*, ed. Peter Kilby (New York: Free Press, 1971), p. 3.

99. Above, pp. 46–51.

100. Peter Marris and Anthony Somerset, *African Businessmen: A Study of Entrepreneurship and Development in Kenya* (London: Routledge & Kegan Paul, 1971), pp. 71–82.

101. David McClelland, *The Achieving Society* (Princeton: Van Nostrand, 1961).

102. E.E. Hagen, *On the Theory of Social Change: How Economic Growth Begins* (Homewood, Ill.: Dorsey, 1962).

on Weber, suggested that the key motivation of entrepreneurs is a need for achievement, which involves an interest in exercising skill in medium-risk situations and a desire for concrete signs of successful performance. This need, moreover, develops in the period of early socialization, when the child is exposed to self-reliance training and high standards of performance; McClelland also argued that the combination of a warm, loving mother with a nondominant father were important in fostering the need for achievement. Most of McClelland's work, and that of his associates, was devoted to measuring the need for achievement as it appears in children's reading books, folklore, and the like, and correlating it with subsequent indicators of economic growth. One study, for example, hypothesized that increases in the need for achievement in British society (as measured by a content-analysis of dramas and sea ballads) would lead to corresponding increases in coal output, with a fifty-year time lag. The authors found strong correlations between their measures and concluded that

> The [need for] Achievement curve reaches its lowest point in the period 1676–1725, while the economic index reaches its lowest point around 1750. The sharp rise in the economic curve during the next two time periods, indicating the full rush of the industrial revolution, is preceded by a sharp rise in the [need for] Achievement curve after 1725. The curves present a pattern of approximate parallel oscillation with roughly a fifty-year time lag between periods, as our original hypothesis predicted.[103]

Presumably the emphasis on achievement (or lack of same) worked its way into patterns of socializing children, who, in the following generation, lived out the results of their own socialization by giving greater (or less) emphasis to economic activity that would generate growth.

Hagen's theory is more complicated than McClelland's, though it also relies on child-rearing patterns and motivation. He argued that stable traditional societies generally employ authoritarian child-rearing practices, which in turn develop passive, noninnovative personality types. When such societies are shaken by external disturbance (such as colonial domination), the first response is a kind of "retreatism," which manifests itself in the family as a decline of the father's status and an enhancement of the mother's status. This in turn "frees" the son from a repressive father in the subsequent generation and releases creative and innovative energies in the economy.

The work of McClelland and Hagen generated much research relevant to their hypotheses. Some of this has revealed positive associations between measures of the achievement motive and various indices such as

103. Norman M. Bradburn and David E. Berlew, "Need for Achievement and English Industrial Growth," *Economic Development and Cultural Change* 10, no. 1 (October, 1961):18.

plans for education for younger children, the extent of planning ahead, and the like;[104] and a number of associations between religious affiliation and occupational achievement in the directions suggested by the Weber-McClelland formulations.[105] On the other hand, their theories have been severely criticized as historically incorrect, theoretically oversimplified, and methodologically flawed.[106] In fact, motivational theories have recently fallen into relative disfavor, and investigators have turned to other questions concerning the supply entrepreneurship.

One theory—that of Young—combines the "drive toward entrepreneurship" variable with a notion of special opportunities for entrepreneurship. His is the theory of "reactive subgroups." Such groups are often ethnic minorities or politically disadvantaged nations whose drive toward creative activity is found in their struggle to overcome their low-status position.[107] If such a group attains a degree of solidarity, it develops a number of characteristics that provide economic opportunities for its members. Enterprising group members may find a supply of capital, advice, and assistance available from other members who trust them. The group may even provide a small initial market for an enterprise.[108]

While Young's theory has not undergone systematic comparative testing, it is possible to cite many instances of entrepreneurial activities that are initiated by deviant or unfavored groups.[109] In addition, a number of studies have uncovered other structural opportunities for (and obstacles to) entrepreneurial success. Alexander's studies revealed that many Turkish and Greek industrialists came from an industrial, mercantile, or trading background—suggesting that they either had initially

104. For an extensive analysis of survey data, see James N. Morgan, "The Achievement Motive and Economic Behavior," *Economic Development and Cultural Change* 12, no. 3 (April, 1964):243–67.

105. For a review of past studies and an attempt to control for variables other than religious preference, see Elton F. Jackson, William S. Fox, and Harry J. Crockett, Jr., "Religion and Occupational Achievement," *American Sociological Review* 35, no. 1 (February, 1970):48–63.

106. A sample of such criticisms can be found in Kilby, "Hunting the Heffalump," section 2, and Sayre P. Schatz, "*n* Achievement and Economic Growth: A Critical Appraisal," chap. 9, *Entrepreneurship*, ed. Kilby.

107. This is the logic used by Gerschenkron in his account of the Old Believers' entrepreneurial outlook. Above, pp. 48–49.

108. Frank W. Young, "A Macrosociological Interpretation of Entrepreneurship," in *Entrepreneurship*, ed. Kilby, pp. 139–49.

109. See Howard R. Smith, "A Model of Entrepreneurial Evolution," *Explorations in Entrepreneurial History* 5, no. 2 (Winter, 1968):145–57; also William P. Glade, "Approaches to a Theory of Entrepreneurial Formation," *Explorations in Entrepreneurial History* 4, no. 3 (Spring/Summer, 1967):245–59.

favorable entry, superior knowledge of demand conditions, accumulated capital, or perhaps all three.[110] In a survey of case studies of entrepreneurship in developing economies. Kilby found a typical pattern of obstacles to entrepreneurial activity. Entrepreneurs in these countries, he concluded, are generally not plagued by unwillingness to risk their own capital, lack of responsiveness to market opportunities, lack of marketing skills, or disrupted relations with staff, suppliers, and the public bureaucracy. The biggest drags on entrepreneurial effectiveness are a lack of technological knowledge and a looseness of management control, both of which make for a competitive disadvantage.[111]

Comparative analysis of entrepreneurship has not been carried far enough to unscramble the precise roles of the several demand and supply factors in entrepreneurial activity. At present they stand as a list of determinants, for each of which certain historical illustrations can be enumerated. Furthermore, the job of unscrambling and reordering the determinants is a formidable one. For example, given some empirical instance of successful entrepreneurship, it is difficult to know whether it was triggered by an augmentation of entrepreneurial effort, some new market opportunity, or the diminution of some institutional obstacle—or by a combination of all three. Given some evidence of entrepreneurial success by embattled minorities, it is difficult to ascertain what aspect or aspects of minority life—repression, superior skills, or blocked political opportunities—are decisive. Such difficulties suggest the need for a comprehensive and systematic program of comparative research, so that some measure of control may be gained over the elusive causes of entrepreneurial success.

The market for consumers' goods. We shall mention only two aspects of the market for consumers' goods—pricing systems and advertising. Many exchange systems rest not on the interplay of supply and demand, but rather on traditional reciprocative and redistributive arrangements with fixed equivalency ratios.[112] When market systems do arise in peasant societies, a typical form of price-fixing is haggling, in which initial offers of seller and buyer are worked downward and upward, respectively, by a somewhat ritualized process of argument. Haggling tends to be most widespread in free, atomistic, competitive markets for

110. Alec P. Alexander, "Industrial Entrepreneurship in Turkey: Origins and Growth," *Economic Development and Cultural Change* 8, no. 4 (July, 1960):349–65; Alexander, "Industrial Entrepreneurship in Contemporary Greece: Origins and Growth," *Explorations in Entrepreneurial History* 3, no. 2 (Winter, 1966):101–19.

111. Kilby, "Hunting the Heffalump," in *Entrepreneurship*, ed. Kilby, pp. 27–40.

112. Paul Bohannan and George Dalton, eds., *Markets in Africa* (Evanston: Northwestern University Press, 1962), pp. 1–18; above, pp. 20–22.

items such as clothing and smallwares. It also occurs in wholesale food markets, but common pricing prevails for foods sold in the units worth the lowest common monetary unit. Furthermore, as marketing units increase in size, haggling tends to give way to more standardized pricing.[113] Haggling persists in some urban settings, for example the Turkish bazaar; in these instances a multiple pricing system prevails, since those unfamiliar with the etiquette of haggling (for example, tourists) or without particularistic links with sellers pay higher prices.

The dominant form of pricing in complex industrial societies is the one-price system; the purchaser may accept or reject the set price but is not normally able to modify it. Two structural features that underlie this one-price system are the depersonalization and complexity of the markets.[114] Three qualifications on this generalization must be entered, however. First, price-bargaining still exists—and is acceptable—in markets where the price of the product is high, such as housing and used cars.[115] Second, products apparently sold for one price go for many different prices in actuality, depending on whether the buyer pays cash or opts for some kind of credit, which is in effect a higher price. Third, the poor—and particularly poor ethnic minorities—whose knowledge of market conditions is limited and who are perhaps more vulnerable to sharp business and credit practices, are charged more for consumer durables than the more affluent.[116]

As the market becomes more depersonalized and complex, advertising arises as a primary means of influencing customers. In one respect advertising is a functional alternative to personal contacts between sellers and buyers. It is a hallmark of capitalist societies and is in evidence in communist and socialist societies as well, even though these societies have

113. Victor C. Uchenda, "Some Principles of Haggling in Peasant Markets," *Economic Development and Cultural Change* 16, no. 1 (October, 1967):37–38.

114. For a contrast of marketing styles, compare the description of (1) the system of marketing alcohol and coffee in the Greek village coffee house, in which purchases take place in the context of the continuous renewal of primary group ties through exchange of news, gossip, and game-playing; and (2) the modern supermarket, frequented by brief, transitory visits by automobile, with little interaction between seller and buyer or among buyers. John D. Photiadis, "The Position of the Coffee House in the Social Structure of the Greek Village," *Sociologia Ruralis* 5, no. 1 (January, 1965):45–56; W.G. McClelland, "The Supermarket and Society," *Sociological Review* 10 (new series) no. 2 (July, 1962):133–44.

115. Some of Garfinkel's students assigned to bargain in supposedly one-price settings in American markets experienced some success in bringing prices down. Harold Garfinkel, *Studies in Ethnomethodology* (Englewood Cliffs, N.J.: Prentice-Hall, 1967), pp. 68–70.

116. David Caplovitz, *The Poor Pay More* (New York: Free Press, 1967).

a tradition of ideological hostility toward it.[117] Despite a great deal of market research on the influence of advertising, much of our knowledge rests on received folklore and the assertions of interested parties. It has been documented, however, that sales of certain individual brands of a product are influenced by advertising campaigns.[118] One line of research, moreover, has yielded insights into the form such influence might take. In an investigation of community buying, voting, and other activities, Katz and Lazarsfeld isolated what they called the two-step flow of influence. Any given community is composed of certain "influentials," who maintain close touch with national and international advertising. The remainder of the buyers, normally out of touch with or uninfluenced by advertising, are nonetheless influenced *personally*, largely through informal contact in the community, by the influentials.[119] A study of the spread of the use of a "wonder drug" also indicated that one of the most important determinants of whether a physician would adopt the drug was the degree to which he interacted with and was influenced by other physicians.[120] Such studies warn against exaggerating the depersonalization of the mass market and suggest that the primary group plays as salient a role in markets for consumers' goods as it does in the productive process.

THE PROCESS OF CONSUMPTION

Economists' Formulations

A convenient starting point for the analysis of consumption is utilitarianism, which dominated economic thought in the early nineteenth century. A dominant feature of this school is that while it held human wants (demand) to be an important determinant in the production and distribution of goods and services, it rested on the assumption that these wants are essentially *structureless*—that is, random in variation in society and to be taken as "given data" for every case of economic analysis.[121]

117. Carter R. Bryan, "Communist Advertising: Its Status and Functioning," *Journalism Quarterly* 39, no. 4 (Autumn, 1962):500–506.

118. K.S. Palda, *The Measurement of Cumulative Advertising Effects* (Englewood Cliffs, N.J.: Prentice-Hall, 1964).

119. Elihu Katz and Paul F. Lazarsfeld, *Personal Influence* (Glencoe, Ill.: Free Press, 1955).

120. James S. Coleman, Elihu Katz, and Herbert Menzel, *Medical Innovation: A Diffusion Study* (Indianapolis: Bobbs-Merrill, 1966).

121. Talcott Parsons, *The Structure of Social Action* (New York: McGraw-Hill, 1937), pp. 60–69.

Much of the history of consumption theory in economics during the past century has been marked by an attempt to read some psychological or social structure (especially the former) into the concept of demand.

One significant modification of the classical position came at the hands of Alfred Marshall (1842–1924). Taking the concept of elasticity, which had developed in past decades in English classical economics, and the concept of marginality, which had been developed by the Austrian school as well as other thinkers, Marshall built some psychological structure into wants. By the principle of diminishing marginal utility, he held that the utility of a product diminishes as an individual acquires more of it.

In addition, Marshall indicated that many human wants are structured in relation to cultural and social patterns. His connection between wants and activities led to this insight. Marshall recognized the existence of certain necessaries for subsistence and for different occupations. But in addition he noted the importance of "activities," in which he included ambition and the pursuit of higher social goals, as themselves part of civilization which systematically generated wants. In effect, Marshall was arguing that something besides residual wants determines demand; wants depend in part on the type of civilization in which the economy is embedded.[122]

Writing about the same time as Marshall, Thorstein Veblen (1857–1929) also suggested, in his theory of conspicuous consumption, that something besides randomly assorted individual wants determine the nature of demand. The very wealthy, Veblen argued, choose their patterns of expenditure to underline, symbolize, and fortify their class position vis-à-vis the rest of the community. Again, this marks the introduction of a social variable into the concept of demand, though Veblen never formalized this insight.[123]

In the past several decades the Marshallian theory of demand has been displaced by preference theory, or indifference curve analysis. Marshall began with an individual's relation to a single product; the indifference curve analyst asks at what rate is the individual willing to substitute one product for another. For two or more individual products, the analyst plots a series of points at which the individual is "indifferent" to the marginal increment of each product; he would just as soon have an increment of either one. This series of points results in an indifference curve, the exact shape of which depends on the substitutability of the

122. Ibid., chap. 4.

123. *Theory of the Leisure Class* (New York: Modern Library, 1934). For an attempt to formalize the Veblen effect, as well as other peculiarities of consumption, see Harvey Leibenstein, "Bandwagon, Snob, and Veblen Effects in the Theory of Consumer Demand," *Quarterly Journal of Economics* 64, no. 2 (May, 1950):183–207.

products and the marginal utility of each. The advantages that economists attribute to preference theory are that it eliminates the measurement problems that arise with notions of diminishing marginal utility, and that it brings more than one product into demand theory. From the standpoint of economic sociology, however, preference theory is essentially structureless, for changes in demand depend ultimately only on changes in income of the buyer and price of products.

The work of Keynes brought into focus the balance between consumption and savings. His theory of consumption and savings rests on what he called a "fundamental psychological law," whereby "when [any modern community's] real income is increased [the community] will not increase its consumption by an equal absolute amount, so that a greater *absolute* amount must be saved."[124] While Keynes admitted that factors other than this may affect savings, he did not give them a formal place in his theory. In the end, all we need to know in order to assess the savings ratio is the total income of society and the distribution of this income.

A serious challenge to the Keynesian postulate is found in Duesenberry's theory of consumption. Basing his case on general sociological and economic evidence, he challenged two of Keynes's assumptions: (1) that every individual's consumption behavior is independent of every other individual, and (2) that people who have recently *fallen* from a higher income level to a given income will spend and save in the same manner as people who have *risen* from a lower income level to the same level. To account for the mutual interdependence of consumers' behavior, Duesenberry developed a utility index incorporating the influence of the expenditure of other individuals. Using this "demonstration effect," he argued that people will not save proportionately more at higher levels of income, but that at every income level the savings ratio will be approximately the same. Duesenberry also argued that people save more when they arrive at their highest income level ever attained than when they have fallen to that level from an even higher one. That is, when income falls, previous consumption needs will continue until spending adjusts to the new income level.[125]

Neither Keynes's nor Duesenberry's theory brings many structural variables to bear on consumption. Keynes's principle allows for the inference that social-structural elements change at the same rate as income changes, or if they change differently, they cancel out in the aggregate. Duesenberry marks an advance insofar as he introduced the effect of one consumer on the other and the effect of the past on the present. But both

124. *General Theory of Employment, Interest, and Money* (New York: Harcourt Brace, 1936), p. 97.

125. James Duesenberry, *Income, Savings, and the Theory of Consumer Behavior* (Cambridge, Mass.: Harvard University Press, 1949).

these effects are "contentless" as far as the social structure is concerned; Duesenberry introduced only a conformity principle and an inertia principle.

Friedman's work on the "permanent income theory of consumer behavior" contains a few sociological variables; he held that the ratio of consumption to permanent (discounted, expected) income is a function of the interest rate, the ratio of assets to permanent income, and "tastes." Friedman also mentioned that the sociological variables of age and composition of family affect tastes.[126] In a similar theory, Modogliani, Brumberg, and Ando held that consumption is a function of current and expected income and assets. Again the expected income is influenced by such factors as age of retirement and the age distribution of the population.[127] And finally, Orcutt and his associates introduced variables such as marital status and duration of marriage, as well as age, education, and race of head of household into probability models of spending and saving behavior.[128] The sociological variables these theories incorporate are limited to gross demographic indices.

From time to time economists have expressed dissatisfaction with deductive theories of diminishing marginal utility and indifference curve analysis. Norris, for instance, argued that consumption theory should not be based on diminishing marginal utility "or any alternative of that theory." Rather, she distinguished among short-term purchases according to type of expenditure: (1) those expenditures that involve no calculation, such as legal obligations (e.g., rent), forced savings for Christmas clubs, income taxes, insurance health plans, and so on; (2) areas in which careful weighing occurs, as in investment in certain stocks on the exchange; and (3) a "dynamic residual," in which the purchaser makes sporadic experimental purchases.[129] While perhaps psychologically more satisfactory than some other theories, this classification marks a movement toward pure description–imitative, rational, and experimental purchases. It does not produce a *theory* of demand.

126. Milton Friedman, *A Theory of the Consumption Function* (Princeton: Princeton University Press, 1957).

127. Franco Modigliani and R.E. Brumberg, "Utility Analysis and the Consumption Function: An Interpretation of Cross-Sectional Data," in *Post-Keynesian Economics*, ed. K.K. Kurihara (New Brunswick, N.J.: Rutgers University Press, 1954), pp. 388–436; Modigliani and Albert Ando, "The 'Permanent Income' and the 'Life Cycle' Hypotheses of Saving Behavior: Comparison and Test," in *Proceedings of the Conference on Consumption and Saving* eds. Irving Friend and Robert Jones (Philadelphia, 1960), pp. 49–174.

128. Guy H. Orcutt et al., *Microanalysis of Socio-economic Systems: A Simulation Study* (New York: Harper & Row, 1961).

129. Ruby Turner Norris, *The Theory of Consumer's Demand*, rev. ed. (New Haven: Yale University Press, 1952), pp. 98–108.

Katona's work presents an even more radical departure from formal economic theory. Unlike economic theorists, he argued that he makes no universal assumptions about economic behavior (such as maximization of some utility). He instead regarded the individual as holding *attitudes* toward economic situations and events that form the basis of his plans and acts. In particular, Katona and his associates chose the attitudes of optimism, pessimism, and uncertainty about the economy as the focus of their interest. The major empirical research undertaken by this group has been to trace changes in consumer attitudes over time, and to demonstrate how these changes have affected buying and saving activities. For example, Katona and Mueller showed how attitudinal responses to a tax cut led to increased spending in the winter of 1963-64 (in anticipation of the cut), generated increased savings immediately after the cut, and led to a substantial increase in consumer spending and borrowing during 1964 and 1965.[130] Katona's major conclusions are that "changes in attitudes serve as advance indicators of the volatile elements of consumer demand," that these attitudes are themselves reactions to economic and political developments, and that they "make a net contribution to the prediction of [spending] after the influence of income has been taken into account."[131] In general, Katona has not developed any generalized or deductive theory of consumer behavior; rather, he has worked with low-level generalizations that relate attitudes to income level and other economic variables. He has occasionally examined social-structural variables that affect consumption; we shall mention some of these presently.

Social Structure and Consumption

Throughout this critique of consumption theory we have noted the dearth of social-structural variables.[132] Behind this critique lies, of course,

130. George Katona and Eva Mueller, *Consumer Responses to Income Increases* (Washington, D.C.: Brookings, 1968); see also Katona's tracking of the major swings in economic attitudes between 1945 and 1963 in *The Mass Consumption Society* (New York: McGraw-Hill, 1964), pp. 92–97.

131. Ibid., p. 97; *The Powerful Consumer: Psychological Studies of the American Economy* (New York: McGraw-Hill, 1960), p. 53. Katona's original theoretical position was outlined in his *Psychological Analysis of Economic Behavior* (New York: McGraw-Hill, 1951), chap. 3.

132. Ferber has noted that "socioeconomic variables remain the stepchild of consumption theory. They are invariably introduced as the extra, though essential ingredient—like pouring salt on french fries—with no theoretical basis except to highlight other relationships. . . ." Robert Ferber, "Consumer Economics, A Survey," *The Journal of Economic Literature* 11, no. 4 (December, 1973):1332. For a promising attempt to assess the effect of the changing effect of married female participation in the labor force, see R. Agarwala and J. Drinkwater, "A Study of Consumption Functions with Shifting Parameters Due to Socioeconomic Factors," Econometrics Group of the Economic Council of Canada, Discussion Paper No. 8, 1970.

our own preference for this kind of demand theory. What kind of theory would this be? We would conceive that consumers classed according to various sociological dimensions (social class, race) are differently involved in social structures; these structures impinge on their spending patterns both at a gross level (for instance, saving-spending ratios) and at a detailed level (for instance, the kinds of consumer items used to symbolize sex roles). Thus, for any given consumer, we would note sex, marital status, age, and position in the class structure, and posit certain *levels* and *kinds* of spending and saving that symbolize his involvement in these social structural contexts. Then, by aggregating these attachments to such contexts, we could produce a series of consumption functions for incorporation into various theories of demand.

Unfortunately such a program is in the visionary stage. No comprehensive consumption function based on such structural variables has been produced. What we possess is a number of empirical studies that show differential savings and spending patterns on the part of persons in different sociological categories. The findings are sufficiently striking, however, that they confirm the advisability of incorporating sociological variables into formal theories of demand. Let us now review a sample of these findings.

For any consumption theory it is important to discard the traditional view of the household as the only significant spender and saver. The government constitutes an enormous percentage of demand for products; further, to understand its "demand schedule" for a category such as defense expenditures, it is necessary to examine fluctuations in American public opinion, the interplay of military and business influences on government decision makers, and the behavior of powerful foreign countries, particularly with respect to their buildup of armaments.[133] Firms, banks, and institutional savers such as savings and loan associations, trust companies, and endowments constitute important forces in determining the balance between consumption and savings. While the savings base for such agencies may rest in part on household decisions, the effective determinants of their decisions to save or spend are in part independent of those decisions.

Turning to the private sector, the broad changes in demand in Western industrialized countries over the past century have been influenced by three historical trends: (a) the increase in per capita disposable income, which makes for generally increasing demand; (b) the continued improvement of technology, which generates ranges of new products (for

133. For evidence of the impact of the changing temperature of the Cold War on defense expenditures in the Western and Communist blocs, see Frederic L. Pryor, *Public Expenditures in Communist and Capitalist Nations* (London: Allen & Unwin, 1968).

example, automobiles, household appliances) available to be demanded; and (c) the shortening of working hours and the accompanying increase in leisure time for most categories of workpeople,[134] which increases the capacity to "consume" various leisure-related products (travel, TV, entertainment).

Sociological and other variables impinge on different kinds of consumption. With regard to food consumption, for instance, the following kinds of social correlates are of interest: (1) Sex and age. Women consume less than men, children less than adults. (2) Ecology. Rural populations consume more than urban populations, product differentiation is greater in urban areas. (3) Economic resources. Those near the starvation level spend almost all their increments of income on food; above this level, "Engel's law" takes effect, and with increments of income a smaller proportion is spent on food; then in the upper reaches, where sedentary occupations dominate, the absolute amount spent for food may actually decrease in some cases.[135] (4) Occupational status of family members. Generally, as the income of family increases at middle-income levels, the proportion of income spent on food diminishes; but if this increase results from the fact that a wife takes a job, the proportion spent on food may *increase*, because of reliance on more service costs on food (for example, restaurant meals and frozen foods).

The impact of the life-cycle and family-cycle on investment in consumer durables is striking. Figures reported by Katona and shown in table 1 indicate a consistent tendency for younger single and older single persons to underbuy on all items (that is, in relation to the percentage "expected" from their proportion among all buyers), whereas younger persons with children consistently overbuy, even though this category is not the most affluent. The effect of income level is shown, however, in the purchase of cars, where the younger persons purchase a higher proportion of used than new cars and older persons with no children reverse this proportion. The impact of having young children on buying patterns is illustrated most dramatically in the purchases of washing machines, where young people with children purchase 56 percent of all washing machines, even though they constitute only 35 percent of total purchasers.

Economists and sociologists have taken a keen interest in leisure spending. Between 1929 and 1960 total measured leisure expenditures in

134. Harold Wilensky, "The Uneven Distribution of Leisure: The Impact of Economic Growth on 'Free Time,'" in *Work and Leisure: A Contemporary Social Problem*, ed. Erwin O. Smigel (New Haven: College and University Press, 1963), pp. 109–13. Max Kaplan, *Leisure in America: A Social Inquiry* (New York: John Wiley, 1960), chap. 3.

135. Carle C. Zimmerman, *Consumption and Standards of Living* (Princeton: Van Nostrand, 1936), pp. 75–117.

Table 1 Differences in Durable Goods Purchases During the Life Cycle (in 1956)

		PROPORTION OF PURCHASERS OF						
LIFE CYCLE STAGE	DISTRIBUTION OF SPENDING UNITS	New cars	Used cars	Furniture	Refrigerator	Kitchen range	Washing machine	TV
1. Younger,* single	10%	6%	9%	5%	3%	3%	3%	5%
2. Younger, married	8	8	11	13	10	17	9	11
3. Younger, with children	35	44	49	50	51	41	56	47
4. Older,* with children	12	14	15	11	11	15	12	12
5. Older, no children	21	23	10	16	18	20	16	17
6. Older, single	14	5	6	5	7	4	4	8
Total**	100%	100%	100%	100%	100%	100%	100%	100%

*Younger means head of family under 45; older, over 45.

**The total of 100 percent does not include all spending units; there are some who do not fit into any of the life-cycle stages and are omitted from consideration.

NOTE: Since, for instance, Stage 3 constitutes 35 percent of the spending units considered but bought 44 percent of new cars, it purchased more than its share.

SOURCE: Katona, *The Powerful Consumer*, p. 166.

the United States increased at approximately the same rate as aggregate disposable income, and slightly more rapidly than aggregate personal consumption expenditures.[136] This finding is surprising, since the popular impression is one of a "leisure explosion." This occurred in some areas, such as foreign travel, boats, TV sets, and books, but this was offset by decreasing proportions of income spent on activities like viewing motion pictures and spectator sports.[137] Social class and occupation are correlated with leisure expenditures; higher-income people, for example, spend more on cultural activities—education, books, and theater—than lower-income people, but the proportion is reversed for activities like baseball game attendance.[138] Professors spend much of their spare time in work, work-connected reading, or recreational reading, whereas people in advertising or dentistry spend more of their leisure time on hobbies,

136. George Fisk, *Leisure Spending-Behavior* (Philadelphia: University of Pennsylvania Press, 1963), p. 80.

137. Ibid., p. 81. See also Joffre Dumazedier, *Toward a Society of Leisure*, trans. Steward E. McClure (New York: Free Press, 1967), pp. 162–69.

138. Katona, *The Mass Consumption Society*, pp. 280–83; Alfred C. Clarke, "The Use of Leisure and its Relations to Levels of Occupational Prestige," *American Sociological Review* 21, no. 3 (June, 1956):301–7.

"family-home" activities, or simply "relaxing."[139] In a piece of spoof-research on the "sociology of ice-cream chimes," Hill illustrated the pervasiveness of social class in consumption. British working-class neighborhoods, he reported, hear military spiels; "transitional" neighborhoods a popular tune from Mendelsohn's "Spring Song"; middle-middle class neighborhoods "Greensleeves" (with academics in these neighborhoods identifying it as Vaughan-Williams's "Fantasia on Greensleeves"); and upper-middle class neighborhoods a tune from a Haydn quartet. Hill speculated that academic-artistic neighborhoods like Chelsea no doubt buy ice cream to the chimes of Schoenberg and Stravinsky.[140]

The expansion of expenditures on leisure has profound economic and social consequences. The expansion of tourism in postwar France, for example, created a crisis for the temporary-shelter industry (hotels, resorts), and a rapidly growing camping industry.[141] Personnel in both industries, moreover, work overtime in holiday seasons and are underemployed for most of the year. Holiday centers are likely to experience magnified effects from economic recessions, since expenditures on travel and holidays are among the first to be cut when economic hardship strikes. Finally, communities that become attractive to tourists are often transformed. Focusing on holiday centers in the Pacific, Forster identified a kind of "popularity cycle" for resort areas. At first, tourists bring money and are welcomed. Land values rise, and handicraft industries for "native products" are greatly stimulated. As time goes on, these products become mass-produced, and the area furnishes a phony "folk culture" for tourist consumption. Areas experiencing invasions of tourists also typically develop new social problems, such as how to control congestion, crime, panhandling, and other by-products of large, transient populations.[142]

Race and class also figure in consumption and savings patterns. Certain products—such as Scotch whisky, butter, and cosmetics—stand out as high-expenditure items among black consumers as compared with whites at similar income levels, but the reasons for these differences are far from clear.[143] With respect to savings, blacks use fewer savings and insurance

139. Joel E. Gerstl, "Leisure, Taste and Occupational Milieu," in *Work and Leisure*, ed. Smigel, pp. 148–49.

140. Michael Hill, "Ice Cream in Contemporary Society," *New Society* 2, no. 43 (July 25, 1963):23–24.

141. Dumazedier, *Toward a Society of Leisure*, pp. 130–35.

142. John Forster, "The Sociological Consequences of Tourism," *International Journal of Comparative Sociology* 5, no. 2 (September, 1964):217–27.

143. James E. Stafford, Keith K. Cox, and James B. Higgenbotham, "Some Consumption Pattern Differences between Urban Whites and Negroes," *Social Science Quarterly* 49, no. 4 (December, 1968):619–30.

services than whites at similar income levels but are more deeply involved in credit and installment buying. These different patterns of financing contribute to the economic disadvantage of black households.[144] Lower-income people use credit cards more for installment buying (in contrast with using them as a convenient, non-interest-bearing form of payment) than do higher-income people—a practice that means, in effect, that the former tend to pay more for products than the latter.[145]

CONCLUSION

What lessons may we draw from this long exploration of the impingement of sociological variables on production, distribution, and consumption? There is little doubt of the *general* strength of such variables. Economic sociology, however, is long on numbers of relevant variables, but short on adequate data, classification of variables, and organization of variables into models. Most sociological studies emphasize some single variable (for example, informal group membership). Little effort is made to show the relevance of this variable to the corpus of economic theory or to other sociological variables. In economic sociology we need not only more research; we also need improved classification schemes that sharpen the differences among sociological variables, and cast them in such a way that they can articulate with economic variables. Only in this way can the field produce more than a proliferation of new variables and bits of insight.

144. S. Roxanne Hiltz, "Black and White in the Consumer Financial System," *American Journal of Sociology* 76, no. 6 (May, 1971):987–98.

145. H. Lee Matthews and John W. Slocum, Jr., "Social Classes and Spending Behavior," *Journal of Marketing* 33, no. 1 (January, 1969):71–78.

CHAPTER 5 SOCIOLOGICAL ASPECTS OF ECONOMIC DEVELOPMENT

In chapters 3 and 4 much of our analysis had a "timeless" character. We were interested in the mutual influence among economic and non-economic variables at the broad societal level and at the level of concrete economic processes. But we seldom asked how this mutual influence leads to cumulative social and economic change over time. In this chapter we open this inquiry.

SEVERAL TYPES OF CHANGE

Perhaps the simplest kind of change is that resulting from the circulation of various rewards, facilities, and personnel in an existing structure. We might refer to this as *social process*. An economic example is the process of allocating goods, services, and money in day-by-day market transactions. Sometimes this gives rise to regularities in the movement of indices—as in inventory cycles, trade cycles, and redistributions of wealth. Outside the economic sphere, similar processes are observable. Social mobility, for instance, often involves the movement of persons through a status hierarchy; it does not necessarily involve structural change in the hierarchy itself. The key characteristic of *process* is that change takes place within an existing structure.

A type of change intermediate between social process and structural change is *segmentation*. This refers to the proliferation of structural units that do not differ qualitatively from existing units. An example is the addition of new firms to the market when demand increases. Another is the creation of new families when the marriage rate increases. Both cases involve the addition of structurally similar units.

Structural change involves the emergence of qualitatively new complexes of roles and organizations. In Berle and Means's analysis of the separation and ownership and control in the modern corporation,[1] for instance, new roles (managers, passive stockholders) and a new *type* of organization (the modern corporation) emerged.

A fourth type involves changes in what we might call the *group structure* of a society. The fact that a society possesses a social structure means that its roles are differentiated in a variety of ways. People occupy different ascribed roles; they are defined socially as women, men, husbands, children, members of a certain tribe, and residents of a certain region. In addition, they may be categorized according to some differentiated economic or social role they have assumed, such as peasant, worker, manager, priest, soldier, student, and the like. These bases of social differentiation provide a series of reference points around which groups may form. Changes in group structure refer to shifts in the composition of groups, the level of consciousness of groups, and the relations among groups in society. Analysis of changes in group (including class) structure are especially relevant to the understanding of political processes, since it is through groups that political influence, conflict, and accommodation are played out.

Though it is possible to separate social process, segmentation, structural change, and changes in group structure analytically, the four are intimately associated empirically. Economic innovations (for example, the establishment of new industries such as railroads) involve structural changes that are of sufficient magnitude to produce, or at least initiate, business cycles. Sometimes the segmentation of family units creates population pressure that is difficult to contain without structural changes in economic production. Structural changes, producing new roles, provide new bases for group membership and the identification of group interests. And groups, through the political process, often influence the direction of all the other types of social change.

In this chapter we shall concentrate on structural changes and changes in group structure, emphasizing those that are associated with economic and social development.

ECONOMISTS' VIEWS OF DEVELOPMENT

Many economists begin with a notion of growth that is limited to an index such as growth of output per head of population, or steel produc-

1. Above, p. 57.

tion, or size of labor force. Such a notion forms the basic dependent variable. The variables that determine rates of growth are found in the factors of production—natural resources, capital for investment, labor, and entrepreneurial talent. Other economic variables immediately involved with the supply of these factors are savings, inflation, balance of payments, foreign aid, size of population, and rate of population change.[2]

Economists also identify a number of structural transformations that accompany the growth of per capita product and increased productivity. Kuznets included among these

> the shift away from agriculture to nonagricultural pursuits and, recently, away from industry to services; a change in the scale of productive units, and a related shift from personal enterprise to impersonal organization of economic firms, with a corresponding change in the occupational status of labor. Shifts in several other aspects of economic structure could be added (in the structure of consumption, in the relative shares of domestic and foreign supplies, etc.).[3]

Subsequently we shall elaborate on such structural transformations, tracing their ramifications into the social order.

SOCIOLOGICAL DETERMINANTS OF GROWTH

Vicious and Beneficent Circles of Growth

For an analysis of how sociological variables impinge on economic growth, we begin with an economic model expounded by Nurkse.[4] Underdeveloped areas, he argued, frequently are caught in a trap of low per capita output—a trap composed of two vicious circles, one on the side of the *supply* of factors of production, and one on the side of *demand* for products.

On the *supply* side capital is scarce because of the low capacity of

2. See Richard T. Gill, *Economic Development: Past and Present*, 3rd ed. (Englewood Cliffs, N.J.: Prentice-Hall, 1973), chaps. 1–2; for discussion of issues relating to capital accumulation, inflation, allocation of resources for investment, etc., see Gerald M. Meier, ed., *Leading Issues in Development Economics* (New York: Oxford University Press, 1964).

3. Simon Kuznets, "Modern Economic Growth: Findings and Reflections," *American Economic Review* 63, no. 2 (June, 1973):248–49; see also P. Sargant Florence, "Economic Trends in Industrial Development," in *Economics and Sociology of Industry: A Realistic Analysis of Development* (New York: Hillary House Publishers, 1964), pp. 1–31.

4. Ragnar Nurkse, *Problems of Capital Formation in Underdeveloped Areas* (New York: Oxford University Press, 1962), esp. chap. 1.

people to save. This low capacity to save is a reflection of the low level of real income. The low level of income is a reflection of low productivity in the economy, which in its turn is due largely to the lack of capital. The lack of capital is a result in part of the small capacity to save, and so the circle is complete.

On the *demand* side, inducement to invest may be low because of the limited buying power of the people, which is due to their low real income. This low real income results from low productivity, which in turn reflects the small amount of capital used in production. The low volume of investment, finally, rests on the small inducement to invest.

Much of Nurkse's exposition is devoted to examining the ways in which these vicious circles can be broken. If it is possible to raise the value of one variable—such as inducement to invest—all the variables will begin to increase, and the result will be a beneficent circle of economic growth. Among the possibilities Nurkse suggested for altering the vicious circles are increasing international trade, diminishing (or at least stopping the growth of) population, removing excess labor from the land, forcing savings, and borrowing internationally. He argued, however, that many of these proposed means are likely to prove ineffective unless entrepreneurs plunge into the economy and augment the variable of "inducement to invest"; in so doing they introduce basic structural changes in the factors of production.[5]

Sociological Determinants of Economic Variables

Nurkse's theory emphasizes the interaction among economic variables, such as savings, investment, consumption, productivity, entrepreneurship, and so on. As economic sociologists we may move behind the immediate interplay and find that the value of each variable is determined in part by sociological variables.

The search for relevant variables has carried in two main directions —first, to identify *external* obstacles or stimuli to development by analyzing the world system of economic specialization, trade, and political domination; and second, to identify *internal* obstacles or stimuli to development that are to be found in societies' religious, kinship, political, and stratification systems. With respect to the former, Myrdal has argued that an international vicious circle operates to keep underdeveloped countries trapped in their internal vicious circles: an international pattern of migration, capital flow, international trade, and regional specialization that widens the inequality gap between rich and poor nations.[6] To ex-

5. Ibid., pp. 154–56.

6. Gunner Myrdal, *Economic Theory and Underdeveloped Regions* (London: Gerald Duckworth, 1957), chap. 5.

tend this line of argument, it could be pointed out that in periods of colonial domination the colonial powers encouraged the development of primary products for export (thus concentrating the labor force in the primary sectors); that colonial domination prevented the emergence of a stable, autonomous political order necessary to foster economic development; that in postcolonial times this skewed specialization has grown even more marked, as industrial countries exhaust their resources and come to depend on—and consolidate—the primary-product industries of the less-developed world; and that the developed countries have closed off emigration opportunities for displaced elements of the population from the less developed countries.[7]

On the side of internal obstacles, sociologists and anthropologists have identified social factors affecting the supply of savings, labor, and entrepreneurship. There is evidence that peasants in traditional societies save a sizeable proportion of their assets;[8] the *form* these savings take, however, does not often encourage their investment. Lambert and Hoselitz, for example, summarized the implications of land-based stratification systems of Southern Asia for saving behavior as follows:

> In all countries of [Southern Asia] land heads the list of approved possessions. . . . Status and power differentials within rural areas are dependent upon land rights and even wealth earned in non-agricultural pursuits must be converted into land holding to be fully legitimized. In part, this overwhelming emphasis on the acquisition of land is understandable since it is the primary agricultural producers goods, but often it is pursued even when the return from it is marginal and when alternative investments are demonstrably more rewarding. . . . One result of this emphasis on land is that with increasing densities and general inflationary trends, the price of land rises rapidly. . . . In 1960 the price of land [was] 8 to 10 times that of 1939 and it [cost] more than can normally be earned on it in 15 to 20 years. . . .
> If accumulation takes place in other items than land, it is in currency or coins, stored in trunks or buried in a corner of the house, in jewelry and precious metals—the lower classes' insurance—and in stores of grain. The latter may be used not only to supply for consumption but to speculate on fluctuation in prices over the growing season.[9]

Such arrangements divert savings into relatively unproductive channels.

7. For reflections on these kinds of international forces, see Kuznets, "Modern Economic Growth," pp. 254–57.

8. Raymond Firth, "Capital, Saving and Credit in Peasant Societies: A Viewpoint from Economic Anthropology," in *Capital, Saving and Credit in Peasant Societies*, ed. Raymond Firth (London: Allen & Unwin, 1964), pp. 22–29.

9. Richard D. Lambert and Bert F. Hoselitz, "Southern Asia and the West," in *The Role of Savings and Wealth in Southern Asia and the West*, eds. Richard D. Lambert and Bert F. Hoselitz (Paris: UNESCO, 1963), pp. 411–13.

Various traditional rituals calling for expenditures on gifts or offerings to the dead also divert wealth from productive investment.[10]

Traditional kinship and other values also have been cited as obstacles to labor commitment in industrial settings. Labor must be brought into a new reward system (wage payments), under a new form of authority (supervision on factory premises), and into a more impersonal market setting. Peasant societies, with their close kinship relations and their attachment to the land, frequently resist recruitment of labor into industrial urban settings. Wilbert Moore has observed of the kinship system in nonindustrial societies: "[It] perhaps . . . offers the most important single impediment to individual mobility, not only through the competing claims of kinsmen upon the potential industrial recruit but also through the security offered in established patterns of mutual responsibility."[11]

This line of argument implies that as such traditional forms are broken down, conditions become more conducive for economic development. Deyrup, for example, has argued that the breakdown of a rigid class structure is "the key to the establishment of a broadly based consumer market which will encourage industrialization." Such a breakdown reduces spending based on local customs and ritual spending and opens the way to the formation of genuinely mass markets.[12]

Some have argued that explanations relying on internal obstacles to the development of the less-developed nations are in contradiction with those relying on external obstacles.[13] This would be true only if (a) external constraints were so powerful that even in the absence of internal obstacles growth could not occur, or if (b) even with plentiful markets and ample international political and economic freedom to develop, internal constraints on factors such as entrepreneurship and labor supply

10. Ibid., p. 397.

11. Wilbert E. Moore, *Industrialization and Labor* (Ithaca: Cornell University Press, 1951), p. 24. For numerous examples, see pp. 24–34. A number of specific case studies are found in Wilbert E. Moore and Arnold S. Feldman, eds., *Labor Commitment and Social Change in Developing Areas* (New York: Social Science Research Council, 1960). For a general characterization of obstacles to development, phrased in terms of sociocultural constraints on the several factors of production, see P. Sargent Florence, "Industrialization of the Underdeveloped Countries," in *Economics and Sociology of Industry*, ed. Florence, pp. 180–86.

12. Felicia J. Deyrup, "Social Mobility as a Major Factor in Economic Development," *Social Research* 34, no. 2 (Summer, 1967):346.

13. This is the argument presented by A.G. Frank, who criticized sociologists and economists who stress internal obstacles to development. Frank himself emphasized the constraints imposed by imperialist practices of the developed nations. *The Sociology of Underdevelopment and the Underdevelopment of Sociology* (London: Pluto Press, 1971).

prevented an economy from developing. But in practice the determination of development (or the lack of it) is more complex. Both external and internal variables are significant in many ways, some of which are constraining and others facilitative for development. Colonial powers, for example, expropriated profits from colonies rather than investing them locally, restricted growth to primary-product industries, and inhibited the development of autonomous polities—all detrimental in some respects to the future development of the colonies. But at the same time they introduced markets and money, systems of wage payments, and systems of administration that were potential resources for future development.[14] With respect to internal obstacles, social scientists have accumulated ample evidence of presumed "obstacles" that turn out to be assets,[15] presumed "obstacles" that do not obstruct, and conditions that facilitate at one stage and obstruct at another.[16] Belshaw's comments on the significance of social structural variables for development seem most appropriate:

> . . . social structure does not in itself either inhibit or promote economic growth. It does, however, have an important bearing upon the forms of organization which are appropriate in given circumstances. . . . The greatest and clearest defect in traditional social structures is that they do not provide sufficient forms of organization for instrumental effectiveness through the complex range of activities necessary for growth to take place. In this sense, certain functions, such as those of banking, credit supply or marketing, are either not performed or are inadequately developed. As discrete tribal and similar groups are brought within the bounds of colonies or new national States, such functions continue to be defective, or are concentrated in particular social groups or geographical areas. . . . The absence of essential functions in an economy as a whole can hold it back, and the social structure must expand in scale and complexity by the creation of new institutions.[17]

Belshaw's remarks suggest a fruitful way of looking at the interplay

14. Gayl D. Ness, "Colonialism, Nationalism and Development," in *The Sociology of Economic Development*, ed. Gayl D. Ness (New York: Harper & Row, 1970), pp. 387–96.

15. Above, pp. 83–84.

16. For two general statements, both of which cite numerous studies, see Joseph R. Gusfield, "Tradition and Modernity: Misplaced Polarities in the Study of Social Change," in *Organizational Issues in Industrial Society*, ed. Jon M. Shepard (Englewood Cliffs, N.J.: Prentice-Hall, 1972), pp. 35–49; Albert O. Hirschman, "Obstacles to Development: A Classification and a Quasi-Vanishing Act," *Economic Development and Cultural Change* 13, no. 4 (July, 1965): 385–93.

17. Cyril S. Belshaw, "Social Structure and Cultural Values as Related to Economic Growth," *International Social Science Journal* 16, no. 2 (1964):221–23.

of external and internal factors. Any external restraint or opportunity must be assessed in the light of existing resources of the affected society—its economic assets, its cultural and institutional framework—and its corresponding ability to respond to the external situation. Any internal factor must be assessed in relation to the contemporary system of opportunities and restraints outside the economy. To regard external and internal factors as continuously changing and evolving in relation to one another suggests a more promising way to understand development than to regard either set of factors as having a fixed significance for development.

STRUCTURAL CHANGES ASSOCIATED WITH DEVELOPMENT

Technological, Economic, and Ecological Aspects of Development

Let us now assume that the vicious circle of poverty has been broken—by what combination of circumstances it does not matter for now—and that economic growth has begun. What happens in the society?

In the first instance the society begins to reorganize its people and other resources in the following ways: (1) With respect to technology, there is a change *from* simple and traditionalized techniques *toward* the application of scientific knowledge; (2) In agriculture, the change is *from* subsistence farming *toward* commercial production of agricultural goods. This means specialization in cash crops, purchase of nonagricultural products in the market, and frequently agricultural wage-labor. (3) In industry, the transition is *from* the use of human and animal power *toward* industrialization proper, or the use of power-driven machines tended by wage-earners and producing goods that are sold for prices in the market; (4) In ecological arrangements, there is movement *from* the farm and village *toward* urban centers. These several processes often occur simultaneously. However, certain technological improvements—e.g., the use of improved seeds—can be introduced without automatically producing organizational changes; agriculture may be commercialized without accompanying industrialization, as in many colonial countries; industrialization may occur in villages; and cities may proliferate in the absence of significant industrialization, as was the case with many medieval trading centers. Furthermore, the specific social consequences of technological advance, commercialized agriculture, the factory, and the city, respectively, are not in any sense reducible to one another.

Variability in the Process of Development

How do these technological, agricultural, industrial, and ecological changes tend to affect the social structure? Or, to put the question in Belshaw's terms, what kinds of institutions are typically invented, borrowed, or adapted, to provide a social setting in which those changes can take place? No simple answer to this question is available, because national differences make for variations in development along the following dimensions:

1. Variations in the *preindustrial conditions* of the country. A society's value-system may be congenial or antipathetic to industrial values. The society may be large or small, tightly or loosely integrated. Its level of market development and national wealth may be low or high. The wealth may be evenly or unevenly distributed. From the standpoint of population, the society may be "young and empty" (for example, Australia) or "old and crowded" (for example, India). The society may be politically dependent, recently independent, or relatively autonomous. Such preexisting conditions make for great differences in national experiences with development.

2. Variations in the *impetus* to development. The pressures to develop may stem from the internal implications of a value-system (as in Weber's theory) from a desire for national security and prestige, from a desire for material prosperity, from pressure on the part of a colonizing country, to develop a primary-product industry in a colony, or from a combination of these.

3. Variations in the *path* toward development. The developmental sequence may begin with light consumer industries. Or there may be an attempt to introduce heavy, capital-intensive industries first. The government may take an active or a passive role in shaping the pattern of investment.[18] The tempo of industrialization may be fast or slow.

4. Variations in the *advanced stages* of modernization. Societies may vary in the emergent distribution of industries in their developed economies. They may vary in the emergent relations between state and economy, state and religion, and so on. While all advanced industrialized have their "industrialization" in common, unique national differences remain. For instance, social class differs in its significance in the United States and Britain, even though both are highly developed countries.

5. Variations in the *content and timing of dramatic events* during development. Wars, revolutions, rapid migrations, and natural catastrophes may influence the course of economic and social development.

Because of these sources of variation, it is difficult to discover empirical generalizations concerning the change of social structures during economic and social development.[19] Nevertheless, it is possible to iden-

18. For an account of the roles of banks and the state in stimulating growth in different national settings, see Alexander Gerschenkron, "Economic Backwardness in Historical Perspective" in his volume with the same title (Cambridge, Mass.: Belknap Press, 1962), pp. 5–30.

19. For a related and overlapping discussion of variations in the path of development, see Bert F. Hoselitz, "Historical Comparisons," in *Approaches to the Science of Socio-Economic Development*, ed. Peter Lengyel (Paris: UNESCO, 1971), pp.

tify some general structural changes that nations experience as they attempt to push their economies forward. The first is *structural differentiation,* or the establishment of more specialized and more autonomous structural units. We shall illustrate this process with respect to economy, family, religion, and stratification. The second is the emergence of new patterns of *integration,* or the establishment of new coordinative structures—especially legal, political, and associational—as the old social order is made more complex and perhaps obsolete by the process of differentiation.[20] Because differentiation and integration proceed irregularly in different spheres of society, however, numerous social tensions are generated, and these eventuate in considerable *disturbance and group conflict.* Let us illustrate these typical concomitants of development.

Structural Differentiation in Periods of Development

Simply defined, differentiation refers to the change from a multifunctional role structure to several more specialized structures. The following are typical examples: (1) In the transition from domestic to factory industry, the division of labor increases, and the economic activities previously lodged in the family move to the factory; the result is a relatively greater split—or differentiation—between domestic and economic roles. (2) With the rise of a formal educational system, the training functions previously performed by the family and church are established in a more specialized unit, the school. (3) The modern political party has a more complex structure than tribal factions and is less likely to be characterized by kinship loyalties, competition for religious leadership, and the like. Formally defined, then, structural differentiation is a process whereby "*one* social role or organization . . . differentiates into *two or more* roles or organization which function more effectively in the new historical circumstances. The new social units are structurally distinct from each other, but taken together are functionally equivalent to the original unit."[21] How does the process of differentiation work out in the various social realms?

Differentiation of economic activities. Typically in underdeveloped countries production is located in kinship units. Subsistence farming

---

128–42. For an extreme statement stressing the heterogeneity of the industrializing process, see Herbert Blumer, "Industrialization and the Traditional Order," *Sociology and Social Research* 48, no. 2 (January, 1964):129–38.

20. The concepts of differentiation and integration occupied a central place in the thought of Spencer and Durkheim. Above, pp. 13–15.

21. Neil J. Smelser, *Social Change in the Industrial Revolution* (Chicago: University of Chicago Press, 1959), p. 2.

predominates; other industry is supplementary but still attached to family and village. In some cases occupational position is determined largely by an extended group such as the caste. Similarly, exchange and consumption are embedded deeply in family and village. In subsistence agriculture there is a limited amount of independent exchange outside the family; this means that production and consumption occur in the same social context. Exchange systems proper are lodged in kinship and community (e.g., reciprocal exchange) in stratification systems (e.g., redistribution according to caste membership) and in political systems (e.g., taxes, tributes, payments in kind, and forced labor).

As the economy develops, several kinds of economic activity are removed from this family-community complex. In agriculture, the introduction of money crops marks a differentiation between the social contexts of production and consumption. Agricultural wage-labor marks the separation of work roles from what previously might have been a family productive unit. In industry, it is possible to identify several levels of differentiation. Household industry, the simplest form, parallels subsistence agriculture in that it supplies the worker's own needs and does not enter the market. "Handicraft production" splits production and consumption, though frequently consumption takes place in the local community. "Cottage industry," on the other hand, frequently involves a differentiation between consumption and community, since production is for unknown consumers in the market and is mediated through wholesalers. Finally, manufacturing and factory systems segregate the worker from his capital and frequently from his family. Why are these new and more specialized forms invented? They are distinctive social-structural responses to the exigencies of large-scale production and marketing with more advanced technology; as larger, more specialized, more specific-purpose roles and organizations, they are more appropriate—indeed efficient—than traditional family and community structures.[22] Employers and workers may rely on traditional obligations to recruit laborers and secure their loyalty and discipline,[23] but this should not obscure the fact that the structure of the productive process has undergone fundamental change.

Similar differentiations appear in the exchange system. Goods and services, previously exchanged on a noneconomic basis, are pulled more and more into the market. Money now commands the movement of more and more goods and services and thus begins to supplant—and sometimes undermine—the religious, political, familial, or caste sanctions that pre-

22. William H. Friedland, "A Sociological Approach to Modernization," in Chandler Morse et al., *Modernization by Design: Social Change in the Twentieth Century* (Ithaca, N.Y.: Cornell University Press, 1969), pp. 61–71.

23. Above, pp. 83–84.

viously had governed economic activity. Insofar as an economy becomes implicated in the international market, an even further differentiation occurs. Exchange is no longer restricted to the citizens of a national polity.

Empirically, we may classify economies according to how far they have moved along these lines of differentiation. Migratory labor may be a kind of compromise between full membership in a wage-labor force and attachment to an old community life; cottage industry introduces extended markets but retains the family-production fusion; the hiring of families in factories maintains a version of family production; the expenditure of wages on traditional items such as dowries also shows this half-way entry into the more differentiated industrial-urban structure. And societies may differ in the degree to which they have developed or been drawn into wider market structures. The reasons accounting for differences in level of differentiation include the resistances on the part of the populace to give up traditional ways of life, the economics of national and international demand for different products, and systems of discrimination against native labor that permit only limited economic participation. In any event, however, the concept of structural differentiation provides a yardstick to measure the degree to which the social structure of the economy has developed.

Differentiation of family activities. One implication of the removal of economic activities from the kinship nexus is that the family loses some of its previous functions, becoming a more specialized agency. The family ceases to be an economic unit of production; one or more members now leave the household to seek employment in the labor market. While many compromise arrangements such as family hiring and migratory systems persist, the tendency is toward the segregation of family functions and economic functions.

Several related processes accompany this differentiation of the family from its other involvements: (a) Apprenticeship within the family declines. (b) Pressures develop against the intervention of family favoritism in the recruitment of labor and management. These pressures often lie in the demands for efficiency. The intervention often persists, however, especially at the managerial levels, and in some cases family ties continue as a major basis for labor recruitment.[24] (c) The direct control of elders and collateral kinsmen over the nuclear family weakens. This marks, in structural terms, the differentiation of the nuclear family from the extended family. (d) One aspect of this loss of control is the growth of personal choice, love, and related criteria as the basis for courtship and marriage. Correspondingly, marriage arranged by elders and extended kinsmen declines in importance. (e) One result of this complex of proc-

24. Above, pp. 83–84.

esses is the changing status of women, who become generally less subordinated economically, politically, and socially to their husbands than under earlier conditions.

These directions of change in the family occur gradually and on a selective basis. Family systems are probably best regarded as rather resilient; they give up certain functions and activities as market opportunities and pressures arise but retain many of their distinctive features. Families, even extended families, retain considerable vitality as bases for urban integration—as havens for support, job placement, borrowing, socializing, and the like[25]—even after they have long ceased to function as a productive unit. In specific instances, moreover, what threatens to produce major family changes often changes very little in actuality.

In 1950, Lambiri studied a small Greek country town (population 16,500) nearby which a cotton factory, employing mostly women, had just been constructed. At that time standards for female comportment were strict and traditional; women were to be "modest, compliant, and domesticated" and girls were to be, "above all, chaste." Only a girl's fiance, brother, or first cousin was permitted to escort her out of doors. To work in the factory meant that women and girls left the town for eight hours a day, mixed with others on the factory premises, and sometimes traveled at night. Initially a wave of alarm spread through the community; fears were expressed for the welfare of the family, and derogatory epithets were coined for women who worked. Yet the women used their wages in traditional ways, especially to increase their dowry; and many traditional attitudes toward women remained. Indeed, the initial alarm and anger may have themselves served as important social sanctions to pressure women to change their traditional sex-role definitions minimally, even though their occupational status was altered significantly. In any event, the "emancipation" occurred within a relatively traditional framework.[26]

However piecemeal and selective the process, however, structural differentiation tends to undermine the old modes of integration in society. The controls of extended family and village begin to dissolve in the enlarged and more complicated social setting, which differentiation involves. And, however resilient, the family cannot serve indefinitely as the dominant mode of integration. We shall look presently at the emergence of new integrative forms.

Differentiation of religious systems. In chapter 3 we explored how

25. Peter Marris, "African Families in the Process of Change," in *Families in East and West: Socialization Process and Kinship Ties*, eds. Reuben Hill and Rene Konig (The Hague: Mouton, 1970), pp. 397–409; above, pp.

26. Jane Lambiri, "The Impact of Industrial Employment on the Position of Women in a Greek Country Town," *British Journal of Sociology* 14, no. 3 (September, 1963: 240–47.

religious and nationalistic belief-systems vary in their effects—as stimuli or obstacles—on economic development.[27] The notion of differentiation permits us to account for some aspects of these contrasting effects. In the early phases of development, many traditional loyalties may have to be weakened in order to establish more differentiated structures. Because loyalties are deeply rooted in the organization of society, a generalized and powerful value commitment is often required to "pry" individuals from their attachments to them. The values of ascetic and this-worldly religious beliefs, xenophobic national aspirations, and political ideologies may provide such a lever. All three have an ultimacy of commitment in the name of which a wide range of sacrifices can be demanded and procured.

The very success of these value-systems, however, breeds the conditions for their own weakening. In a perceptive statement, Weber noted that by the beginning of the twentieth century, when the capitalistic systems was highly developed, it no longer needed the impetus of ascetic Protestantism.[28] Capitalism had, by virtue of its conquest of much of Western society, established an institutional base and a secular value-system of its own—economic rationality.

The development of differentiated values such as economic rationality constitutes one facet of the secularization of religious values. In this process, other institutional spheres—economic, political, and scientific, among others—come to be established on an independent basis. The values governing these spheres are no longer sanctioned by religious beliefs, but by autonomous rationalities. Insofar as such rationalities replace religious sanctions in these spheres, secularization occurs.

Similarly, nationalistic and related value-systems undergo a process of secularization as differentiation proceeds. As a society moves toward more complex social organization, diffuse nationalism gives way to more autonomous systems of rationality. The Soviet Union, for instance, as its social structure grew more differentiated, has appeared to introduce more "independent" market mechanisms, "freer" scientific investigation in some spheres, and so on. These measures are not, moreover, directly sanctioned by an appeal to nationalistic or communistic values.

Thus the paradoxical element in the role of religious or nationalistic values: Insofar as they encourage the breakup of old patterns of commitment, they may stimulate economic development; insofar as they resist their own subsequent secularization, however, the very same values may become a drag on structural change.

Differentiation of systems of stratification. In discussing stratification

27. Above, pp. 46–51.

28. Max Weber, *The Protestant Ethic and the Spirit of Capitalism* (London: Allen & Unwin, 1948), pp. 181–82.

in chapter 3, we noted the importance of ascription-achievement in classifying ranking systems. We also asserted that collective forms of mobility are typically associated with ascribed systems of stratification.[29]

Many less-developed societies are characterized by ascribed systems of stratification and correspondingly by collective forms of mobility. Under conditions of economic development, moreover, structural differentiation involves a change in both characteristics:

1. Other evaluative standards intrude on ascribed memberships. Castes, ethnic groups, and traditional religious groupings do not necessarily decline in importance in every respect during periods of development. As we shall see presently, they continue to be important as political interest groups or reference groups for diffuse loyalties. As the sole bases of ranking, however, ascriptive standards become more differentiated from economic, political, and other standards.
2. Individual mobility through the occupational hierarchies increases. This signifies the differentiation of the adult's functional position from his point of origin. In addition, individual mobility is frequently substituted for collective mobility. Individuals, not whole castes or tribes, compete for higher standing in society. This phenomenon of increasing individual mobility seems to be one of the universal consequences of industrialization. Many obstacles to it remain, however—such as the continuation of patterns of inheritance of wealth, the persistence of racial discrimination[30]—and patterns of class symbolization and class ideology continue to differ among developed countries.

The Integration of Differentiated Activities

One of Durkheim's insights concerned the role of integrative mechanisms under conditions of growing social heterogeneity. One of the concomitants of a growing division of labor (differentiation), he argued, is an *increase* in mechanisms to coordinate and solidify the interaction among individuals with increasingly diversified interests.[31] Durkheim found this integration reflected mainly in the legal structure, but it is possible to identify similar kinds of integrative forces elsewhere in society.

Development proceeds as a contrapuntal interplay between differentiation (which may be divisive of established society) and integration (which attempts to unite differentiated structures on a new basis). Paradoxically, however, the process of integration itself produces more differentiated structures—e.g., trade unions, associations, political parties, and a mushrooming state apparatus. Let us illustrate this complex process.

29. Above, pp. 91–93.

30. Above, pp. 87–88.

31. Above, pp. 15–17.

Economy and family. Under a simple kind of economic organization —subsistence agriculture or household industry—there is little differentiation between economic and family structure. All reside in the kinship structure. The *integration* of these diverse but unspecialized activities also rests in the local family and community structures, and in the religious traditions that fortify both of these. Under conditions of differentiation, the social setting for production is separated from that for consumption, and productive roles of family members are isolated geographically, temporally, and structurally from their distinctively familial roles. Such differentiation immediately creates integrative problems. How is information concerning employment opportunities to be conveyed to workpeople? How are the interests of families to be integrated with the interests of firms?

As indicated above, the family often continues as an important integrative mechanism:

> . . . ties of kinship may provide a unique source of knowledge about people, and of sanctions to enforce economic contracts. The family may be your only source of credit for a business venture, for they alone know what you are worth, and how to bring pressure to bear if you fail to meet your obligations. You may choose to employ relatives for the same reasons, irrespective of the claims of kinship. All that gives the family its unalterable importance.[32]

In an interview study of 240 unemployed men in Nairobi and Lagos, Gutkind found that men who migrate to these cities to seek employment "almost invariably stay initially with close or distant relatives." A young man typically stays with—and is supported by—one kinsman until his welcome is exhausted and then moves on to another for a limited time. Moreover, he often relies on these kinsmen for information about jobs and influence in seeking jobs. This familial integrative mechanism, however, is a fragile one. Gutkind found many instances of ill will developing between guest and host and some cases of economic exploitation of relatives; older unemployed interviewees, with a history of job-seeking, preferred relying on friends rather than relatives because of unpleasant personal situations that arise with the latter. Moreover, reliance on family alone is often not an effective means of securing employment, because of the family's limited information about and control over employment opportunities.[33]

Side by side with the old integrative structures arises a host of new

32. Peter Marris, "African Families in the Process of Change," pp. 402–3.

33. Peter C.M. Gutkind, "The Energy of Despair: Social Organization of the Unemployed in Two African Cities: Lagos and Nairobi," *Civilizations* 17, no. 2 (1967): 202–3.

institutions and organizations—labor recruitment agencies and exchanges, labor unions, government agencies to allocate labor, welfare and relief arrangements, cooperative societies, and savings institutions. All these involve agencies that specialize in integration, reflecting the fact that the older modes of integration and allocation that were based on kin and community are not sufficient to cope effectively with the scale and complexity of an impersonal market situation.

Community. Among the most conspicuous features of expanding urban areas in the developing countries is the appearance of a variety of voluntary associations—churches and chapels, unions, schools, halls, athletic clubs, bars, shops, mutual aid groups, and the like. Some of their functions are economic; in his study of the unemployed, Gutkind found that individuals seeking work frequently became involved in networks of friendship, or joined an ethnic or recreation association, a church, or political party, thereby extending their network of information and contacts and increasing their probabilities of landing jobs. Informal social organizations arose among the unemployed as well.[34] More broadly, these associational ties give the individual a basis for informal social interaction for personal identity, and for building relations of trust with others.

Early in the stages of development the criteria for association may be common tribe, caste, or village of origin.[35] But as development proceeds, as communication networks become more complex, and as people's interests become more diverse, there arise new types of formal volunteer associations based on economic, political, recreational, esthetic, or other interests. In a comparative study of eleven nations, ranging from developed to underdeveloped, Smith found the number of formal volunteer associations to be strongly and positively correlated with measures of development such as urbanization, per capita gross national product, literacy, and proportion of labor force in industrial occupations.[36] Voluntary associations appear to be appropriate forms of "community" integration in societies that have grown large-scale, mass, and heterogeneous in structure.

Political Structures

In the less-developed setting political integration is typically fused with kinship position, tribal membership, control of the land, or control

34. Ibid., pp. 381–88.

35. See Peter Marris's characterization of the strength of tribal-associational ties in Africa; *African City Life* (Kampala: Transition Books, 1968), pp. 12–17.

36. David Horton Smith, "Modernization and the Emergence of Volunteer Organizations," *International Journal of Comparative Sociology* 13, no. 2 (June, 1972):113–34.

of the unknown. Political leaders include chieftains, kings, councils of elders, and powerful landlords and oracles.

As social systems grow more complex, political systems are modified accordingly.[37] Several decades ago Fortes and Evans-Pritchard identified three types of African political system, which they listed according to their degree of differentiation from kinship lineages: (a) small societies in which the largest political unit embraces only those united by kinship; (b) societies in which the political framework is the integrative core for a number of kinship lineages; (c) societies with an "administrative organization" of a more formal nature. Such systems moved toward greater differentiation, moreover, as population grew and economic and cultural heterogeneity increased.[38] In colonial and recently independent African societies, political systems have evolved much further, with the appearance of parties, congresses, pressure groups, parliamentary systems and national governments. Sometimes this wider political integration, like community integration, is based on an extension and modification of an old integrative principle. Many of the most politically significant organizations in some African societies are tribal associations,[39] and caste has persisted as one of the bases for political lobbying in India.[40] These traditional forms, persisting alongside civil-service bureaucracies, parties, and trade unions, present a broad array of integrative efforts that are fashioned as a society undergoes development and structural differentiation.

At various points in this book we have indicated the economic and social-structural bases for expecting government to assume a more salient role as societies become more developed and complex. We might review them here:

> 1. On the economic side, governmental planning and activity are required in rapidly developing societies to direct saving and investment, to regulate incentives, to encourage entrepreneurship, to control trade and prices, and so on.
>
> 2. Undifferentiated institutional structures frequently constitute primary social barriers to development. Individuals refuse to work for wages because of traditional kinship, village, tribal, and other ties. Invariably a certain amount of political pressure is required either to pry individuals

37. For a glance at some comparative evidence on this point, see above, pp. 71–73.

38. Meyer Fortes and E.E. Evans-Pritchard, eds., *African Political Systems* (London: Oxford University Press, 1940), pp. 1–25.

39. Marris, *African City Life*, pp. 14–17.

40. T.N. Madan, "The Changing Political Functions of Caste in India," in *Social and Economic Change*, eds. Baljit Singh and V.B. Singh (Bombay: Allied Publishers, 1967), pp. 208–76; Richard D. Lambert, "Some Consequences of Segmentation in India," *Economic Development and Cultural Change* 12, no. 4 (July, 1964):416–24.

loose from their ties or to redefine them so that they may be used as resources in the development of new institutional forms.

3. The process of growing complexity associated with development continuously makes archaic earlier modes of integration that are too localized or too limited in scope to be appropriate for such complexity. The "net" of responsibility for families to provide for kinsmen who might be economically deprived fails to "catch" all that experience economic hardship in the vicissitudes of a market system of wage labor. Accordingly, systems of welfare and support develop as adjuncts to the more informal forms. This entails, of course, an expansion of governmental activities.

4. As we have seen, the process of development generates structural conditions that precipitate a large number of different types of groups that are, in part, integrative in their significance—clubs, labor unions, religious sects, tribal and caste associations, and other voluntary associations based on like interests. But another significance of these groups is that they are potentially—and sometimes actually—mobilizable for political causes. The growing complexity of group life adds to the burdens of political integration of the society—to regulate conflict, to accommodate a diversity of demands, and to effect compromises. We shall expand this point presently when we discuss social conflict and social disturbances.

Up to this point we have sketched some structural consequences of technological advance, agricultural commercialization, urbanization, and industrialization. We have analyzed these consequences in terms of differentiation and integration. The structural changes are not, it should be remembered, a simple function of "industrialization" alone. Some of the most far-reaching structural changes have occurred in countries which have scarcely experienced the beginnings of industrialization. For instance, colonialism—or related forms of economic dominance—creates not only a differentiation of cash products and wage labor but also a vulnerability to world price fluctuations in commodities. Hence many of the structural changes described above—and many of the resulting conflicts and disturbances to be described presently—characterize societies which are still technically "preindustrial."

Discontinuities in Differentiation and Integration: Social Disturbances and Conflict

The structural changes associated with economic development are likely to be disruptive to the social order for the following three reasons:

1. Differentiation demands the creation of new activities, norms, and sanctions—money, political position, prestige based on occupation, and so on. These often conflict with old modes of social action, which are frequently dominated by traditional religious, tribal, and kinship systems.

2. Structural change is, above all, *uneven* in periods of development. In colonial societies, for instance, the European powers frequently revolutionized the economic, political, and educational frameworks but simul-

taneously encouraged or imposed a conservatism in traditional religious, class, and family system.

> The basic problem in these [colonial] societies was the expectation that the native population would accept certain broad, modern institutional settings . . . and would perform within them various roles—especially economic and administrative roles—while at the same time they were denied some of the basic rewards inherent in these settings. . . . They were expected to act on the basis of a motivational system derived from a different social structure which the colonial powers and indigenous rulers tried to maintain.[41]

Under noncolonial conditions of development similar discontinuities appear. Within the economy itself rapid development, no matter how coordinated, bites unevenly into the established social and economic structure. Unevenness may characterize the rates of development of different sectors of society as well. For example, political elites may encourage merchants and entrepreneurs, but their efforts may be frustrated by traditional value-systems that afford little status to commercial roles; in this example the discontinuity is between the change in the economic system and the change in the stratification system. Or, an educational system may produce more trained personnel than can be absorbed by a flagging economy.[42]

The myriad of contending political groups that emerge as societies develop unevenly pose problems of conflict-regulation for political authorities, who themselves may be struggling to find a legitimate place for themselves in society:

> . . . in consequence of . . . structural differentiation, specific and functional organizations emerge. . . . At the same time, however, . . . tribal and communal organization is resurrected, which shows much ingenuity in adapting to new conditions by redefining its former, now obsolete functions and taking on new ones. The general development of the periphery, which contains enclaves with a participant social orientation, is such as to speed up its access to the political arena. The elite is frequently unable to regulate and direct the masses that flood it with their demands and threaten to sweep away the power center. Typical of most of these [developing] countries is the emergency [*sic*] of big new social enclaves consisting of incongruent status groups. The older enclaves consisted of ethnic minorities that monop-

41. S.N. Eisenstadt, "Sociological Aspects of Political Development in Underdeveloped Countries," *Economic Development and Cultural Change* 5, no. 4 (July, 1957):298.

42. These and numerous other examples of unevenness are cited in Moshe Lissak, "Some Theoretical Implications of the Multidimensional Concept of Modernization," *International Journal of Comparative Sociology* 11, no. 3 (September, 1970):195–207.

olized economic key positions but were socially despised, while the new enclaves consist of educated and semi-educated.[43]

An important instance of unevenness is what might be called the lag between economic differentiation and integrative inclusion. Vallier described this lag—and its consequences—in his study of an Israeli kibbutz's adaptation to a labor shortage. The kibbutz was a highly integrated organization, and its integration was based in part on an ideological commitment to the mission of collective farming. Under pressure to produce more, the kibbutz found itself facing the dilemma of recruiting and socializing new full-time members into the collective farm or relying on hiring students and unemployed immigrants for wages. In the end they opted for the latter, hiring but making no effort to integrate the wage-laborers into the collective life of the community. The hired hands, for their part, maintained an instrumental orientation to the kibbutz, kept socially distant from its members, and found intimacy and solidarity with their own numbers.[44]

This kind of situation has arisen repeatedly as foreign immigrants or previously low-status ethnic groups are brought in as laborers during periods of expansion. It is the story of many minority groups who migrated to America, and of laborers from Turkey, Yugoslavia, and elsewhere who have been brought in as guest laborers in the Western European economies since World War II. The migration brings higher remuneration to the group than it had previously enjoyed. Political, social, and cultural assimilation lags, however, and sets the stage for a vicious circle of discrimination against and withdrawal of the new group, and potential ethnic-political polarization of the groups.[45]

3. Dissatisfactions arising from such discontinuities are sometimes aggravated by attempts to overcome them. Some of the discomforts arising from the discontinuities of development may be cushioned by effective political parties and institutions, which provide a locus for accommodating political conflicts. Such political forms are often opposed, however,

43. Ibid., p. 205. Huntington has argued that the key source of instability in modernizing societies is that numerous politically significant groups are formed in the process of attempting to mobilize the society for development, but that political mechanisms for accommodating these groups lag in their own development. This constitutes a special form of unevenness of development. Samuel P. Huntington, *Political Order in Changing Societies* (New Haven: Yale University Press, 1968).

44. Ivan Vallier, "Social Change in the Kibbutz Economy," *Economic Development and Social Change* 10, no. 4 (July, 1962):337; 352.

45. For documentation of this cycle in a quite different setting, see Wesley R. Hunt, Jr., "The Urbanization of the Yankton Indians," *Human Organization* 20, no. 4 (Winter, 1961–62):226–37.

because the new forms of integration compete with older, undifferentiated systems of solidarity. Because of this competition, new political forms often rest on unsteady legitimacy and support. The result of all these discontinuities is a three-way tug-of-war among the forces of tradition, the forces of differentiation, and the new forces of integration.

One should therefore regard political conflict arising from discontinuities as an endemic feature of development—a feature amply documentable in the continuing history of the developed societies as well as in the contemporary situation of the developing ones. The ultimate outcome of this disturbance and conflict, however, is variable. Furthermore, the following factors seem to be the most decisive in the genesis and shaping of disturbance and conflict:

1. The scope and intensity of the social dislocation created by structural change. In general, the greater the tempo of the change, the greater the integrative problems that are generated.
2. The structural complexity of a society at the time when development begins. In the least-developed societies, where "the language of politics is at the same time the language of religion," protest and conflict more or less immediately take on a religious cast. In colonial Africa, for instance, utopian religious movements appear to have had relatively greater appeal in the less-developed regions, whereas the more secular types of political protest such as trade union movements and political parties clustered in the more-developed areas.[46]
3. The access of political groups to channels of influencing social policy. If such groups have access to those responsible for introducing reforms, conflict tends to be relatively peaceful and orderly. If this access is blocked, either because of the isolation of the groups or the intransigence of the ruling authorities, demands for reform tend to take more extreme form and move in the direction of challenging the legitimacy of the authorities.
4. The overlap of interests and lines of cleavage. Those societies in which economic, political, and ethnic cleavages coincide are likely to produce more diffuse kinds of conflicts and social movements than societies in which these cleavages crisscross.
5. The kind and extent of foreign infiltration and intervention on behalf of political groups.

In this chapter we have tried to sketch, in ideal-type terms, the ways in which economic and social development is related to social structure. We have centered the discussion around three major concepts—differentiation, which characterizes a social structure moving toward greater complexity; integration, which in certain respects balances the divisive character of differentiation; and social disturbances and conflict, which result from the discontinuities between differentiation and inte-

46. Thomas Hodgkin, *Nationalism in Colonial Africa* (New York: New York University Press, 1957), pp. 95–150.

gration. To this analysis must be added three qualifications: (a) For purposes of exposition we have presented the three major categories in a certain order—differentiation, integration, and disturbance and conflict. We should not assume, however, that any one of them takes causal precedence in the analysis of social change. Rather they form an interactive system. Conflicts and disturbances, for instance, may arise from discontinuities created by structural differentiation, but they may also shape the course of future processes of differentiation. (b) Even though the three sets of forces are closely linked empirically, we should not "close" the "system" composed of the relations among them. Differentiation may arise from sources other than economic development; the requirement of integration may arise from conditions other than differentiation; and the sources of social disturbance and conflict are not exhausted by the discontinuities between differentiation and integration. (c) The "all-at-once" character of the transition from less-differentiated to more-differentiated societies should not be exaggerated. Empirically the process evolves gradually and influences the social structure selectively. The emphasis on various half-way arrangements and compromises throughout the chapter illustrates this gradualness and irregularity.

EPILOGUE: THE CASE FOR ECONOMIC SOCIOLOGY

To close our account of the sociology of economic life, we shall indicate, in a few sentences, where we have been in this volume. We began with the notion that social life can be separated analytically into a number of "aspects"—the economic, the political, the legal, the religious, and so on. Even though analytically separable, however, these several aspects influence one another empirically. In this volume we selected the economic aspect as a focus, but, unlike economists who often study this aspect in relative isolation, we elected to examine the interaction among the economic and noneconomic aspects.

We began this examination by isolating some themes in the history of economic and social thought. Economic theorists, such as Adam Smith, Karl Marx, and John Meynard Keynes, ventured different assumptions about the relations between the economy and the rest of society. These assumptions often made a great difference in how these thinkers conceived the operation of the economy. Social theorists, such as Emile Durkheim, Max Weber, and Bronislaw Malinowski, systematically demonstrated how political, familial, and legal forces shape economic processes. Finally, economists, sociologists, and anthropologists in modern times have developed new theories and types of research to assess the relations between economic and noneconomic variables. The history of thought presents a strong case for needing to observe the interaction among the several aspects of social life to gain an adequate account of any one aspect.

But this case, resting as it does on the unsystematic accumulation of thought of diverse writers through the ages, is only a very general one. It is necessary to become more specific and detailed in drawing out the interrelations between economic and noneconomic variables. We attempted to introduce the detailed case for economic sociology in four ways:

1. We systematically compared the disciplines of the economist and the sociologist. We asked what kinds of assumptions each makes about the other's subject, what kinds of questions each asks in his own field, how each goes about answering these questions, how the fields overlap, and how they might be integrated theoretically.
2. We considered each aspect of social life as a subsystem of society. We then asked how each subsystem influenced and was influenced by the economy. Taking kinship as an example, we suggested that certain kinds of family structure have a greater "strain toward consistency" with wage and factory labor than other family structures. Turning to religion, we explored on the effects of different religious beliefs on economic activity. Similarly, we reviewed the economic implications of research on the political system and the stratification system.
3. We asked how noneconomic variables condition various types of economic activities—production, distribution, and consumption. In this operation we incorporated many of the findings of industrial sociology, the research on comparative exchange systems, and the work of economists and sociologists on the determinants of spending and saving.
4. We asked how economic and noneconomic variables affect one another during periods of social change. Concentrating on economic development, we first observed some of the ways that social factors facilitate or impede the effort to modernize. Then we showed how a rapidly developing economy brings about a proliferation of changes in the social structure. The case for economic sociology is particularly striking in the analysis of change, since many of the economists' simplifying assumptions are inapplicable when the economy's social environment is in flux.

An advantage of this multi-sided approach to the sociology of economic life is that we are able to locate the field's weaknesses as well as its strengths. We have discovered not only what we know, but also what we do not know. We have attempted throughout to identify the gaps and uncertainties in our knowledge. As these are overcome gradually by the efforts of scholars, the field of economic sociology will come to play a unique role, contributing to the development of both the fields it encompasses.

SELECTED REFERENCES

These notes are intended to launch the student on a search through the available writings on economic sociology, rather than provide him a comprehensive bibliography.

For the discovery of sociological elements in economic thought, it is best to go through the classics. Important ones are Adam Smith, *Inquiry into the Nature and Causes of the Wealth of Nations* (New York: The Modern Library, 1937); Karl Marx, especially *Communist Manifesto* (London: Allen & Unwin, 1948, and many paperback editions) and *Capital* (New York: The Modern Library, 1936); Alfred P. Marshall, *Principles of Economics,* eighth edition, especially Books III and VI (New York: Macmillan, 1920); and John Maynard Keynes, *General Theory of Employment, Interest, and Money* (New York: Harcourt Brace, 1936). A modern secondary treatment of the history of economic thought is Eric Roll, *A History of Economic Thought,* fourth edition, revised and enlarged (London: Faber & Faber, 1974). Joseph A. Schumpeter's *History of Economic Analysis* (New York: Oxford University Press, 1954), is an enormous and challenging work.

Classics in the history of sociological thought include the aforementioned works of Marx; Emile Durkheim, *The Division of Labor in Society,* translated by George Simpson (Glencoe, Ill.: Free Press, 1949); Vilfredo Pareto, *The Mind and Society*, translated by Andrew Bongiorno and Arthur Livingston (New York: Harcourt Brace, 1935); Max Weber, *The Protestant Ethic and the Spirit of Capitalism*, translated by Talcott Parsons (New York: Scribner, 1930), and *Economy and Society*, edited by Guenther Roth and Claus Wittich (New York:

Bedminister Press, 1963), 3 vols. More recent works of broad theoretical scope are Talcott Parsons, *The Structure of Social Action* (New York: McGraw-Hill, 1937); Talcott Parsons and Neil J. Smelser, *Economy and Society* (Glencoe, Ill.: Free Press, 1956); and Karl J. Polanyi, C. M. Arensberg, and H. W. Pearson, eds., *Trade and Market in the Early Empires* (Glencoe, Ill.: Free Press, 1957).

Students interested in the economic life of nonindustrial and nonmarket economies should consult Bronislaw Malinowski's *Argonauts of the Western Pacific* (London: Routledge & Kegan Paul, 1922) and *Coral Gardens and their Magic* (London: Allen & Unwin, 1935). Other sources are Marcel Mauss, *The Gift,* translated by Ian Cunnison (Glencoe, Ill.: Free Press, 1954); Raymond Firth, *Primitive Polynesian Economy,* second edition (London: Routledge & Kegan Paul, 1965), and *Malay Fishermen: Their Peasant Economy,* third edition, revised and enlarged (London: Routledge & Kegan Paul, 1966). More recent sources include George Dalton, *Economic Anthropology and Development: Essays on Tribal and Peasant Economies* (New York: Basic Books, 1971); Raymond W. Firth, ed., *Themes in Economic Anthropology* (London: Tavistock, 1967); Edward E. LeClair, Jr., and Harold K. Schneider, eds., *Economic Anthropology: Readings in Theory and Analysis* (New York: Holt, Reinhart & Winston, 1968).

In the field of industrial sociology, the single most significant work is F. J. Roethlisberger and William J. Dickson, *Management and the Worker* (Cambridge: Harvard University Press, 1947). The broader aspects of the "human relations" approach are explored in Elton Mayo, *The Social Problems of an Industrial Civilization* (Boston: Graduate School of Business Administration of Harvard University, 1945). Modern comprehensive treatments are found in Delbert Miller and William Form, *Industrial Sociology,* third edition (New York: Harper & Row, 1971); Eugene V. Schneider, *Industrial Sociology,* second edition (New York: McGraw-Hill, 1969); and Jon M. Shepard, ed., *Organization Issues in Industrial Society* (Englewood Cliffs, N. J.: Prentice-Hall, 1972). On occupational roles see Peter L. Berger, ed., *The Human Shape of Work: Studies in the Sociology of Occupations* (New York: Macmillan, 1964); and Clifton D. Bryant, ed., *The Social Dimensions of Work* (Englewood Cliffs, N.J.: Prentice-Hall, 1972). The student interested in industrial relations and industrial conflict should refer to Walter Galenson and Seymour Martin Lipset, eds., *Labor and Trade Unionism* (New York: John Wiley, 1960); Arthur M. Ross and Paul T. Hartman, *Changing Patterns of Industrial Conflict* (New York: John Wiley, 1960); and Everett M. Kassalow, *Trade Unions and Industrial Relations: An International Comparison* (New York: Random House, 1969).

For the analysis of economic development, see Richard T. Gill, *Economic Development: Past and Present,* third edition (Englewood

Cliffs, N.J.: Prentice-Hall, 1973); Bert F. Hoselitz and Wilbert E. Moore, eds., *Industrialization and Society* (The Hague: UNESCO-Mouton, 1963); Gerald M. Meier, ed., *Leading Issues in Development Economics* (New York: Oxford University Press, 1964); Gayl D. Ness, ed., *The Sociology of Economic Development* (New York: Harper & Row, 1970), and S. N. Eisenstadt, *Tradition, Change, and Modernity* (New York: John Wiley, 1973). The journal *Economic Development and Cultural Change* contains many studies of the social aspects of economic growth, as does the journal *Explorations in Entrepreneurial History.*

Other important volumes on various aspects of economic sociology are Reinhard Bendix, *Work and Authority in Industry* (New York: John Wiley, 1956); Robert Blauner, *Alienation and Freedom* (Chicago: University of Chicago Press, 1964); William J. Goode, *World Revolution in Family Patterns* (New York: Free Press, 1963); Alvin W. Gouldner, *Patterns of Industrial Bureaucracy* (Glencoe, Ill.: Free Press, 1954); Robert L. Kahn et al., *Organizational Stress: Studies in Role Conflict and Ambiguity* (New York: John Wiley, 1964); George Katona, *The Powerful Consumer: Psychological Studies of the American Economy* (New York: McGraw-Hill, 1960), and *The Mass Consumption Society* (New York: McGraw-Hill, 1964); Delbert C. Miller, *International Community Power Structures: Comparative Studies of Four World Cities* (Bloomington: University of Indiana Press, 1970). Journals containing many studies in economic sociology are *American Sociological Review, American Journal of Sociology, British Journal of Sociology, Administrative Science Quarterly,* and *American Journal of Economics and Sociology.*

SUBJECT INDEX

NAME INDEX

The volumes in the ***Prentice-Hall Foundations of Modern Sociology Series*** are designed to cover all major areas in the field of sociology. Each book, written by an outstanding specialist, introduces a particular sub-field within the discipline. The unifying feature of the series is the systematic study of groups and societies. In each book one major aspect of social life is analyzed, with special reference to its role in the development, functioning, and change of larger social systems; the history of theory and research in this sub-field is reviewed; and the current state of knowledge and research is summarized. These findings are combined to lend both historical depth and comparative breadth to the series.

PRENTICE-HALL
FOUNDATIONS OF MODERN SOCIOLOGY SERIES

Alex Inkeles, Editor

THE SCIENTIST'S ROLE IN SOCIETY, *Joseph Ben-David*

DEVIANCE AND CONTROL, *Albert K. Cohen*

MODERN ORGANIZATIONS, *Amitai Etzioni*

SOCIAL PROBLEMS, *Amitai Etzioni*

THE FAMILY, *William J. Goode*

SOCIETY AND POPULATION, second edition, *David M. Heer*

WHAT IS SOCIOLOGY? AN INTRODUCTION TO THE DISCIPLINE AND PROFESSION, *Alex Inkeles*

THE SOCIOLOGY OF SMALL GROUPS, *Theodore M. Mills*

SOCIAL CHANGE, second edition, *Wilbert E. Moore*

THE SOCIOLOGY OF RELIGION, *Thomas F. O'Dea*

SOCIETIES: EVOLUTIONARY AND COMPARATIVE PERSPECTIVES, *Talcott Parsons*

THE SYSTEM OF MODERN SOCIETIES, *Talcott Parsons*

THE AMERICAN SCHOOL: A SOCIOLOGICAL ANALYSIS, *Patricia C. Sexton*

THE SOCIOLOGY OF ECONOMIC LIFE, second edition, *Neil J. Smelser*

FOUNDATIONS OF MODERN SOCIOLOGY, *Metta Spencer/Alex Inkeles*

SOCIAL STRATIFICATION: THE FORMS AND FUNCTIONS OF INEQUALITY, *Melvin M. Tumin*